Understanding the School Curriculum

D1613000

At a time of rapid social change and numerous policy initiatives, there is a need to question the nature and function of school curricula and the purposes of formal public education. Comparing curriculum developments around the globe, *Understanding the School Curriculum* draws on a range of educational, philosophical and sociological theories to examine the question 'What is a curriculum for?' In considering different answers to this fundamental question, it explores a range of topical issues and debates, including:

- tensions and dynamics within curriculum policy;
- the implications of uncertainty and rapid social change for curriculum development;
- the positive and negative influence of free market ideologies on public education;
- the impact of globalisation and digital technologies;
- arguments for and against common core curricula and state control.

It examines the possibility of a school curriculum that is not shaped and monitored by dominant interests but that has as its founding principles the promotion of responsibility, responsiveness, a love of learning, and a sense of wonder and respect for the natural and social world.

Understanding the School Curriculum is for all students following undergraduate and Masters courses in curriculum, public policy and education-related subjects. It is also for all training and practising teachers who wish to combine a deeper understanding of major curriculum issues with a critical understanding of the ways in which ideologies impact on formal state education, and to consider ways of producing school curricula that are appropriate to the times we live in.

Alex Moore is an Emeritus Professor at the Institute of Education, University of London, UK.

'[H]ow much can be hoped for within the framework of values in a capitalist and autocratic…system? This is a great source of my wonder. It is a wonder about how to keep the great curriculum questions alive, the ones too seldom asked by policy makers: What is worthwhile? What is worth knowing, experiencing, needing, becoming, being, overcoming, sharing, and contributing? What life is worth leading? Who does it benefit and who needs to benefit more? How could they be enabled to benefit more? How can I become my own curriculum director?'

(William H. Schubert 2011: 19)

'Nietzsche reminds us that the recognition that the social order is conventional – constructed – grants us a great deal of creative agency in relation to the world in that we can strive to reconstitute it along new and innovative lines; the constructed character of our existence, rather than being a source of anxiety or concern, should empower us to engender fresh meanings, values, and modes of life. After all, the most effective way to transcend outdated or oppressive conventions is to counter them with better ones.'

(Mari Ruti 1999: 21)

'Education in its deepest sense and at whatever age it takes place, concerns the opening up of identities – exploring new ways of being that lie beyond the current state…Education is not merely formative – it is transformative…[I]ssues of education should be addressed first and foremost in terms of identities and modes of belonging and only secondarily in terms of skills and information.'

(Étienne Wenger 1998: 263)

Understanding the
School Curriculum

Theory, politics and principles

Alex Moore

Routledge
Taylor & Francis Group

LONDON AND NEW YORK

First published 2015
by Routledge
2 Park Square, Milton Park, Abingdon, Oxon OX14 4RN

and by Routledge
711 Third Avenue, New York, NY 10017

Routledge is an imprint of the Taylor & Francis Group, an informa business

© 2015 A. Moore

The right of A. Moore to be identified as author of this work has been asserted by him in accordance with sections 77 and 78 of the Copyright, Designs and Patents Act 1988.

All rights reserved. No part of this book may be reprinted or reproduced or utilised in any form or by any electronic, mechanical, or other means, now known or hereafter invented, including photocopying and recording, or in any information storage or retrieval system, without permission in writing from the publishers.

Trademark notice: Product or corporate names may be trademarks or registered trademarks, and are used only for identification and explanation without intent to infringe.

British Library Cataloguing in Publication Data
A catalogue record for this book is available from the British Library

Library of Congress Cataloging in Publication Data
Moore, Alex, 1947-
Understanding the school curriculum : theory, politics and principles / Alex Moore.
pages cm
1. Education–Curricula. 2. Public schools. I. Title.
LB1570.M625 2014
375'.001–dc23
2014008312

ISBN: 978-0-415-63056-6 (hbk)
ISBN: 978-0-415-63057-3 (pbk)
ISBN: 978-0-203-09759-5 (ebk)

Typeset in Bembo Std
by Saxon Graphics Ltd, Derby

MIX
Paper from
responsible sources
FSC® C013604   Printed and bound by CPI Group (UK) Ltd, Croydon, CR0 4YY

Contents

Contents

Acknowledgements

In addition to those other writers, too numerous to mention, whose work has continued to enthuse and encourage me over the years and whose presence is very visible in the pages that follow, I owe huge debts of gratitude to my colleagues Gwyn Edwards, who was largely instrumental in inducting me into the field of Curriculum Studies at Goldsmiths College in the 1990s, and Paddy Walsh and Denis Lawton, who continued that induction when I joined the Curriculum Studies Group at the Institute of Education in 2000. I must also thank Helen Pritt at Routledge for her confidence in my existing work, for suggesting that I write a new book on the school curriculum, and for persuading her colleagues that such an enterprise was worthwhile; Stephen Ball, Gunther Kress and David Halpin all for sharing their wisdom and for their friendship, encouragement and infectious positivity over the years; my wife Anna for her boundless love and support, as well as for keeping me up to speed with developments and experiences on the ground; and all those colleagues who contributed to an earlier, edited book, *Schooling, Society and Curriculum*, whose structure and themes have very much influenced the shape and content of this current book – in particular, Bridget Somekh for persuading me that Curriculum Studies was a discipline worth fighting for at a time when I was probably ready to throw in the towel. Finally, I want to acknowledge the influence on my thinking and teaching of my late friend and colleague Robert Kwami, whose premature death at the age of 50 was such a loss not only to the academic community but to those many, many people whose lives, like mine, he touched so generously with his patience, his wisdom and his love.

Acknowledgements

Chapter 1

Introduction

'A curriculum for the future'

> We look back because, in part, learning is about taking on the heritage of our culture and learning about what has made us who we are. We look forward because we know the world is going to be different than it was and we accept the challenge of making the best judgments we can about what that world will look like.
>
> (The International Middle Years Curriculum: Making Meaning, Connecting Learning, Developing Minds 2013: 3)

> The future cannot be known, but we must debate its possible shapes.
>
> (Coffield and Williamson 2011: 17)

Cha(lle)nging times

The question 'What's it for?' or 'Why are we doing this?' is frequently asked by school students of their teachers (and indeed by teachers themselves, though perhaps less vocally); less so, one suspects, by politicians and policymakers, for whom the answers may seem self-evident. There is always, of course, a rationale to be found – either explicitly or implicitly – for both education in general and for the school curriculum in particular: in, for example, the countless pages of Education Acts, White Papers, and National Curriculum Guidelines. However, the curriculum itself, in England as in many countries (though particularly, perhaps, in England), has arguably changed very little over the last 100 years or so, either in terms of its officially stated purposes or in basic curriculum content and design, despite considerable changes in the wider socio-economic and physical worlds.[1]

In his book *The Curriculum of the Future*, published in 1998, Michael Young argues, as others have done, that whatever reasons for 'doing this' or 'doing that' may have applied in the past, the times in which we are now living and into which we are now moving render many of those reasons defunct or at best tenuous, and that a radical reappraisal of what we are doing in formal mass education – of what we are asking young people to do – is itself in need of radical reappraisal. Identifying a number of changed contexts in which public education is designed and practised, Young placed particular emphasis on global (or rather 'western') *economic* changes; on the similarities and differences between (and the implications of) education-for-work and education-for-its-own-sake in a much changed global workplace; and on what we understand by, and what we value in *knowledge*: that is, what 'counts' as knowledge. As Young put it:

> [I]f new concepts of work and production are emerging, albeit under specific conditions, and they do represent possibilities for the future...then such seemingly commonplace and uncontentious notions as qualification, skill and knowledge, and the traditional division between academic and vocational learning, *can never be the same again.*
>
> (emphasis added, Young 1998: 3)

Young's particular interest in the so-called 'academic–vocational divide' in formal education (particularly in relation to post-compulsory education) and in the need for education to prepare learners not just for the 'specific conditions' of the *present* but for a future which is in part planned and in part unpredictable, led him to an endorsement of lifelong learning in the 'learning society' entailing a new relationship between 'school and non-school learning', and in the continuing promotion of 'situated learning': that is to say, a principle that formal learning cannot and should not be (though very often *is*) 'abstracted from the contexts in which it takes place so that it can be a topic for specialized psychological study' (ibid.: 2).

In exploring the curriculum implications of such a perspective, Young took as a starting point, as others have done (see, e.g., Giroux 1992: 241; Ross 2000: 11), another principle: that the curriculum we construct today should not just concern itself with the perceived needs of today or even the imagined individual and collective economic needs of the future, but should also be constructed around a *vision* or 'concept' of the kind of *future society* we might wish our education systems to help bring about: 'The curriculum debate thus becomes a debate about the different views of the kind of society we want to see in the next century and how they are embedded in different curriculum concepts.' (ibid.: 6)

Young's concern with the future, *and* with revising and constructing present curricula with the future (or perhaps '*a* future') much more clearly in mind, suggests the need critically to revisit both curriculum theory and curriculum practice in relation to radically altered circumstances in the wider socio-economic world as well as to ongoing changes in the way we understand ourselves as social, cultural, ethical beings in a world (I would argue) whose future is increasingly uncertain and difficult to predict.

I have dwelt on Young's book partly because the themes I have highlighted are also central to *Understanding the School Curriculum*, partly by way of introducing some important differences between the two books: books which, I hope, readers will find complementary rather than oppositional. To begin with the similarities, many of the key underlying issues, questions and arguments raised by Young are also present in *Understanding the School Curriculum*, albeit with a somewhat different inflexion. In addition to those aspects already referred to (situating the curriculum debate within considerations of wider economic changes; recognising the importance of [re]producing 'learning societies', of valuing and promoting 'situated learning', of exploring, understanding and developing new relationships between 'school and non-school learning', of curricula both reflecting and resisting the educational changes prompted by those wider socio-economic changes), other common strands across the two books include: recognising, exposing and debating the general 'arbitrariness' of formal curricula (that is, their grounding in selections which self-present as 'natural', 'obvious', and 'essential' rather than as choices which may reflect and promote certain interests – inevitably at the expense of others); the consequent need to return to fundamental curriculum *principles* (as opposed to tinkering around the edges of what we already have and do) and of exploring new 'forms of knowledge' and new relationships within and between such forms (a concern which is part of a wider common theme, of emphasising the importance of *context* in making sense of, critiquing and developing curricula); and underpinning all of this, a concern to speak up for and develop curricula that are both forward-looking (that is, concerned with shaping some imagined future society – or perhaps future world) and simultaneously questioning of existing curricula that remain, despite much rhetoric to the contrary, locked into a time and a mood when education was principally aimed at a small élite.

Some of the differences between *Understanding the School Curriculum* and *The Curriculum of the Future* are what we might call superficial: differences, for example, in the selection and use of references (partly a matter of personal preference). Others are more substantive, concerning, largely, matters of emphasis. Young's book, for instance, is more concerned with developments in post-compulsory education (more his field than mine) and on the boundaries and relationships between subjects and subject disciplines in those educational phases (for example, Young's book goes into far more detail than I have done in relation to moving forward an existing academic–vocational debate). *Understanding the School Curriculum*, by contrast, focuses exclusively on the compulsory phases of education (though without too much difficulty, most of the debates can very easily be transferred to the discussion of issues in the post-compulsory phase), and puts the emphasis not so much on issues of knowledge itself and what 'counts' as knowledge (a key debate in Young's book) as on:

1   the way in which ubiquitous neo-liberal discourses of self, alongside just-about-compatible conservative discourses of tradition, have dominated – and continue to dominate – curriculum development and design in England, the USA and some Western European countries in particular;
2   the ways in which some countries are beginning to question such discourses and their operationalisation in national school curricula; and
3   the implications for curriculum design and development in England and elsewhere once that revised stance is adopted and carried through into state-supported education systems.

What kind of future? And Who Decides?

Alasdair Ross (2000: 11) has wisely and helpfully observed, reminding us perhaps that school curricula should *begin* with principles, aims and rationales, rather than appending them at some later date:

> Once a policymaker grasps that the act of defining the curriculum is a conscious selection of which culture shall be transmitted to the next generation, then it becomes possible to reverse the process: to decide what form of culture (or society) will be desirable in the future, and to ensure that it is this which is included in the curriculum.

'The policymaker' can come in one of many guises (and is *almost* certainly part of a policy 'team' of some sort), and can be the bearer of any number of ideologies, theories and biases. Ross' point, however, remains an important one. Let us imagine for a moment that policymakers decide that they – whether reflecting their own views or seeking to synthesise and work on those of others – would like education principally to help bring about a future in which everyone in the nation (or perhaps in the world) might be equally capable of living a fulfilling life in which poverty is nationally and globally eliminated; in which everyone is entitled to the same quality and availability of medical care; in which racism, sexism, sectarianism and homophobia are eliminated; in which everyone is valued equally, regardless of their specific skills and interests and the work they do (and this is reflected in the distribution of income); and in which the world generally is a safer place ecologically and politically. What kind of curriculum would be required to bring about such an undertaking? What attitudes might it seek to foster? What knowledge and skills might it need to prioritise? And to what extent could it realistically hope to bring about the achievement of all of these aims through education alone? (Clearly, at the very least, other policies – perhaps some new or revised laws – would be required to, for example, redistribute wealth or reduce carbon emissions, and the education policy espousing this particular future might need to be embedded in a much bigger politics of radical socialism.)

Then let us imagine a group of policymakers who take a different view: who might agree, for various reasons, with some of these other priorities, but who, either because they have a preferred alternative vision or because they feel the first set of alternatives is unattainable, would like to help bring about a future characterised by other priorities, such as free competition, an unfettered national and global marketplace, and the continuation of hierarchies of job status and income within some version of an 'organic society' (more on which later). What kind of curriculum might *they* need to establish? And how easy or difficult might *this* be in relation to that bigger politics outside public education?

In a sense, curriculum always has, and always has had, some kind of a future orientation, underpinned by some kind of vision (however flimsily articulated) of that future. As Clarke points out, public policy in whatever field has 'imaginary dimensions' in which it 'envisages certain models of society and seeks to bring into being particular types of individuals ideally suited to populating this imagined world' (Clarke 2012: 3) – an envisaging which typically, Clarke suggests, homes in on 'values' and on 'the identification of a population that *lacks* [those values]' (my emphasis). In reflecting specifically on curriculum reform in the context of the 'globalisation' of education policy, Rizvi and Lingard echo Clarke, in their talk of how such reform 'has been linked to the reconstitution of education as a central arm of national economic policy, as well as being central to the *imagined community the nation wishes to construct through schooling*' (Rizvi and Lingard 2010: 96, emphasis added).

Apart from decisions about what aspects of any 'imagined' or 'envisaged' future politicians and policymakers might seek to prioritise or lend differential weight to (for instance, the perceived needs of a current and future national economy, or the development of 'social cohesion'), there is always another immediate decision to be made, as Clarke (ibid.) argues, in relation to *values*: that is to say, do we design a curriculum that validates, promotes and protects certain 'current values' into the future (which, in addition and in any event, may not be everyone's values but those of a small élite), by 'passing them on' to new generations (characteristic of what I shall call, after Bourdieu, the *reproductive curriculum*)? Or do we seek to encourage in, or draw out of our young people some previously less validated values – or perhaps apply different emphases to existing values – with the intention of bringing about a significantly *different* (e.g. more socially just) society (what I shall call the *[r]evolutionary curriculum*)? To what extent do we (for example) follow the lead of the Finnish national 'Basic' curriculum in seeking to balance reproduction and innovation, to respect the past and to prepare for the future – to ape a curriculum 'mission' advising us that:

> In order to ensure social continuity and build the future, Basic education assumes the tasks of transferring cultural tradition from one generation to the next, augmenting knowledge and skills, and increasing awareness of the values and ways of acting that form the foundation of society. It is also the mission of Basic education to create new culture, revitalize ways of thinking and acting, and develop the pupil's ability to evaluate critically.
>
> (Finland: *National Core Curriculum for Basic Education* 2004: 12)

Either way, a matter of great importance is: Who decides what kind of society 'we' want – and in whose interests, and with what mandate? In the broadest sense, should this be a matter for the State to determine (by which, effectively, is meant whatever political party and attendant ideology are in the ascendancy at any given time – or even, as in England currently, a single Minister *of* State capable of shaping a national curriculum as a one-person enterprise)? Or should it be more a matter for local or 'de-centralised' decision-making of some sort? The former option certainly makes it much easier to control the curriculum and to ensure, if 'we' so desire, a high degree of equity and uniformity in its distribution across society; however, if it is overly explicit it can also lead to the deprofessionalisation of teachers (by, for example, reducing opportunities for school-based curriculum development), to stagnation, 'sameness' and dullness (through a lack of local diversity and a curtailment of curriculum 'conversations'), and to the kind of policy overload that in recent years in England and some other countries has driven so many teachers to the brink of exhaustion and despair. The latter option (the decentralisation of curriculum design) might enable a school's curriculum to rise above political ideologies, to promote the development of curricula that are more reflective of the interests and needs of local communities, and that perhaps are more inclined to incorporate educational research and theory into their considerations. However, it might equally put learners at the mercy of ill-prepared teachers and ill-informed school principals (particularly, perhaps, in the case of less stringently regulated 'free schools') and, if it does succeed, does so patchily, inconsistently and unfairly.

It is precisely this aspect of the 'Who Decides' question that makes me somewhat nervous when it comes to suggesting a 'curriculum for the future', and, I hope, explains a certain tentativeness in the suggestions put forward in the final chapter of *Understanding the School Curriculum*. I certainly am not nominating myself to take on this monumental task, nor to offer specific recommendations as to who else might do so, beyond endorsing a broad view that the more that relevant 'stakeholders' can be involved in such decisions the better.

Whose future is it that the curriculum is seeking to prepare young learners for, in any event? Can our desire as educationalists of whatever kind become so overly concerned with 'the future' as to turn it into an obsession that loses sight of the past or – more importantly, perhaps – of the *present*, including young learners' *experience* of the curriculum in the present they inhabit? What do we make of Keck's observations (below) about contemporary schooling more broadly, on the way in which policy's determination to bring about a particular future can impact negatively, conservatively and in a constraining manner on *both students' and teachers'* curriculum experience, compelling present activity to be aligned always to the achievement of that imagined future?

> Whether schooling looks backwards, forwards, or both, it is…rarely occupying the present richly, deeply. Generally speaking the problem of tense is managed through the domination of the present as the emergent is forced into alignment with the past-future continuum. …To be effective within the past-future continuum of schooling the teacher must be able to *harness* the present, and this generally involves minimizing and/or aligning all the interactions of the classroom. …The classroom is to be on-task, whether this be listening to the teacher (traditional) or doing group work (progressive). In short, teachers are responsible for exercising control, either through the orchestration of the 'voices' of the classroom toward a goal, or through authoritarian approaches, or both. This question of temporality is a fundamental problem for all teachers. To which temporality do they owe allegiance? In which tense is education to be conducted? Which time is education responsible for sustaining?
>
> (Keck 2012: 150; see, too, Dewey's assertion, 2009: 36, that education 'is a process of living and not a preparation for future living')

Regardless of whether it is 'the State' that is charged with designing the curriculum, or groups working independently of central control, or a mixture of both, one thing that is clear is that it is invariably – some might argue inevitably – adults (very often, relatively 'old' adults) who are making the decisions for and on behalf of young learners who must, whether they want to or not, agree to them. All well and good, we might say, and we would surely be doing our young people a disservice by denying them access to our own accumulated knowledge, wisdom and experience – until we remind ourselves that, very often, it is also adult *teachers* who may find themselves on the 'receiving end' of major curriculum decisions, that the 'experienced' are as liable to have their judgements influenced by vested interests as the inexperienced, and that (to develop an earlier point) without some kind of genuine consultation process involving all stakeholders, curriculum becomes not just a matter of the imposition of 'adult values', 'adult interests' and an 'adult vision of the future' on to a disenfranchised and largely unconsulted young, but of the values, interests and vision of a very specific group of adults with a very specific orientation to existing socio-economic arrangements in the nation and in the world. To quote Keck again:

> Schooling, from the ground of its status quo, does not cease to be utopian in that it claims to be preparing the coming generations to take their place in a history of ceaseless economic and social progress: *the present of the child must be rigorously framed and qualified by this adult future.*
>
> (emphasis added, ibid.: 149)

Curriculum tensions

The idea that the school curriculum needs to take full and appropriate account of changes in the wider world, as well as endeavouring to keep pace with them, is not a new one. Almost 100 years ago, in the Preface to his then very influential book *The Curriculum*, the American educationalist Franklin Bobbitt, whom we shall meet again in future chapters, made the following observation, which I think is as relevant in the early years of the twenty-first century as at the beginning of the twentieth:

> Since the opening of the twentieth century, the evolution of our social order has been proceeding with great and ever-accelerating rapidity. Simple conditions have been growing complex. Small institutions have been growing large. Increased specialization has been multiplying human interdependencies and the consequent need of coordinating effort. Democracy is increasing within the Nation; and growing throughout the world. All classes are aspiring to a full human opportunity. Never before have civilization and humanization advanced so swiftly.
>
> (Bobbitt 1971: iii)

Bobbitt continued (ibid.):

> As the world presses eagerly forward toward the accomplishment of new things, education must also advance no less swiftly. It must provide the intelligence and the aspirations necessary for the advance; and for stability and consistency in holding the gains. Education must take a pace set, not by itself, but by social progress.

More recently, other influential curriculum theorists have echoed Bobbitt's analysis – a reminder, perhaps, that relatively little has been achieved in the field of curriculum policy to heed such advice! Here, for example, is Jerome Bruner, observing a similar situation, and proposing a similar curricular response, towards the *end* of the twentieth century:

> Should schools aim simply to reproduce the culture [...] Or would schools, given the revolutionary changes through which we are living, do better to dedicate themselves to the equally risky, perhaps equally quixotic, ideal of preparing students to cope with the changing world in which they will be living?
>
> (Bruner 1996a: ix)

Elsewhere, Gibbs has argued that education should allow students the time to strive forward into the unknown in order that they might prepare themselves for uncertain futures – to enable young learners to 'confront the *anxiety* of the future with confidence, creativity and criticality' (Gibbs 2011: 61), while more recently still, the current UK Secretary of State for Education, generally very conservative in his views, has advised:

> Over the next ten years the world we inhabit will change massively. We are at an inflection point in the economic and educational development of nations. Technology will change out of all recognition how individuals work, how we teach and how students learn. Millions more across the globe will go onto higher – and post-graduate education. Globalisation will see the number of unskilled or low-skilled jobs in this country [sic] diminish further and the rewards to those with higher-level qualifications continue to soar further ahead. We cannot ignore, wish away or seek to stand aside from these developments. Not least because they promise a dramatic step forward in the unleashing of talent, the fulfilment of human potential and the reach of our creativity. So we need to have an education system equipped for that world – one that equips young people for all its challenges and opportunities. We need to cultivate

higher order thinking skills and creativity. We need to be adaptable and fleet-footed. We need to welcome innovation and challenge as a way to ensure we lead rather than meekly follow.

(M. Gove, Speech to ASCL 24 March 2012 Birmingham)

If the similarities between Bobbitt's and Gove's takes on human progress, separated as they are by almost a century, might lead us to conclude that nothing has changed and that curriculum development has always been – and perhaps always will be – faced with the challenge of responding to wider social, economic and environmental change that is in danger of perpetually threatening its existing shelf-life, we might justifiably argue that we really are currently living in times of unprecedentedly rapid change and a higher degree of global uncertainty and opportunity than we have ever experienced before. This presents curriculum not with a qualitatively *different* challenge but arguably one on a more serious, potentially radicalising scale; one that renders particularly compelling a related debate that is never far from centre stage in ongoing curriculum discussions – not just the question of who should be entrusted to make the key curriculum decisions, but that other persistent curriculum question regarding how far our curricula should be forward looking, how far they should concern themselves with preserving traditional knowledge and values 'from the past', and what the relationship and 'balance' should be between these two aspects of curriculum content and design.

Two particular changes, which might be seen as pivotal in terms of the ways in which human beings understand themselves and their world and interact with one another, are explored in some detail in Chapters 5 and 6. These changes are, first, the impact on our lives of the development of digital information and communications technologies and second, the not unrelated phenomenon of globalisation in its various forms and guises. Each of these developments reminds us, in relation to any desire we might have to 'shape' our future via formal education, that however worthwhile such a project might be, the future might not be as easy to shape or as easy to predict as we might like to believe, and that in addition to seeking to 'shape' it we might also need to develop the skills and aptitudes to respond to and 'manage' it.

The possibility that an uncertain, unpredictable future, rather than (or perhaps as well as) spreading panic and alarm, can open up exciting personal and collective possibilities, choices and opportunities, including pedagogic ones, and a radical challenge to the ways in which school curricula are currently conceived as managed entities, is summarised by Elliott (2000) who, after Posch (1994), talks of the

growing complexity of the economic and social conditions which impinge on people's lives, and the inability of centralized agencies to control their impact. In this context the latter depend on individual citizens to exercise more control over these conditions at the point of impact i.e. at the "grass roots" level. The challenge for teachers is to develop in their pupils those abilities which will enable them, as future citizens, to cope with the "unstructured situations" of everyday living. This will entail a learning process which engages pupils in making sense of the practical problems and issues such situations present, in making decisions about appropriate courses of action, and accepting responsibility for them.

(Elliott 2000: 254)

Žižek, as is his custom, takes the wider argument a little further, suggesting that present uncertainties and the unpredictability of the future – which can be very frightening, and can perhaps lead us to an unhelpfully defensive obsession with the present and the past – actually create the circumstances for us to effect *change in response to change:* 'I'm a pessimist in the sense that we are approaching dangerous times. But I'm an optimist for exactly the same reason. Pessimism means things are getting messy. Optimism means these are precisely the times when change is possible.' (Slavoj Žižek interview, Aitkenhead 2012)

One of the underpinning arguments of *Understanding the School Curriculum* is precisely that the rate and scale of change in the wider socio-economic world has brought us to a place from which we can – and perhaps must – contemplate some radical curriculum possibilities and changes (indeed, some countries are beginning to do this already): a set of circumstances that offers us what I am calling 'the clarity of radical choice' (see also Chapter 5). One very specific aspect of such choice regards our orientation toward 'knowledge', our definition of what we understand by knowledge that is 'useful' and 'powerful', and our considerations about knowledge that might have specific 'local' value and importance, as opposed to knowledge that we might believe has universal value and importance. (It is for this reason that I have decided to devote an entire chapter to issues around 'Knowledge'.) As Elliott continues, in his own analysis of a social world in which uncertainty is embraced rather than avoided – and indeed may be positively inflected as 'risk':

> [There is] an increasing consciousness on the part of citizens that they live in a "risk society" where the consequences of technological innovation for human well-being are ambiguous, context-bound, and beyond the power of science to predict with certainty. In the "risk society" scepticism and doubt about the use of science grow with increasing dependence on it. In this paradoxical situation definitions of what constitutes useful scientific knowledge can no longer be left to "central authorities" and scientific experts if public confidence in science is to be maintained. They need to be negotiated with those whose well-being may be affected in particular localities. Social processes for establishing "local truth" within our risk society will need to be established in ways which can handle differences and conflicts of perspective among citizens at the local level.
>
> (Elliott 2000: 254, summarising Posch 1994)

Elliott concludes his summary of Posch's argument:

> The challenge the "risk society" presents for teachers is to "develop both an appreciative and critical stance towards scientific knowledge", through inducting pupils into social processes within their own localities and communities aimed at establishing "local knowledge" about the impact of technology on their own and others' well-being.
>
> (ibid.)

We need to remember, of course, that, as Power (2007: 3) observes, the concept of risk remains elusive, contested and 'inherently controversial'. Just as uncertainty and rapid change can open up new possibilities and new ways of seeing and doing things, so they can also provide, so to speak, a market opportunity for those quick to capitalise on the notion that where there is uncertainty and change there is another profitable possibility, i.e. of its 'management'. Such a situation, Power suggests, offers us not radical change in the face of uncertainty, but rather the possibility that uncertainty can (and perhaps must) be 'organised', providing consumers with a 'fantasmatic source of reassurance and certainty in the face of an unruly and chaotic world' (Clarke and Moore 2013: 493). In relation to what uncertainty might mean for the school curriculum, it can, thus, result either in radical change or in a conservative resistance to change: to make early use of a metaphor to be introduced properly in Chapter 2, a 'paranoid', regulatory response to change, to uncertainty, and to their social and cultural implications. Referring to the controlling, conservatising impact of neo-liberalism's 'risk management' policy on public education, and to look ahead to issues of curriculum selection in Chapter 7, Power (ibid.) thus argues: 'In a short period of time the dominant discourse of risk management has shifted from the logic of calculation to that of organization and accountability.' (See also Touraine 2000: 27; Bates 2005: 102; Clarke 2012; and Hacking 1990, 2006.)

That is to say, while the initial thrust of risk management in response to uncertainty might essentially have been one of reducing the possible negative consequences of events and actions by way of making careful, balanced judgements regarding likelihood and potential severity, and of weighing up the pros and cons of any proposed course of action, risk management has extended its brief and its influence to require organisations and individuals to account for and justify any significant future actions they might intend to complete, including any potential financial consequences, potentially holding them responsible and accountable for any 'misjudgements' that might be adjudged to have occurred. The effects of such a risk management culture in terms of time and management will be all too familiar to many school principals and senior leaders. There is clearly a sense too, however, in which the effects of such a culture are experienced within classroom practice and curriculum policy – in, for example, the obsession of some politicians and policymakers with measurable, quantifiable educational 'outcomes', and in enforced pedagogies that focus more on achieving high grades for their students than on promoting critical, creative, autonomous learning, and that promote target-oriented, 'risk-free' learning rather than the kinds of open learning that are envisaged in and central to some of the proposed future oriented curriculum proposals that we have thus far considered. As Coffield and Williamson (2011: 24) wisely observe, the future does not simply threaten physical challenges which may be hard to overcome unless we learn the skills and develop the orientations effectively to do so, but the very act of centrally managing such threats by managing the populace's understanding of and orientation toward them (effectively, to deny the potential severity of such threats, delimiting it and 're-branding' it as manageable 'concern' to be responded to via individual actions and personalised 'responsibility') threatens democracy itself. 'As times change', Coffield and Williamson argue, and as 'new threats to democracy emerge', we have to 'think in innovative ways to overcome them'. Whether a curriculum of – or for – the future based on knowledge acquisition and the reproduction of dominant cultural forms and interests will be up to such a task is debatable, and inevitably, as with the other issues highlighted in this introductory chapter, is a question that will resurface regularly in the pages that follow.

An invitation

I have already said that (and explained why) my own suggestions as to what a curriculum 'for' (rather than 'of') the future might look like are necessarily tentative – and the curriculum 'alternatives' examined in the book's final chapter are presented more by way of supporting discussion and debate than didactically offering some kind of definitive curriculum answer. They are unapologetically informed by my own views and opinions, just as anyone else's reading of and approach to education will be (who but a fool would claim that such views were not infused with a specific, preferred philosophy, ideology and politics?) – and they are based on a personal view of what a fulfilling life might be and a vision of what I consider a better world to be (essentially, one that is manifestly and considerably more socially just, more inclusive, safer, happier, less violent and more friendly than the one I experience today). They will also draw on my own experience as a teacher, as a teacher educator and as an academic working in the field of Curriculum Studies: practical experience – within the terms of my own vision and philosophy, but also to a considerable extent within those of other people who might not altogether agree with me – of what 'works', along with more theoretical experience based on a little over 40 years of reading and doing education research and theory.

Inevitably, both my analyses and my suggestions are in part constructed out of my own politics and sensibilities (albeit by no means mine alone) and my persistent *questioning* of current curriculum policy in England and elsewhere – of holding it to account, so to speak – marks the book out as consciously and overtly political. In relation to the 'understanding' of the book's title, for example, the intention is that this should be a critical, potentially subversive and endlessly unfinished understanding, that is, an understanding of the fundamental political and ideological debates that underpin curriculum theory, policy and design, rather than simply the development of a knowledge of curriculum theory and curriculum models per se – based on a view that understanding is seldom 'complete' anyway, that social structures and institutions are never above critique and change, and that understanding is itself, at some level, a political choice no matter how vehemently we might protest to the contrary. Nor does the book propose any 'grand curriculum theory' of its own, choosing instead to offer the reader what my Australian colleagues might call a series of 'provocations'; indeed, the very suggestion, argued throughout the book, that curriculum is appropriately contestable and endlessly dynamic (unless this itself counts as a grand theory!) resists such theorising.

I'm aware also that, almost without noticing it, I may have slipped into an easy elision between 'curriculum' and 'national curriculum'. This is not surprising, perhaps, given the irresistible recent rise of national curricula around the globe. However, I do not want to create the impression that the issues I am inviting us to (re-)explore apply only to national curricula and to those obliged to follow them, or indeed to those non-compulsory aspects of the minimum national curricula that many nation states are blessed with. We are always being advised in England (e.g. DfE 2011) that there is a difference between the school curriculum and a national curriculum, and quite rightly so. For those of us working in England, this distinction has become somewhat blurred given the high levels of prescriptive content in our national curriculum. However, in many – perhaps most – other countries, as indeed in the private education sector in England, schools and teachers continue to have considerable autonomy in curriculum content and design, and it is my hope and intention that the issues raised in *Understanding the School Curriculum* will be of use and interest just as much to practitioners engaging in their own curriculum development and design as to those wishing to explore and critique imposed elements of the national curricula to whose demands they are working, or indeed the nature and influence on school-based curriculum development of the syllabuses and criteria of the examination boards whose demands, ultimately, both they and their students are required to meet. (Partly for this reason, and partly because it makes more sense in terms of the logic and broader structure of *Understanding the School Curriculum*, I have resisted the temptation to include a separate chapter on national curricula, opting instead to allow specific national curriculum issues to emerge in the discussion of various broader issues. Such specific issues arise particularly in Chapter 4 [on 'Knowledge'], Chapter 6 [on 'Globalisation' and on curriculum 'internationalisation'] and Chapter 8 [on curriculum decision-making]. For similar reasons, I have eschewed the option of writing a separate chapter on the implications of 'uncertainty' and 'change' on curriculum, or of the curriculum balance of past, present and future orientations – both topics again being re-cast as themes which cut across every other discussion and issue.)

I don't imagine for one moment that all readers will agree with the political stance of *Understanding the School Curriculum*, but all will, I hope, agree that the questions raised and explored have an enduring relevance and are worth raising, whatever our political, philosophical, theoretical or ideological perspective. This prompts me to extend an 'invitation' to readers to agree, if we can, on some very broad territories (which in themselves might also be described as 'principles') that might underpin our thinking in relation to designing a 'curriculum for the future' – if, indeed, we agree that such a project is worthwhile.

1   First of all, I'm hoping we might agree, broadly, that a curriculum for the future needs to address the *here and now* and to reflect what the policymaker identifies as essential or desirable knowledge and skills for all students to enable them to engage productively, happily and harmoniously with the social and natural world in which they find themselves immediately living and are likely to find themselves in the short term on finishing their formal education. (This is akin to what is sometimes referred to, these days, misleadingly perhaps, as 'cultural literacy'. We might disagree over these identifications, and we might argue about how broadly we interpret some of our terms – such as 'social and natural world'; however, the principle remains.) The emphasis on the here and now also relates to each student's *experience* of school and the curriculum, embracing the fostering of positive attitudes to learning and 'finding out', to exploring and more fully understanding oneself and others, to expressing oneself creatively, therapeutically and communicatively in a variety of ways (including through physical activity) through a variety of media, and to enjoying, understanding and appreciating the expressions of others.

2   The curriculum of the future needs to recognise that to an extent our future – as individuals, as groups, as nations, as a species – can be *shaped and directed* by what we do and learn in the present. Though the 'we' may be up for grabs, the question remains the same: 'What sort of future society – what sort of future world, of a future national and global citizenry – do we want, and how do we bring it about?'

3   Our curriculum for the future also needs to take account of the *unpredictable aspect of the future,* of the fact that some things happen regardless of our best laid plans, and of

the fact that our future citizens, whoever they might be and whatever job they might (or might not) have, are likely to have to deal with crises and take advantage of opportunities on an unprecedented scale in the very rapidly changing world in which we live. The curriculum for the future therefore needs to arm its students with the generic skills to tackle problems and opportunities individually and collectively which may be broadly though perhaps not precisely predictable, in addition to others which may well arrive with very little or no warning. An inevitable consequence of this is that the curriculum also needs to be flexible, dynamic, evolving and reflexive in nature – the very concept of 'curriculum' remaining endlessly open to interpretation and contestation.

I am going to suggest that all three of these elements need to be embedded in the school curriculum – that, effectively, we begin to understand and conceive of *any and all curricula as curricula for the future but also for the present*. Each element comprises knowledge, skills and values, and underpinning all three elements are the important, indispensible aims of ensuring that learning is enjoyable and rewarding, of helping students see a value in what they do, and – to borrow that rather over-used expression from the marketplace – of giving young students a genuine sense of 'ownership' of their learning.

Putting it all together

None of these discussions about – and analyses of – current curricula and proposed alternatives can take place without some shared interest and knowledge of key curriculum issues. Given the numerous overlaps between such issues, the business of organising them in the most helpful and coherent way has, if I am allowed a brief personal note, proved remarkably difficult and time-consuming, frequently bringing me to the brink of despair. After a great deal of consideration, I have finally organised the book into nine chapters which, as it were, 'speak' to one another and tell a story, but which can also be read in isolation and in any order. (The same is true, to an extent, of individual sections within chapters). There are at least three ways of reading a book of this kind: the traditional way (from start to finish); the non-sequential or partial chapter-by-chapter way (in which some chapters grab the attention before others); and the subject-search way, using the book's Index to locate and explore theories and topics of particular interest. *Understanding the School Curriculum* has been designed to be read in any or all of these ways, and to facilitate this I have, unusually, undertaken the indexing of the book myself.

Given its agreed length, I have been unable to include everything I might have wished to, but the decisions I have made about what to keep and what to shelve for future use have not been taken lightly and I hope represent a judicious choice. (The same applies in relation to the various chapter notes.) It is worth adding that I have been particularly exercised by the content and positioning of the chapter that immediately follows this one, entitled '*Curriculum dynamikos*'. I am still unsure whether this chapter is appropriately placed near the beginning of the book, on the basis that it establishes a key theme of the following text, or whether it appears 'too early' and might be better placed at the end, where it can draw retrospectively on the issues and examples that precede it. On balance, I have decided to leave it where it is, hoping that if readers do decide to skip it they may feel inclined to return to it later. For such readers, it might prove useful to know that the key theme it seeks to clarify concerns (what I am suggesting is) a need for the concept of curriculum to remain an open one that embraces and thrives on – rather than becoming stagnated or straitjacketed by – a certain overriding tension that exists not only within curriculum policy and practice itself but indeed in how we experience and manage our lives more widely. That tension is between two interacting, sometimes competing, sometimes symbiotic forces in the conduct of social and economic life, akin to Sigmund Freud's notions of the id, the ego and the superego and their relationships and interactions in the psychic nature and experience of the individual: one force which is freely creative, exploratory, developmental, iconoclastic, revolutionary, and excited by unpredictability and change; the other which is more regulatory, circumspect, controlling – the voice that always says to us 'Hang on a minute. Let's not be too hasty. Why change things if we don't need to?'

As is my practice, in each chapter I have, in addition to including as many of what I take to be the major theories and theorists of education as I can, endeavoured to invite readers to explore a number of theorists and ideas with which they may be less familiar, by way of encouraging new ways of looking at issues and circumstances that may have become dulled by familiarity. It goes without saying that these are the same theories and theorists that have helped *me* to look at things differently, often providing or suggesting a 'new language' for doing so. While in previous books I have included, at some length, references to Bourdieu, Lacan, Žižek and Sigmund Freud, in *Understanding the School Curriculum* I have drawn more substantially on the writings of Deleuze, Guattari, Bernstein, Ruti (whose work is surprisingly under-celebrated outside North America) and Rancière with the same purpose in mind.

I have also made use from time to time of some curriculum *metaphors*, mostly purloined from other social commentators. These include Holland's metaphor, after Deleuze and Guattari, of jazz music and the symphony orchestra; Deleuze and Guattari's own metaphor of schizophrenia and paranoia; and the artist Maurizio Cattelan's very powerful and eloquent visual metaphor 'Charlie Don't Surf'. None of these metaphors works perfectly in relation to the arguments I am putting forward, nor, in all probability, do they say anything that could not be said without them. I have chosen to use these metaphors, however, precisely because I believe they can help us to think differently about things – or (a phrase that will be known to anyone familiar with qualitative social research methodology) to 'make the familiar strange'. This is a particularly useful approach – even a necessary one, perhaps – when the thing we are trying to see differently (in this case, 'the curriculum') is so resistant to change, so self-justifying, and made so familiar over a period of time: a concept so 'deadened by routine use' as Lacan (1977: 33) put it, as to have effectively naturalised itself in our collective consciousness. Unlike much academic language, metaphors also have the capacity to render a text more 'writerly': that is (Barthes 1990) to invite the reader into a provocative but non-didactic discussion space in a way which encourages interpretive, idiosyncratic readings, rather than an attempt to (Rancière 1991) offer the reader some kind of 'explication'. I hope you enjoy your own interpretive, idiosyncratic engagement with the rest of the book.

Note

1 This statement itself is in need of some qualification. When I say the curriculum has (in most countries that have had a formal curriculum) changed very little over time, I am referring to its basic structure, to much of its actual content, and to its broad rationale. Many school curricula have changed in some ways, of course, for example, in recent tendencies to ape neo-liberal, post-Fordist philosophies, policies and practices in the wider socio-economic environment. Such developments may not have posed a significant threat to standard, subject-based curricula or to the viability of the subject disciplines themselves, but have resulted in a marked increase of *emphasis* on economic-related curriculum aspects such as preparing young people to contribute to the so-called 'knowledge economy'.

Chapter 2

'Curriculum dynamikos'

[H]ow we understand the world is inevitably mediated by the language we use to represent it. This suggests that many of the things that we take to be "real" and "commonsensical" are merely social constructs that have become so deeply ingrained in our psyche that we have lost track of their constructed status and come to regard them as unquestionably true.

(Ruti 2009: 20)

Curriculum design and review is a continuous, cyclic process.

(New Zealand Ministry of Education 2007: 37)

Unfinished business: Curriculum as contestable

In his book *Curriculum Theory: Conflicting Visions and Enduring Concerns*, Michael Schiro observes: 'concerns about education are not new, and we need to realize that many of today's new issues and "fads" are related to enduring educational concerns that have long been debated' (2013: xv) – adding a little later: 'As individuals, we are constantly disagreeing with each other – and with ourselves – about what we should be doing in our schools' (ibid.: 2).

In *Understanding the School Curriculum* I want to elaborate a little on each of these points. For one thing (and this is substantially the content of Chapter 3), I want to consider some of the different ways in which we might – and others have sought to – identify and define curriculum, to answer the question 'What is it?' In doing so, we must always keep in mind Bates' observation (2005: 96) that curriculum 'is a tricky word as it has both a general meaning (everything that goes on in an educational situation) and a specific one (the content of what is taught), as well as a variety of meanings in between'. A pressing reason for engaging in such an activity, however, is neatly encapsulated in a recent remark of Olof Olafsdottir's (2010): 'What is education for? And what is the role of teachers? Surely these questions are unnecessary; after all, everyone knows the answers. Yet far too often it would seem that education and teachers are taken for granted.'

An underlying premise of *Understanding the School Curriculum* is that we must never 'take education [or teachers] for granted', and should never stop questioning its purposes and practices, regardless of efforts that others might make to encourage us to do so. I shall argue in this chapter that rather than seeking out a definitive answer to the question 'What is it?' (posed in the following chapter), we should rather be conceptualising curriculum as endlessly unfinished and evolving, asking ourselves instead 'What is it *now*?', '*Why* is it as it is?', and 'What else might it be, now or in the future?' We might even, as some have done, take our questioning a step further and cast our quest as something of a *political* project – one that aims to remove curriculum decision-making away from powers that might seek to deny curriculum's contestability, and restoring it to the hands of powers more inclined, and perhaps better positioned, to reassert its openness and flexibility. As Pinar puts this proposition to an academic audience, though it is readily transferable to an audience of teachers:

> We must work to understand what curriculum is and might be. And this means we must focus on education, not just on schooling. We must labour to remain and/or become intellectuals, not just professors (i.e. employers of increasingly corporatized institutions). In doing so, we must encourage our students – prospective and practicing teachers – to become intellectuals as well, finding in their various locales sites of resistance to top-down, business-style reform, opportunities for solidarity with their colleagues and with students, to reassert their academic freedom, their jurisdiction over curriculum content and the means by which its study is assessed.
>
> (Pinar 2004: 180)

Abiding issues

If an argument for what I shall call 'curriculum dynamism' – and therefore for ongoing curriculum development – is a central purpose of this opening chapter, an additional, related aim (and this is, essentially, the rationale for the first part of the chapter) is to attempt to identify and to look more closely at some of Schiro's 'enduring educational concerns that have long been debated'. I will do this partly by way of introducing themes which will appear and reappear in the discussions that take place throughout the remainder of the book, partly by way of introducing what we might call some of the main 'sites' within which curriculum discussion and disagreement, and its dynamic potential, are likely to be located. I am calling these 'abiding issues' simply on the basis that they have been around for such a long time, continuing to exercise us as they reappear in various (dis)guises in educational landscapes that, at least on the surface, are themselves constantly shifting. In some later chapters (specifically, Chapters 5 and 6), I will invite readers to look more closely at three very specific 'current' issues for education and curriculum, which I think do not qualify for the title 'abiding' even though they may be seen as providing fresh contexts for some issues which are. These are: the impact of digital technologies on learning and on how we understand learning and teaching; the questions that 'globalisation' in its various manifestations might ask of national school curricula; and, embedded within these considerations, the rapid pace of change generally in the world, and its implications for human life. Setting aside for now these 'newer' issues, what, then, are some of the curriculum issues that do 'abide' so persistently?

Let's begin, for the sake of argument, with a premise that every school, its students, its teachers, *needs* a curriculum in the most general sense of the word: that is to say – to leap ahead for a moment – it needs to have an agreed, principled plan of what teachers should teach and students should learn, that this should include, at some level of specificity, an agreed (and 'demonstrable') set of skills and items of knowledge, that there should be a structure and strategy for putting the plan into practice and monitoring its success, and that without such an arrangement schools would not be schools at all but simply detention centres or glorified play-centres.[1] Let's go further, and say that in order to ensure a degree of fairness and equity, every *country* needs a kind of *national curriculum* that all state sector schools (and perhaps even all schools) should subscribe to.

Most, if not all, of us can probably accept some such premises without too much difficulty. The problems arise, however, when we are very quickly confronted by a number of key questions arising from them – for instance:

- On what basis do we decide what is important and what is less so? How do we set about identifying 'useful' and 'powerful' knowledge and skills? How do we define 'useful' and 'powerful' anyway?

- How often do we revisit our curriculum (or curricula), and to what extent do we seek to keep it/them 'up to date' with changing circumstances in the wider world which may impact on changes in our learners' needs? (Or do we, rather, see the curriculum as having a more regulatory function – of providing some kind of *balance to* or *critique of* some of those changes?)

- How do we *structure* our curriculum, and how does that structure relate to how we understand learning, knowledge and human development? Do we divide it into traditional subjects or disciplines? Do we tie it to a developmental pattern such as that proposed by Piaget, so that students move incrementally from 'easier' to 'more difficult' concepts, skills and materials – from 'concrete' to more 'abstract' learning? Or might we consider a topic-based approach as our basis for curriculum design, that, in terms of most existing arrangements, would represent and demand a more cross-curricular approach: something approaching, perhaps, Bruner's 'spiral curriculum' (Moore 2012)? Or might we consider something broader still, that begins not with 'disciplines' at all (though these may continue in a more subservient role) but with a radical return to those most fundamental of curriculum questions 'What do we want the curriculum – education – to achieve? And how do we plan to achieve it?'

- Do we require all learners to follow exactly the same curriculum – whether within a school or classroom or country? Or some of the same curriculum? Or have completely or partially different curricula for different (groups of) students? What account do we take of student/parent/teacher/school selection and choice? How do we square the circle of valuing and promoting individual freedom while at the same time ensuring some uniformity and equality of access in our curriculum offer? If we have a centrally mandated 'national curriculum', how much of it should constitute a compulsory 'core' and how much be left to local choice? And if there is a National Core Curriculum, '[W]hat are the subjects most worthy of study? Who is to determine which subjects are best?' (Eisner 1979: 55). Should we have national curricula at all? And at which point – if at all – should student choice take precedence over commonality and compulsion? (For example, within the subject-based curriculum should students be given some choice, albeit limited, of which subjects to specialise in at a certain age followed, perhaps, by opportunities for further specialisation later on, as is the case in many countries still using public examination systems like the UK's GCSEs and 'A levels', or is it preferable to adopt programmes such as the International Baccalaureate in which students must continue to study a wider range of subjects throughout their school careers?)

- If our curriculum incorporates different curriculum goals (for example, geared toward meeting the country's economic needs, preparing young people for the world of work, helping young people become creative, socially confident, respectful and tolerant citizens, promoting lifelong learning skills), how mutually compatible are they, and how do we address any actual or potential *in*compatibilities?

- Should our curricula seek to promote actively *critical* citizens, willing and able to recognise and seek to address any perceived shortcomings in the society in which they live? Or do we want to produce a more compliant citizenry, which simply 'buys into' existing dominant values and socio-economic arrangements and so reproduce them? (Where do we stand in relation to Finkelstein's [1984: 277] assertion that [public] education should 'arm the nation's young with the intellectual wherewithal to criticize, reconstruct, or reform the society they will enter as adults'?)
- How do we understand and approach issues of culture and cultural difference, including culture-related *values*, in our curriculum? How do we avoid the imposition of 'dominant' cultures and values on our (perhaps reluctant) students? And in any event, is it wrong to attempt to do so?
- What steps do we take to ensure an appropriate fit between our curriculum aims and the ways in which the curriculum is actually taught and experienced?
- How do we *assess* the success of the curriculum, as well as the success of learners in completing it and teachers in mediating it? How do we balance what is most effective with what is economically and logistically viable?

Even as we struggle, individually, collectively, nationally with such questions, yet others begin to emerge:

- If we decide we ought to have a *national* curriculum, do we mean by this a curriculum aimed mainly at promoting national interests and culture (what we might, in its more extreme forms, call a national-*ist* curriculum) – or do we simply mean an 'entitlement' curriculum to which everyone in the nation has access? If the latter, to what extent do we seek to 'internationalise' our curriculum, attempting to prepare 'global citizens' with an understanding of and a sense of responsibility toward the planet as a whole and its inhabitants? If the former, how do we manage to combine the perhaps competing demands of inclusion, entitlement and commonality, of 'sameness' and 'difference'? In an effort to ensure the 'same for everyone', is there a danger of overlooking the idiosyncratic, contingent nature of teaching, learning and schooling, or the idiosyncratic needs, wishes and talents of individual students, whose appropriately nurtured richness might benefit both the individual and society? How do we ensure that in our efforts to offer the same access to 'key' knowledge and skills to all students we do not, at the same time (perhaps through our efforts to assess the efficacy of our stated aim), fall foul of Foucault's 'triadic elision', whereby 'conformity becomes the reigning norm', leading to 'an ever more finely tuned streamlining and ranking in accord with that norm', resulting in the construction of 'normal' (included) and 'deviant' (excluded) learners? If we decide, instead, to focus on the individual, on the idiosyncratic, how might we avoid doing so at *the expense of* promoting collaboration and co-operation, consideration for others and selflessness, community consciousness and internationalisation?
- If our curriculum is more 'about and for the nation' rather than simply available to all young people *in* the nation, what balance do we consider appropriate between on the one hand recognising, valuing and perpetuating all that [we as curriculum

designers think] is good from our past (our 'heritage'), and on the other hand adopting a more forward-looking, 'prospective' or evolutionary position, aimed both at shaping what we may feel is a better future world (the search for agreement on which will give us yet more food for thought and cause for argument!) and at preparing young learners for what might be an uncertain, unpredictable future?

• And underlying all our thoughts about the *means* by which our broad curriculum – whatever we may decide it is and for whatever purpose(s) – is actualised, what do we mean when we talk about curriculum 'content'? Are we simply referring to so-called (and largely pre-specified) 'knowledge content' (as I think is often the case)? Or can we also envisage and produce curricula which are based, for example, on values and processes, or which perhaps go little further than elaborating very broad aims and principles to be interpreted and fleshed out by schools and teachers as they see fit? Would such a curriculum – which could clearly be constructed so as to satisfy the very broad criteria outlined at the start of this section – have to be described as 'content free'? Or might we argue that it still *has* content, albeit of a different character: i.e. that the values, processes, aims and principles *represent* the content?

'Curriculum dynamikos'

Given the number of questions we have already asked of the curriculum – and the complexity with which each one of them is imbued – it would be surprising, and indeed somewhat worrying, if there was universal agreement regarding every answer. Indeed, two of the principal arguments in this book, as each abiding issue re-presents itself, are as follows:

1   The curriculum – let us say, the 'future curriculum' – should be both dynamic and contested: that is to say, its potential for evolution, its creativity, even its 'betterment' are sustained by its not standing still, by its resistance to 'completion' (even as it might purport to seek out such completion), by its *embracing* of discussion, debate and disagreement over what it 'is' and what it might look like, i.e. curriculum policy should welcome rather than shy away from big questions like 'What is it for?', 'Do we really need it?', 'If so, who needs it? And why?' In support of this, I have proposed the term 'curriculum dynamikos' by way of acknowledging the Greek roots of our word 'dynamic', and in the hope that this grammatically heretical act (attaching a Greek adjective to a Latin noun) will not engender too much grief in those for whom such things matter. It is important to note in this regard that in its original meaning 'dynamic' refers not just to movement, to development, to argument and debate, to an ongoing capacity for change, as it is very often understood these days, but also to 'strength'; in short, what we might call 'strength-through-development' and 'strength-in-development'.

   Such a view of curriculum understands curriculum development as the endless pursuit (deliberate and 'knowing' perhaps at one level, though seldom acknowledged as such) of something that can never be 'perfect' and can only ever *approach* perfection contingently in relation to the particular place and time within which it is located: one which will always please some and disappoint others and that will always be shaped by certain interests and specific circumstances in the ever-evolving world in which it is embedded. It is important to state immediately and unequivocally that this does *not* signal support for the somewhat manic outpouring of curriculum policy directives that schools and teachers have had to deal with in England in recent years, whereby no sooner has one policy initiative been put in place than another, often contradictory, initiative arrives hot on its heels. Teachers, schools and learners clearly need a certain degree of *stability* within ongoing curricular development and debate if they are to function effectively and happily, and the notion of the curriculum dynamikos should not be seen as an enemy of such stability. This is largely a matter of time and timing. The curriculum dynamikos speaks of a conversation, a debate that unfolds over time, that may introduce practical change but that does so via a process of discussion, negotiation and debate, and, where it does result in change of a more radical nature (as in some instances described in the book's final chapter, in countries as diverse as China, Singapore and Sri Lanka), gives that change a fair, transitional wind both to embed itself and to test out its efficacy. The more genuinely engaged and engaging approach to curriculum development and practice implicit in the idea of the curriculum dynamikos is, I would argue, one that is particularly appropriate to societies which perceive themselves as – and/or strive to be – *democratic*. As Hoggett (2004: 84) has very persuasively argued with reference to differences of opinion over public policy more widely, some such differences in democracies are inevitable and should be welcomed; rather than avoiding dialogue and disagreement, we should perhaps embrace and value the psychic *energy* that argument reflects and generates: 'Group desires and interests will always at some point collide, and without such conflict there can be no energy for further development. We must learn to enjoy our conflicts; it is only when we are afraid of them that the trouble begins' (Hoggett: ibid.). In any event, as Eisner (1979: 275–6) points out, education is far too important a subject for us *not* to have disagreements, arguments and debates about!

To approach curriculum in this way should not represent any major difficulty. It is, after all, reflective of understandings and experiences that we are very familiar with in our daily lives more broadly, both inside and outside the world of formalised social institutions. There is a particularly apposite passage from Mari Ruti's book *The Summons of Love* which, apart from its specific and particular relevance to issues concerning uncertainty and change (issues that will be returned to, particularly in Chapters 8 and 9), bears ready translation to our understandings of curriculum more generally – and to not just the impossibility of 'completeness' (that is, of curriculum being finally and universally defined) but also to the important developmental role of believing in and seeking out such completeness:

> [T]he tension between what we are and what we yearn to become is what is what lends human life much of its innovative energy. Because this tension keeps us from feeling fully satisfied with our lives, it compels us to reinvent ourselves on a regular basis. It repeatedly pushes us into cycles of personal renewal that guarantee that we do not become emotionally stagnant or complacent; it prevents us from becoming bored with ourselves by supplying us with an endless array of new aims, aspirations, and preoccupations. It is, in short, the underpinning of everything that is *creative* about our lives.
>
> (Ruti 2011: 2, emphasis added)

Just as in the case of our individual lives, so in the case of school curricula we might surmise that it is the experience and commitment to (endless) 'becoming', to the constant pursuit of wishes and goals that might always leave us wanting more, rather than a seeking out and endeavouring to settle on some definitive 'being', that fosters innovation and creativity. This is an important concept, and one which will re-emerge later in discussions of what I will call *the tyranny of The Answer* – that is to say, the way in which not simply the curriculum taken as a whole but also its constituent elements so often exist in thrall to the notion of completion (complete understanding, 'right answers', defined, itemised and legitimised knowledge) rather than embracing in-completion and 'The Question'. Such a re-emergence will effectively lead us to another very important proposal – that, in addition to dynamism and disagreement lending energy and strength *to* the curriculum, the curriculum itself might have a responsibility to *foster* dynamism and disagreement in those for whom it is designed: not to (re)produce a citizenry that is gratuitously confrontational and self-wearyingly hyperactive, but one in which conflict(s) can, at least in some circumstances, be drawn upon positively and creatively if not always 'enjoyed'.

2   Despite, and in seemingly permanent tension with, the need for curriculum to be dynamic, flexible, provisional and contingent, I will also be arguing that there is, globally, to one degree or another, an abiding, pervasive *resistance* within much centralised education policy to the possibility and desirability of curriculum's dynamism and contestability, and that even when 'change' is implemented it might more appropriately be described as the modification of existing models, constructed within existing dominant ideologies – currently, to flag an issue to be returned to shortly, the ideology of neo-liberalism. (Such resistance, as will become evident, is much stronger in some countries' national curricula than in others.) It is a resistance, which, following on from Ruti, we might also experience in more general terms in our personal and private engagements with social life, and one which exerts a powerful gravitational pull toward curriculum stasis and definition. To play a little with Fukuyama's terminology (Fukuyama 1992), rather than remaining open to the idea of genuine curriculum development and evolution, there is, for all the talk we often hear in public policy pronouncements of the school curriculum 'needing to keep pace with change' and 'needing to be appropriate for the 21st century', a dangerous, inhibiting discourse at large which effectively speaks of *The End of Curriculum* (thereby threatening to bring about *The End of Curriculum Studies*) – a discourse which proclaims 'This, finally, after years of experience, discussion and trial, is what we can say the definitive school curriculum, albeit in broad terms, will always look like': a claim curiously supported sometimes by the 'evidence' that precisely because school curricula have changed so very little over the many decades of public education they must inevitably be fundamentally 'right'.

This essentially conservative tendency toward stasis is, I believe, born essentially of a *fear of change*: in particular, fear of a radical change in the social and economic status quo within the nation state, or even *between* nation states, some of which remain prosperous while (and perhaps because) others remain poor. Such a view helps to explain a phenomenon that curriculum theorists have often commented on: that is to say (see, e.g., Tseng 2013; Gee and Lankshear 1995; Mahoney and Hextall 2001), that while changes in the workings of national economies within globalised, post-Fordist capitalism have pressed – often very hard and often with great success – for parallel changes in education, with demands (for example) for the prioritisation and development of specific work-related knowledge and skills in what have come to be known as 'knowledge economies', the actual 'look' of school curricula globally has changed remarkably little over the last 150 years: broadly speaking, the same division of knowledge and skills into the same subject disciplines, examined and taught in much the same way now as then. A metaphor I shall be borrowing from Deleuze and Guattari's project of 'schizoanalysis' (1977, 2004), which re-applies the pathologising language of psycho-analysis to a critique of global Capitalism (within which, of course, almost all public education is currently situated), to describe such resistance is that of *paranoia*.

If the above summarises what I see as comprising a central debate and a central difficulty for curriculum study, curriculum development and curriculum design (also, naturally, of great relevance to the curriculum *experience*, for both students and teachers) – that is to say, a set of issues around the desirability or otherwise of curriculum dynamism versus curriculum 'solutions' or curriculum *stasis* – it also finds embedded within it a potential difficulty, perhaps even a contradiction, for *Understanding the School Curriculum* itself: one that will perhaps become more apparent as its argument unfolds. This concerns the fact that on the one hand, *Understanding the School Curriculum* counsels against 'final' curriculum definitions and models, while on the other hand it is clearly underpinned by agendas of its own – suggesting, perhaps, that it has a definitive curriculum model of its own in mind: one including, for instance, the very imperative that curriculum *should always have* the capacity to be readily flexible and willing to evolve.

One can only come clean about this and confess that while no specific model of curriculum is being proposed in *Understanding the School Curriculum*, and no specific curriculum content championed, the book does have a position of its own in an ongoing curriculum debate whose continuing existence it supports and believes in. The point here is that a desire to keep our definitions of curriculum open is not equivalent to sacrificing some genuine educational principles that we might have in our approaches to curriculum development and design: in my own case, for example, a desire for curriculum to promote social justice, and never to favour, either deliberately or incidentally, the interests and talents of some students over others. Nor does it imply dispensing with, as permanently unattainable, some social and political *goals* that we might wish public education broadly to incorporate and to bring about. Underpinning any desire that resists and refutes completion, we can – and perhaps must, if I may risk appearing presumptuous – pursue and foster an educational agenda that does not have to be overly detailed or prescriptive in terms of content and content 'delivery', but is *principled* and fundamentally *ethical*: that is to say, to propose and to work with some 'principled principles' that might underpin a curriculum for the future as construed from a particular vantage point in a particular present. It is for this reason that I have been disinclined in this book to commit to specific details regarding what a 'curriculum for the future' might look like, but have placed greater emphasis on the matter of curriculum 'vision'. For if we do not have some vision of 'the good curriculum', if we do not enter the curriculum debate, we cannot really hope to contribute, either, to the curriculum's ongoing evolution.

But it is time to turn in a little more detail to the nature of the dynamism I am suggesting, and to the social, economic and psychic forces – in the wider 'public' world of social and economic policy, philosophy and ideology, but also in the 'private' world that additionally demands reference to the individual's and social group's 'psychic economy' – that might either promote or impede it. My approach in this regard is to offer three similar but subtly different versions of a tension or, more accurately, a set of tensions between two interconnected positions of – broadly speaking – freedom and constraint, in the hope that readers will take some of the abiding issues highlighted in the first part of this chapter and re-examine them independently within the contexts offered by these three versions, the first of which concerns a global political tension between policies of conservatism and policies of what has come to be known as neo-liberalism.[2]

Policy tensions I: Conservatism and neo-liberalism

In his book, *Educating the Right Way: Markets, Standards, God and Inequality* (2006), Michael Apple analyses the conservatising influence on public education in the USA of a loose but powerful alliance between the political Right, located within discourses and ideologies of conservatism and neo-liberalism in central government, and discourses of *neo*-conservatism located largely within the (extremely influential) religious Right. Such an analysis views neo-liberalism as principally concerned with maintaining the *economic* status quo within the nation, defending and endorsing free-market capitalism by rendering it more effective in terms of global competition, while conservatism and neo-conservatism, driven by fears of social breakdown and disintegration, are more concerned with curriculum initiatives such as 'character education' that seek to defend and endorse particular elements of a particular version of a past (understood as a 'better time') in which people are imagined to have generally behaved in more neighbourly and respectful ways both to one another and to the nation and its 'core values'. The *neo*-conservatism of the religious Right, which includes a moral crusade to spread a form of fundamentalist Christian capitalism around the globe by whatever means it takes, is a force that is perhaps rather more influential in the USA than in most other countries – certainly than in England, where the influence of the Christian Church has waned considerably since the turn of the century.[3] However, I want to suggest that the same kinds of policy tensions described by Apple in the USA between conservatism and neo-liberalism are also found in England and, no doubt, in many other nations around the world; that their impact on school curricula (as indeed on formal education more widely) is profound; and that that influence is more likely to inhibit curriculum dynamism and evolution than to promote or facilitate it.

Another way of putting this is to say that in their respective ways both conservatism (which depends on high levels of state control) and neo-liberalism (which promotes a reduction in centralised control and greater decision-making power to various 'markets') are fundamentally conservatis*ing* in nature when it comes to public school curricula (and not *just* public school curricula) – but that they are conservatising in different ways. Conservatism itself, for example, is interested in preserving and promulgating the status quo of a nation's dominant cultures, or in attacking those elements of the status quo that it finds threatening in relation to perceived values and social relations (including what might be termed 'power relations') of the past. It is therefore particularly concerned with the preservation and passing on of certain traditions (and the marginalisation or exclusion of others), of the educational celebration of historical national figures selected as heroic, and of (mainly national) historical events selected as exemplary. Though conservatism may claim to be concerned with the interests of individuals, its emancipatory rhetoric might conceal a rather less altruistic purpose. That is to say, a conservative education, rather than providing young learners with the tools to construct their freedom and expand their life choices, might be more concerned in reality with 'preservation or reproduction of what has been attained [in the past]…[so that] it becomes conservation *for the purpose of preventing anything new*' (Bernfeld 1973: 83, emphasis added; see also Keck 2012: 99).

Unlike 'small c' political conservatism, neo-liberalism is an ideology and a theory of social, political and economic practices espousing a belief that (Harvey 2007: 22) 'human well-being can best be advanced by the maximization of entrepreneurial freedoms within an institutional framework characterized by private property rights, individual liberty, unencumbered markets, and free trade' – a theory in which '[t]he role of the state is to create and preserve an institutional framework appropriate to such practices' (ibid.). Neo-liberalism is thus more concerned with an education that is essentially a preparation for individual and national participation in an unchallenged but constantly evolving global free market – ensuring, so to speak, that the educated citizenry is able to work with that evolving system in ways that preserve the *economic* status quo or render it more advantageous to the nation in question. Its prime curriculum thrust is therefore less concerned with personal enrichment or the preservation of certain 'enduring' cultures, values and traditions, than with 'fill[ing] students with the knowledge that is necessary to compete in today's rapidly changing world' (Apple 2006: 4). In this, neo-liberalism may be seen to be similarly duplicitous in its education policy as conservatism, and indeed may share conservatism's tendency to conceal controlling and conserving practices behind rhetorics of personal empowerment and emancipation.

Seen thus, the sometimes antagonistic, sometimes cautiously collaborative forces of conservatism and neo-liberalism in *curriculum policy* can be understood to have something very important in common with each other despite their obvious differences of emphasis and approach – one dishing out compulsory prescriptions and vaccinations to a 'sick' society, the other peddling compulsory self-help. This commonality is that they both represent, in their respective ways, existing dominant interests, both place a perceived (and highly idiosyncratic) 'national interest' above individual human development, and both may thereby be characterised, in terms of curriculum content and design, as essentially *reproductive*. Conservatism, that is, is reproductive of old (in the case of England, some might say 'colonial') traditions and perceived values, of the status of certain cultural tastes and artefacts over others, of a particular, traditional view of and approach to the teaching and learning of clearly defined and officially sanctified subjects or disciplines, while neo-liberalism is equally reproductive in validating, lauding and placing beyond criticism the practices and values of (often very weakly regulated) free-market capitalism.

A problem in countries such as England, which have political parties calling themselves 'Conservative', is that such parties very often place reduced state control and more freedom for 'the Market' at the heart of their policies, suggesting that they are often more neo-liberal in their approach than conservative. Their 'conservatism' in the sense I have indicated here resides in their simultaneous insistence on and prioritisation of the perpetuation of dominant cultures, traditional values, existing laws and, in broad terms, existing socio-economic hierarchies. This project, unlike the contemporaneous neo-liberal one, demands a relatively high level of state control, as may be witnessed in education policies demanding highly prescriptive national curricula and increased powers for education ministers. The extent of such centralised state control over education in England is starkly outlined by Coffield and Williamson (2011: 63) in their excellent book *From Exam Factories to Communities of Discovery*. They report:

Since 1960, through legislation, secretaries of state in England have acquired around 2,500 new powers. Despite all the rhetoric from the [current UK government] about returning power to the people, Michael Gove, the current Secretary of State for Education in England, is taking 50 additional powers in the Education Bill which is, at the time of writing in June 2011, being debated in Parliament.

In opposition to the reproductive curriculum of conservatism and neo-liberalism, and to introduce another term to be returned to later on, I want to posit the idea of the *[r]evolutionary curriculum*: a curriculum, that is, which keeps itself open to development and change and is prepared to challenge the status quo both of the curriculum itself at any given point in time *and the wider social arrangements within which it is* situated – evolutionary in its more tentative forms, when it is happy to engage dialogically with development as a longer-term, more open-ended project; *r*evolutionary when it seeks to address more fundamental questions (Do we need a curriculum at all? Should learning really be organised 'sequentially', via subject disciplines and 'bodies of knowledge'? Should curricula encourage or permit '*non*-compliance', and/or promote 'critical literacy'?) in a more radical way as a matter of urgency, with curriculum *alternatives* rather than simple curriculum improvements or modifications in mind. Unlike the reproductive curriculum, the [r]evolutionary curriculum is more likely to celebrate difference, to focus on individual well-being within contexts other than the purely economic, and to be guided by the social-liberal ideologies of many teachers as referenced above.

Policy tensions 2: Bernstein's policy 'dislocations'

The same tension identified by Apple in regard to education policy in the USA, between on the one hand a conservative focus on 'tradition' (and what Apple calls 'compliance') and, on the other hand, an obsessive (neo-liberal) concern that education should contribute to maintaining national competitiveness in a global marketplace, is highlighted by the English sociologist of education Basil Bernstein in his analysis of late twentieth-century educational policy and reform in the UK. Referring to the same differing policy directives in terms of a 'complementary relation' (indicating, perhaps, that both directives are essentially on the same conservative 'side', if pulling in somewhat different directions), Bernstein points to a specific tension between what he sees as a persistently conservative *school culture* (particularly in terms of power relations between teachers and students, and within staffing hierarchies) which is supported by conservative policy with its emphasis on 'pupil discipline', 'traditional', centrally designed and mandated curricula, and teacher and school evaluation linked to pay and resourcing, and more recent neo-liberal policy in which the State publicly distances itself from school and classroom practice by (for example) devolving previously centrally-managed budgets to schools, by encouraging schools to weaken their links to the Centre through developing (financial) relationships with businesses and charities, and in an emphasis on the economic demands on the nation of an evolving global marketplace which does not, however, undermine so-called traditional values.

In Bernstein's political theory, the expressions 'retrospective pedagogic identity' and 'prospective pedagogic identity' are employed to describe the different ways in which education policy seeks to preserve a (perhaps mythic) past, or to somehow project a particular version of past-and-present into the future, typically drawing on 'some central, often considered national discourse' (2000: 66): for example, the discourse of the shopkeeper nation, the enterprise nation, the Christian/churchgoing nation, the tolerant nation, the nation of good neighbours, and so on. Bernstein's use of the terms 'pedagogic' and 'identity' can thus appear somewhat confusing. They refer to how schooling is conceived and constructed in official policy, rather than to the 'identities' of classroom practitioners or to what teachers actually do.

While Bernstein's terms do not equate exactly with conservatism and neo-liberalism (both of which terms he also uses), they nevertheless do share some significant common characteristics. The retrospective identity, for example, has much in common with conservatism, while the prospective identity has more in common with neo-liberalism. The difference between the two 'identities' is also subtle. In the case of the retrospective pedagogic identity, the emphasis in educational terms is upon preserving a particular version of the past by 'recontextualising' it in present and future practices: that is to say, to somehow 'stabilise' that past (ibid.: 67) or to prevent its potential demise (the 'fear factor' in conservatism, referred to earlier on in this chapter). In curricular terms, this means exercising tight control over curriculum *inputs* to ensure that they support rather than challenge the version of the past (and indeed of the present) that those responsible for designing and mandating the curriculum *wish* to 'stabilise', perhaps in the face of perceived threats to such stability (for instance, the emergence of a radical politics that challenges existing socio-economic relations, or of a mode of communication such as the internet which might be seen as resisting the central control upon which the stabilisation of the past depends). Although Bernstein asserts that the retrospective pedagogic identity is primarily concerned with curriculum 'inputs' rather than 'outputs' (the latter, in the form, say, of public examination grades, being arguably of more use to the individual than to the country as a whole), we might argue that it is nevertheless important for the successful establishment of the retrospective pedagogic identity that, in addition to these curricular inputs, a pedagogy and assessment regime is imposed through which to ensure that curricular control is not weakened. Consequently, retrospective identities are formed (ibid.: 66) 'by hierarchically ordered, strongly bounded, explicitly stratified and sequenced discourses and practices'.

Reminding us of their equally conservatising nature, prospective identities are, Bernstein advises us, also 'formed…from the past'. However, 'it is not the same past [as in the case of retrospective identities]' (ibid.: 67). While conservative retrospective identities are concerned to preserve very broad traditions, values, philosophies and ideologies ('narratives') from the past by finding new homes for them in the present and in the unfolding future, prospective identities are more concerned with drawing on *elements* of past narratives, both to ensure their continued existence and to support the development of that unfolding future in ways that validate and promote such change where it relates to concerns with the nation state's perceived economic well-being. As Bernstein puts it, such identities are constructed 'to deal with cultural, economic and technological *change*. …[They] are shaped by *selective* recontextualising of features of the past to defend or raise economic performance' (ibid.). Two examples of 'prospective' selections in the wider arena of UK politics – one relating to Thatcherite, the other to Blairite 'New Labour' policy – are provided by Bernstein as helpful illustrations. Within Thatcherism, Bernstein argues, 'features of the past were selected which would create what were considered to be appropriate attitudes, dispositions and performances relevant to a *market culture and reduced welfare state*', whereby a 'new collective base was formed by fusing [discourses of] *nation, family, individual responsibility and individual enterprise*'. Blair's prospective approach, on the other hand, while it also drew selectively on elements of a perceived past, drew on distinctively different ones: that is to say, '[a]n amalgam of notions of *community*...and *local responsibilities to* motivate and restore belonging in the cultural sphere, and a *new participatory responsibility in the economic sphere*. Thus the underlying collective of New Labour appears to be a recontextualising of the concept of the *organic society*'. (Bernstein 2000: 68, emphases added; for a gloss of 'organic society', see Chapter 3).

Rather than necessarily working harmoniously together as implied in the term 'complementary relation', Bernstein points to less helpful 'dislocations' within central education policy, in which, for example, the attempted 'embedding' of 'a retrospective pedagogic culture into a prospective management culture' (2000: 61) is characterised by curious internal contradictions. For example:

> Ideally, the neo-liberal position [with its emphasis on reduced State control, freedom of choice, and the marketisation of education] would be against a centralised national curriculum. However, if we look at the contents and organisation of the educational reform this would appear to have emanated from the *retrospective* [conservative] position, as it consisted (with an occasional new subject) [and despite vocational insertions in the curriculum] of the segmented, serial array of subjects, on the whole departmentally organised, typical of the past and [including] a focus upon "basic skills".
>
> (ibid.: 71)

It is not difficult to see how Bernstein's initial analysis of the tensions in broad curriculum policy between retrospective and prospective identities, and between conservative and neo-liberal ideologies and demands, might be expanded to a closer consideration of the curriculum itself. Thus, while, as Bernstein argues, the retrospective, essentially conservative approach seeks to protect traditional subject boundaries and traditional subject knowledge, the prospective, essentially neo-liberal approach might be more concerned to develop transferable *skills*, including a range of communication skills and skills related to entrepreneurialism. And while the retrospective/conservative approach might give greater weight to the academic, 'cultural' aspects of formal education, the prospective/neo-liberal approach might have a greater interest in developing vocational programmes of study. There are also, however, likely to be areas of agreement between each approach, and it could be argued that a danger for curriculum development is that these areas of agreement can become overly prioritised, first in public rhetoric and then in public policy – returning the curriculum debate to what is effectively a squabble over leftovers. (Current *victims* of such squabbles within English national curriculum policy might include, centrally, its creative and expressive aspects.) Although Bernstein references a conservative emphasis on 'the basics', for example, this same emphasis is also very evident in the neo-liberal approach – albeit for a different set of reasons. We might surmise that from the conservative point of view an emphasis on basic (literacy and numeracy) skills has the happy effect of reducing the spaces for school and teacher choice regarding other, potentially more contentious matters within subjects such as Art, Drama, Social Studies and English that might, if allowed, promote a non-compliant citizenry. From the neo-liberal perspective, on the other hand, the emphasis on 'the basics' is made on the understanding that 'employers' are (so we are told) complaining about the lack of basic literacy and numeracy skills in new recruits, which is therefore impacting negatively on the nation's economic competitiveness.

Another difficulty occurs when the alliance between conservatism and neo-liberalism itself becomes factionalised and oppositional. Just as the conservative/neo-liberal alliance contributes to stagnation and obstructs dynamism when it is working (within its own terms) relatively harmoniously, so it can have a not dissimilar effect when it finds itself locked in internal strife – resulting not so much in ongoing curriculum evolution as in a seemingly endless war of attrition: a curriculum equivalent of trench warfare, in which the battle itself is in danger of becoming more important than the initial cause and nature of the disagreement, and all that prospers (again) is a status quo of enduring, unresolved oppositions punctuated by brief periods of uneasy truce.

Policy tensions 3: 'Schizophrenia' and 'paranoia'

Before returning to Bernstein, whose theory offers us a helpful way in to the consideration of another set of curriculum tensions – not just within official curriculum policy but within curriculum *practice* and *between* curriculum policy and curriculum practice – the final bit of theory I want to introduce in relation to tension and dynamism comes from Deleuze and Guattari's so-called 'schizoanalysis' of capitalist society to which I have already briefly referred, and in particular their anti-psychoanalytic metaphorical reconfigurations of 'schizophrenia' and 'paranoia' (Deleuze and Guattari 1977, 2004).

Deleuze and Guattari's 'schizoanalysis' essentially comprises an appropriation of psychoanalytical terms and concepts through which to analyse the wider socio-economic system, specifically, that system which has become dominant throughout most of the world: free-market capitalism. Deleuze and Guattari use the terms 'paranoia' and 'schizophrenia' to describe two forces, not entirely unlike conservatism and neo-liberalism or Bernstein's retrospective and prospective pedagogic identities, that are in permanent tension with one another: forces which, within human societies, find their most sophisticated manifestation in the form of two competing '*poles of desire*'. These two forces or poles of desire are:

1   a creative, unfettered, we might say completely unethical force that in classic Freudian psychoanalytic theory we might compare to the desire of the selfish, pleasure-seeking 'id' (this force or pole is Deleuze and Guattari's 'schizophrenia');
2   a controlling, cautious, regulatory, interrupting force that might be compared to the regulatory desires of the Freudian 'ego' (related to our developed sense of what is 'socially acceptable' and our desire to be 'accepted') and 'superego' (related to our internalised sense of morality and perhaps to feelings we may have of guilt or shame: Deleuze and Guattari's 'paranoia').

In relation to their schizoanalysis of capitalist societies, the free market of the private sector is presented by Deleuze and Guattari as predominantly 'schizophrenic', while the State generally takes on a more regulatory 'paranoid' or 'repressive' character.

As far as the study of school curricula is concerned, Holland's summary of the difference within schizoanalysis of schizophrenia and paranoia is particularly useful, inviting us to consider the ways in which both schizophrenia and paranoia can impact on how curriculum is conceived and constructed, and of the very complex nature of the curriculum dynamic: an approach that can be over-simplified by a consideration of the inter-relations of neo-liberalism, conservatism and classic liberalism alone, useful though it is:

> If we understand schizophrenia...to designate unlimited semiosis, a radically fluid and extemporaneous form of meaning, paranoia by contrast would designate an absolute system of belief where all meaning was permanently fixed and exhaustively defined by a supreme authority, figure-head, or god....*[P]aranoia represents what is archaic in capitalism, the resuscitation of obsolete, or traditional, belief-centred modes of social organization, whereas schizophrenia designates capitalism's positive potential: freedom, ingenuity, permanent revolution.*
>
> (emphasis added, Holland 1999: 2–3)

A not dissimilar account is offered by Bogue (1989: 103):

> the intensified despotism of capitalism represents the paranoiac, fascisizing tendency of desire to assemble entities in molar aggregates and to impose on them a centralized, unified organisation, whereas capitalism's accelerated deterritorialization of flows represents the schizophrenic, revolutionary tendency of desire to form molecular, non-systematic associations of heterogeneous elements.

Holland's references to the 'unlimited semiosis' (endless development and re-interpretation of language and meaning) of schizophrenia, in which the inbuilt obsolescence of definitive meanings (not to mention 'values') renders them as vulnerable to market forces as the latest electric toothbrush or mobile phone, and Bogue's account of the 'molar aggregates' (the obsession to classify, to pigeonhole and to 'tie down') favoured by paranoia, in which 'molecular' difference and diversity are eschewed in favour of forced 'molar' similarities and sameness, provide a helpful starting point in thinking about how Deleuze and Guattari's schizoanalysis of capitalism might be re-applied and re-configured in terms of one of capitalism's most successful inventions: the universal compulsory curriculum set within the universal compulsory education system. They also, to anticipate once again the final section of this chapter, help to reveal the complexity of the tensions that teachers and school principals have to negotiate as curriculum directors who must mediate between the curriculum they are 'given' and the curriculum as they practise it and as it is experienced by their students.

The idea of 'unlimited semiosis', for instance, appropriately modified so as to deal with its potential excesses, may be understood as descriptive of a curriculum model and theory which sets itself oppositionally to an education dominated by the quest for 'right answers', by 'final assessments', and by securing a certain basic knowledge and skills set, in favour of a more open-ended, questioning education in which answers are always looked upon as having a degree of provisionality and a function of setting the learner forth in the pursuit of further questions. It might also suggest a related pedagogy involving teachers working collaboratively and cooperatively in 'non-systematic elements'. On the other hand, (if we do not moderate it appropriately) it might equally be used in support of rejecting a curriculum founded upon principles, ethics or cherished values, in favour of an anything-goes relativism and a pot-luck access to existing knowledge and skills that is heavily dependent on the education provision that is geographically (and perhaps economically) most readily available to young students. Similarly, the 'paranoid' orientation and approach might be 'old fashioned', obsessed with the past and with preserving the status quo, forcing 'molar aggregates' – in the form of overly prescriptive, one-fit-for-all National Curricula or examination syllabuses and assessment criteria, or sanctified, fundamentalist models of staged 'human development', or clearly specified and incontrovertible roles and identities for 'teachers' and 'learners', fearful or suspicious of change – but it might also be seen in terms of its capacity to resist the kinds of schizophrenic excesses described above, and in preserving cherished social values (relating to, for example, equity, pluralism or social justice) in the face of the sometimes less humanitarian, more pragmatic values of the market.[4]

Just as in the case of Bernstein's 'prospective and retrospective pedagogic identities', and related understandings of neo-liberalism and conservatism, it is important to acknowledge in relation to our current discussion that Deleuze and Guattari's 'poles of desire' produce oppositional *tendencies*, which will always be compromised or modified to an extent by the magnetic pull of the opposing pole, and that consequently their manifestation in practice may thus be temporary and even illusory. The 'schizophrenic' freedom, choice and creativity suggested by decentred school management and the development of 'free schools', for example, might simply end up or be a contributing factor in promoting the paranoid, *status-quo* reproduction of a wider neo-liberal politics and ideology, while (as Bernstein has argued elsewhere) student-centred, exploratory, progressive *pedagogic* developments in schools and classrooms might simply represent another way of perpetuating the existing interests of a dominant middle class. To *sustain* a truly schizophrenic trajectory might be another matter altogether.

The point is that it is the endless interplay of these potentially competing forces, their interactive relationship, that lends curriculum its dynamism and ensures its flexibility and capacity to evolve, but that problems occur (as in the case of specific political ideologies) when either force becomes overly dominant, or when the tension and interplay between them turns into fundamentalist deadlock rather than discussion and debate. It is thus (to underscore an earlier point) the active interplay, the creative potential of the tension that I am invoking when I champion the 'curriculum dynamikos', not the rapid, seemingly endless, rarely consulted modifications and changes that characterise some central curriculum policy at the present time, that have schools and teachers rushing around endeavouring to keep up with each new 'initiative' in a way that denies the degree of stability required for constructive development and change to take place at a sensible pace, and that effectively *excludes* genuine dynamism by excluding key contributors from the curriculum debate.

Central and local policy and practice: 'Official and pedagogic recontextualising fields'

Thus far, I have focused on tensions and interactions *within* central curriculum policy. There is, however, another potential source of tension – and indeed dynamism – *between* central policy and the practices, beliefs, principles, ideologies, theories and 'unofficial' curriculum policies of school principals and classroom practitioners: for insofar as they are charged with the actual implementation of curriculum policy, which can never, despite what politicians themselves might believe and hope and wish for, be uni-directional, they are as much policymakers as anyone else.

As others have pointed out, and as I have already suggested, there may be a significant mismatch between the policies of those designing school curricula for national use and the policy views of those responsible for putting them into practice. Ozga (2000: 14), for example, argued some years ago that 'policymakers tend to emphasise the economic function of education, while teachers align themselves with education as a vehicle for equalising opportunities and/or enriching experience'. One way of looking at this difference of emphasis and opinion might be to suggest that whereas central policy tends to remain locked within the conservative/neo-liberal alliance referred to earlier, a significant number of teachers are more likely to align themselves with 'social liberalism', which does not necessarily oppose free-market policy but emphasises the need for greater equity and social justice within it, or various forms of socialism, which is more critical of free-market policy and more likely to hold it responsible for many of the inequities and social injustices that already exist in the world. Each of these potential philosophical–political mismatches is likely to present a challenge for teachers and school principals – and, furthermore, one which they encounter and manage every day of their working lives. On the one hand, it could be argued (in the case of England, for example) that the neo-liberal devolution of budget management to schools in the public sector, the growing support for private and 'free' schools, the encouragement for schools to opt out of state control, and the imposition, for those who choose to 'stay in' the State system, of a highly detailed and prescriptive school curriculum, almost *necessitates* the translation-into-practice of neo-liberal and conservative policy at the local level (including 're-branding' activities aimed at attracting 'high-quality clients', or active competition for student numbers with neighbouring schools, not to mention the requirement to get students safely to negotiate the hoops and hurdles of national attainment tests). However, it is also the case that teachers and school principals are unlikely to forget or readily abandon the (liberal/ socialist) social and educational *principles* that brought them into the profession in the first place, or the pedagogies and curricular inputs they might associate with such principles. While public policy might often highlight the *national economy* in terms of curriculum content, it is rare to hear a teacher claim they entered the profession in order to help make the nation more economically competitive in a global marketplace – even though they might acknowledge that this is one of several important curricular aims. Indeed, in the absence of a social liberal or socialist central government, we might suggest that teachers and schools themselves potentially offer a more powerful moderating force to neo-liberal policies than those currently available within the official policy context itself. Unlike conservatism, whose main interest in the individual is to promote the compliance and conformity necessary for continuity of the socio-economic and cultural status quo, or neo-liberalism, whose interest in individual development is mainly concerned with the uses to which such development can be put in serving the national economy, the social liberal and socialist agendas exhibited in the testimonies of a great many teachers (see, for example, Moore 2004) is more likely to begin with a desire to promote the individual's wishes, talents and interests, to help them develop as a happy, 'well rounded', socially and expressively confident adult, to prioritise equity, social justice and individual rights within a context of inclusivity and mutual respect, and to take a greater interest in pedagogies that might promote such a project than in those concerned almost exclusively with curriculum 'content' and student examination and grading. In relation to curriculum itself, this social liberalism might be reflected in the teacher's choice of materials, where such choice exists (for instance, histories and accounts of racial and gender oppression and civil rights movements in English Literature and the Humanities) and, in relation to pedagogy, in student-centred approaches which respect difference and which engage learners themselves in establishing appropriate working relations.

Bernstein, to whose theory I will return for much of the remainder of this chapter, frames this tension between central policy and local practice (including, also, local interpretations, implementations and mediations of such policy) in terms of the 'Official Recontextualising Field' or 'ORF' (of central policy) and the 'Pedagogic Recontextualising Field' or PRF of 'classroom practice, departments of education, specialised journals [and] private research foundations' (Bernstein 2000: 33). As Bernstein points out, the potential for dynamism and dialogue between these two fields, including the capacity for schools and teachers to influence curriculum policy and design as well as being influenced *by* it, to engage in school-based curriculum development (Skilbeck 1984) and to translate broad curriculum directives into locally relevant practice, can be severely restricted when the quantity and detail in centrally designed policy – as well as the strength of its mandate – becomes overly dominant. Thus, in a critique of the National Curriculum for England (as relevant today as in 2000), Bernstein argues:

> If the PRF can have an effect on pedagogic discourse independently of the ORF, then there is both some autonomy *and* struggle over pedagogic discourse and its practices. But if there is only the ORF, then there is no autonomy. [...] Today [in England] the state is attempting to weaken the PRF through its ORF, and thus attempting to reduce relative autonomy over the construction of pedagogic discourse and over its social contexts.
>
> (Bernstein 2000: 33)

Bernstein's account of the stagnation that can ensue when teachers and schools, along with their more liberal, progressive stance toward public education, are effectively written out of discussions about the nature and content of the school curriculum is an important one, pointing, again, to the way in which genuine curriculum development and debate can all too easily be replaced by curriculum in-fighting. It also leaves us wondering what a curriculum might look like if it was constructed less centrally on principles of conservatism and neo-liberalism, and more on principles of social liberalism or socialism, and the extent to which such a curriculum might survive and prosper within free-market capitalist societies. What we can say is that not all countries have developed quite the same relationship between the 'ORF' and the 'PRF' as in England. In some countries, for example (Finland and Singapore being two cases in point), it is not unusual for schools and teachers to be presented with an outline national curriculum (sometimes referred to as a 'minimum curriculum') fashioned in the 'ORF' of central government policy, in which there is plenty of scope for local interpretation in schools and school districts as the policy moves from one 'context' (the central, policymaking context) to another (the local, putting-into-practice context). In the national curricula of these countries, it is not only seen as *desirable* for school-based curriculum development and innovation to take place, but something of a *necessity* and a *requirement*. In such instances, there is ample opportunity for the thriving of the curriculum dynamikos, in that just as official policy has the scope – we might say, the intention – of influencing what happens in school classrooms, so what happens in school classrooms can, as it were, speak 'back to' and influence public policy dialogically. Not only that, but the space that the outline curriculum opens up for schools and teachers is also opened up for education theorists and local policymakers, so that dialogue and debate concerning educational and curricular *principles* do not just take place but remain open.

Liberal and conservatising organisation and practice: Pedagogic 'codes', 'competence' and 'performance'

The umbrella term used by Bernstein to describe curriculum content, pedagogy and assessment deployed to support education policy as it is still most widely conceived and practised around the globe – which may have a stronger allegiance to conservatism than to neo-liberalism but cuts across both and stands counter to social liberal and socialist positionings – is that of the '*collection code*' (Bernstein 1971a, 1971b). The 'collection code' describes a theory and manner of curriculum and pedagogy that most of us will be readily familiar with, which separates learning and knowledge into collections of distinct, clearly separated and broadly autonomous subject areas: essentially, what Bernstein refers to as '*strong classification*' in relation to curriculum content and perceived forms of knowledge, indicating the strength of the boundaries between subject disciplines. Within each subject area, a body of knowledge and skills is identified and strictly policed, so that any changes in it must come with authoritative force from the 'ORF' of central policy and public testing and examination systems. This restriction on possibilities for meaningful negotiation in relation to curriculum content is in turn supported by the promotion of pedagogies rooted in 'traditional', 'transmissive', front-of-class teaching, giving extremely limited power to *students* in regard to lesson content and conduct (referred to by Bernstein as '*strong framing*') – and is likely to favour externally-mandated, single-mode, end-on assessment processes.

In opposition to the collection code (though Bernstein points out that the two codes are not mutually exclusive and can co-exist to some degree at any time, even within the same educational establishment), Bernstein posits the 'integrated code'. In this code, there is a deliberate and principled weakening of traditional subject boundaries, enabling greater cross-curricular teaching and learning (in Bernstein's terms, '*weak classification*'), and a greater emphasis on student-centred, enquiry-based learning, mixed-ability grouping, wider choice for students, multiple-mode assessment (including coursework/teacher assessment), and a more interpersonal mode of teacher guidance of students: a set of approaches that Bernstein calls '*weak framing*', and that we might associate with less autocratic, more democratic classrooms.

If the integrated code might appear in many ways to be most readily compatible with neo-liberal approaches to education and curriculum, it is likely to be less so when it comes to the matter of measurable 'outputs' and so-called 'success criteria'. In Bernstein's account, neo-liberalism and the 'prospective pedagogic identity' have a particular concern both to prescribe curriculum content and to demonstrate the successes of a curriculum that is geared very much to meeting the perceived demands and requirements of the nation's economy and of its businesses and industries. Such an approach tends towards what Bernstein calls a 'performance' pedagogy: that is to say, a pedagogy similar to that espoused within conservatism which 'places the emphasis upon a specific output of the acquirer, upon a particular text the acquirer is expected to construct and upon the specialised skills necessary to the production of this specific output, text or product' (Bernstein 2000: 44). Such a pedagogic orientation suggests, in turn, the continuation and refinement of a universal, one-fits-all approach to educational *assessment* – one, furthermore, which (despite another economy-focused imperative to develop different skills in different students) under-privileges student *difference* through assessing individuals against common norms or 'standards': one which, in Bernstein's own words, privileges 'absences' (what is 'missing' or wrong in a student's observable outputs) rather than 'presences' (what the learner *can do*).

In contrast to this performance-oriented pedagogy, which may or may not find support within the ORF, Bernstein offers a 'competence' pedagogy, linked to pedagogic 'progressivism', which would seem immediately more appealing to and compatible with the social liberal and socialist orientations that many teachers will bring to their work. When Bernstein uses the term competence, it is significantly different from the meaning we very often encounter these days in relation to the idea of 'training'. Bernstein effectively resurrects an earlier understanding of the term, in which competence refers to what might be called a student's 'natural' or extra-formal-educational abilities, talents and leanings: that is to say, those 'intrinsically creative... procedures for engaging with, and constructing, the world' which are acquired 'tacitly... in informal interactions' – and which formal education can work on and with but does not, so to speak, create (Bernstein 2000: 42). Bernstein suggests that the 'social logic' of this conceptualisation reveals a number of underpinning understandings, intentions and possible consequences for formal education generally and for formal pedagogies in particular, comprising:

> an announcement of *a universal democracy of acquisition* [in which] all [learners] are inherently competent and all possess common procedures. There are no deficits; the subject is active and creative in the construction of a valid world of meanings and practice. Here there are differences but not deficits...
>
> (ibid.: 42–3, emphasis added)

Competence-based approaches to pedagogy are related to 'liberal, progressive and even radical [educational] ideologies'.

As with 'paranoia' and 'schizophrenia', history suggests that at different points in time either performance pedagogies or competence pedagogies may be supported or refuted by central governments, as of course within broadly neo-liberal politics. Indeed, a significant aspect of the recent history of curriculum development and reform in England has been a shifting in the ORF from a support for performance pedagogies, which largely predominated up until the late 1960s, to a grudging acceptance of competence pedagogies, largely developed and promoted within the PRF, up until the mid 1980s, back to an increasingly aggressive insistence on performance pedagogies, linked in to a wider 'performativity' discourse, up until the present day. To repeat an earlier point, such to-ing and fro-ing, while indicative of curriculum's insistence on remaining open to challenge and contestation, is not, however, indicative of the kind of 'dynamism' for which I am arguing. This is mainly because of its fundamentally non-dialogic, horn-locking nature. It illustrates the difference between dynamism geared toward endless evolution and a repeated shuffling from foot to foot which gets us nowhere in terms of forward momentum.

The all-knowing 'master' and the 'ignorant' teacher

In the Introduction to Jacques Rancière's fascinating and provocative book *The Ignorant Schoolmaster*, Kirstin Ross echoes Bernstein's competence pedagogy in asking: 'What would it mean to make equality a *presupposition* rather than a goal, a *practice* rather than a reward situated in some distant future?', citing the proposition (as a starting point for the teacher): 'All people are equally intelligent' (Ross 1991: xix).

The notion of finding, praising and building on what students already 'bring with them' into the classroom, rather than simply validating certain knowledge, preferences and skills as superior to others and expecting students to internalise that knowledge, to develop those skills, and to be successful in demonstrating that they have done so, seeks not solely to 'judge' students and to allocate them a place in educational hierarchies in comparison with externally fixed, apparently immutable norms, but rather to produce pedagogies, assessment processes and sufficiently 'open' curricula to enable students to show us what they can do as intelligent, creative, idiosyncratic people. As such, it has very clear implications regarding not only the way we design curriculum but – to anticipate much of the discussion of the following chapter – our understanding of what the curriculum *is*. Such pedagogies are reminiscent of those outlined by Rancière in *The Ignorant Schoolmaster*, in which he proposes, and exposes, what he calls the 'pedagogical myth' of 'explication' – a myth in which (Rancière 1991: 3):

> the essential act of the master [is] to *explicate*: to disengage the simple elements of learning, and to reconcile their simplicity in principle with the factual simplicity that characterizes young and ignorant minds…to transmit learning and form minds simultaneously, by leading those minds, according to an ordered profession, from the most simple to the most complex.

As Ross (1991: xx) elaborates:

> The pedagogical myth divides the world into two: the knowing and the ignorant, the mature and the unformed, the capable and the incapable…[A] world divided into knowing minds and ignorant ones, ripe minds and immature ones, the capable and the incapable, the intelligent and the stupid.

Challenging notions of 'deficit' (students as possessing 'lacks' which the rescuer teacher must fill), Rancière proposes that we need to acknowledge the intelligence of all those (teachers and students) engaged in the educational process, going so far as to suggest that the teacher needs not to be the knowing master-explicator at all, but may well be – or perhaps feign to be – 'ignorant' in terms of subject knowledge, adopting the role of facilitator or (in *the e-ducare* sense made famous in the 1969 film *The Prime of Miss Jean Brodie*) the leader-out of students' learning – thereby re-casting learners not as disenfranchised or in need of salvation, but as intelligent human beings capable, under appropriate guidance, of teaching themselves and, through that self-teaching, of achieving intellectual emancipation. (As we shall see in Chapter 5, this is an argument not dissimilar to that proposed by Bridget Somekh in relation to the potential offered by new digital technologies in relation to active, independent learning.)

Describing the pedagogic journey of a much earlier educator, Jacotot (a schoolteacher working in the early days of the French Republic), Rancière illustrates how, even within so-called progressive pedagogies and inclusive rhetorics, the notion of the teacher as master or as explicator can act against the best interests of the students it claims to help, by establishing in them a mode of being in which, even after they have left school, they continue to perceive themselves as inferior or deficient (see e.g. Rancière 1991: 107). We might add that, within this perception, their own capacity for dynamic development is curtailed by the illusory but powerful conviction of identity 'completion'. (For an obvious and unambiguous contrast with this view, see Hirst 1998: 259, in an analysis that combines 'mastery' with a version of situated learning and a belief in the importance and centrality of 'knowledge'. Hirst argues: 'Acquiring knowledge of any form is…to a greater or lesser extent something that cannot be done simply by solitary study of the symbolic expression of knowledge, it must be learnt from a master on the job.')

Whatever we may feel about Rancière's analysis, which itself becomes increasingly (and deliberately) ambiguous as his argument develops, the propositions and provocations he puts before us raise some important questions for curriculum theory and development – especially for 'universal' national curricula. For example, do we begin (in practice or as a matter of belief and policy) with a curriculum that assumes not simply different needs but also different abilities? If so, do we privilege some abilities over others – and on what bases? Do we (in policy or in practice) use the curriculum as a means of planning for and perpetuating this particular kind of difference – preparing students for some version of the 'organic society' in which each person is deemed to have a particular skill or skill set that they need to hone and develop for their own and for society's benefit, rather than seeking or expecting to find broader enrichment? How do we understand *knowledge*, and how it is 'acquired' and 'developed'? Is our curriculum constructed on a notion of deficit and absence (that is, aimed at rectifying an identified 'lack' or correcting an identified delinquency), or is its aim to build on existing abilities and interests? And on what bases do we judge 'good teaching'? It is hard to imagine Rancière's ignorant schoolmaster going down very well with Ofsted inspectors in today's England – or, for that matter, with a school's Senior Leadership Team who are themselves constrained by the desperate need to achieve competitive results in public examinations devised according to an essentially performance-oriented pedagogy.

Working with tensions and contradictions: The pedagogical balancing act

I'm conscious once again that talk of curriculum dynamism and student-centred learning is likely to raise a wry smile on the faces of many practising teachers, who may feel far more involved in having to manage more negatively-inflected curriculum *tensions* – in particular, those embedded within central policy itself and those between central policy and personal–professional preferences – than taking an active and welcomed part in public discussions about curriculum theory or in developing their own progressive pedagogies. As has been previously pointed out, this is a particular problem for teachers who may find themselves in the situation described by Bernstein in which they experience, on a daily basis, an attempted reduction on the part of central government 'to reduce relative autonomy over the construction of pedagogic discourse and over its social contexts' (ibid.).

The impact of such conservatising, reproductive forces on curriculum *work* may indeed be seen itself as anti-dynamic, placing restrictions on teachers' capacity for experimentation and innovation, that can be plotted along a continuum of 'modest' to 'severe'. At the 'severe' end, when, for example, tensions between conservative and neo-liberal policy results (as seen recently in England) in cycles of ideological skirmishing manifesting themselves in a constant barrage of frequently changing policy initiatives and u-turns, teachers and school principals can find themselves having to devote so much time and energy to managing these externally created tensions and trying to render them workable in practice as to have very little left for initiatives of their own. Indeed, that they carry out such management so effectively may be seen as a tribute to their resilience, as well as an indicator in its own right of the energy and creativity available for more productive ends. As Fisher (2009: 25–6) observes, in an argument that contains loud echoes of Bernstein's 'policy dislocations':

> Teachers are now put under intolerable pressure to mediate between the post-literate subjectivity of the late capitalist consumer and the demands of the disciplinary regime (to pass examinations etc)…Teachers are caught between being facilitator-entertainers and disciplinarian-authoritarians…Ironically, the [teacher's] role of disciplinarian is demanded of educators more than ever at precisely the time when disciplinary structures are breaking down in institutions.

But teachers and school principals, like everyone else, are not only theoretical, ideological beings; they are also psychic beings, and this recognition is equally important in our understandings of curriculum and its implementation, raising as it does the possibility of another set of tensions, this time at work *within the individual practitioner*. In her elegant summary of Sartrean existentialism, Mari Ruti (2009: 22) writes:

> Sartre proposes that the subject is always torn between two warring modalities of being in the world. On the one hand, there is a creative and future-oriented aspect to the self that is capable of transcendent acts of self-overcoming. On the other, there is the self of bad faith, a non-creative and stagnant self that remains mired in immanent forms of life with no possibility of change or growth. The latter is plagued by a hopeless sense of emptiness and meaninglessness that undermines its ability to reflect on the meaning and future direction of its life.

We can hardly fail to be struck by the similarities between this brief account of Sartrean existentialism as it relates to the individual in society, and the schizoanalysis (with its references to 'schizophrenia' and 'paranoia') of Deleuze and Guattari as it relates to (capitalist) society and its structures and practices. In Ruti's/Sartre's account, it is as if we internalise those wider creative-emancipatory and restrictive-incarcerating forces and tendencies at work in the wider socio-economic system – or perhaps are infused with them independently, as if neither as individuals nor in the social systems we construct we can avoid them. In fact, one of the reasons and advantages of adopting schizoanalysis instead of or in addition to more traditional sociological or political theory as a way of looking afresh at curriculum policy and practice is precisely because it locates the forces of fundamentalist conservatism and unfettered liberalism (and all that goes between) within 'desire' – indicating its active or latent presence in both public and private, collective and individual, policy and practice.

Ruti's and Sartre's accounts are, it must be added, concerned with the operations of the human psyche independently of the paid work we do and the ways in which we experience it, and perhaps do not bear straightforward translation into the domain of Curriculum Studies. They serve to remind us, however, that just as there may be both creative, adventurous, risk-taking forces at work in the socio-political world in which we live and work, in tension with other forces that are cautious, regulatory and perhaps constraining, so as individuals we experience on a daily basis, in our private and in our more public lives, a tension between and a navigation through adventure and caution – more often than not resisting the temptation to implement actions and to pursue directions that might prove dangerous, either by reconfiguring them as more modest proposals or by sublimating them through fantasy and the imagination. Certainly, as teachers it is unlikely to be the constraints of externally-imposed policy alone that impose limits on what we might wish to do or what we might seek to achieve; it is our own sense as well of the consequences to ourselves and to others that our actions may bring the complications, the extra work, the toes we might tread on, the self-inflicted punishments should our bolder schemes and intentions founder. Thus, in addition to constraints that we can quite clearly locate as 'external', there are others – whether or not we perceive their origins to be external to ourselves – that are experienced as 'internal' or self-imposed. We might say, to conclude this brief account of some of the tensions and issues that may encourage or inhibit curriculum dynamism, that we have to consider another set, involving another balancing act; this time between pragmatism (what we feel we can do in the circumstances) and desire (what we would choose to do if free of perceived constraints). To its cost, the field of Curriculum Studies has too rarely taken on this difficult but important set of understandings related to curriculum practice and experience.

Making connections

To round off this chapter, and by way of leading us forward into the next, we are now in a position to bring together some of the ideas thus far introduced and explored. Figure 2.1 represents an attempt to do this, taking Deleuze and Guattari's metaphors as a starting point and considering the likely influences and more commonly found characteristics of each force on the three curriculum areas of: the curriculum 'itself' ('what' is taught); pedagogy (how it is taught – and how we expect it to be learned); and assessment. Stationed between these two I have consciously left a gap, to be used – or not – by readers as they see fit, having resisted the temptation myself to fill it in with some kind of 'balanced' yet provisional curriculum proposals.

I appreciate that it is important to approach such summaries with caution, not least because they can oversimplify things to the point of misrepresentation or obscurity (it is important to keep in mind her that 'paranoia' and 'schizophrenia' are being seen as representing competing tendencies rather than representing straightforward binary opposites); nor am I offering 'balance' as some kind of ideal state, either in the grid as presented here or in any alternative grid which might, for instance, be indicative of a less draconian and ideologically driven paranoia or of a less theory-based schizophrenia. A devolved, localised, 'molecular' curriculum, for instance, might still require some degree of 'paranoid' regulation and repression in order for its dynamism to be sustained and in order for equity across the system to be ensured.

The grid may also have more immediate relevance to the current educational situation in some countries than in others; it owes much, for instance, to debates about and developments in the English school curriculum in recent history. As has already been suggested – and to refer back to the not-always-productive tensions between neo-liberalism and neo-conservatism, between 'schizophrenia' and 'paranoia' – it is the case that in England during the course of the last half-century two dramatic swings in education policy and practice have taken place, first away from didactic pedagogies operating within externally-fixed, normative, end-assessed curricula toward more student-centred pedagogies operating within partially school-constructed, criteria-referenced, continuously assessed curricula, and then back again – with the result that what might be called a 'creative balance' with dynamic potential has never been achieved, as the over-reactive, full-on force of current political paranoia (growing exponentially since the 1990s) has reined in what many of us saw (and still see) as the creative, developmental ('schizophrenic') initiatives of the 1970s and the 1980s. While such a scenario will be familiar (or perhaps will become familiar) to readers operating within the curriculum arrangements of other nations, this inherent 'Englishness' will need to be taken into account, and translation and modifications undertaken as necessary.

'schizophrenia'			'paranoia'
Curriculum			
Devolved, localised, 'molecular'		Centralised, national, 'molar'	
General, principled, interpretable		Detailed, subject-based, prescriptive	
Cross-curricular initiatives encouraged; classification weak		Subject/discipline boundaries conserved; classification strong	
Diversity and difference (cultural, linguistic, cognitive) celebrated		Promotion of conformity, sameness, 'correctness'	
[R]evolutionary		Reproductive	
Teaching			
The 'ignorant schoolmaster'; student-centred; 'progressive' framing weak		The 'explicator'; teacher, examination and textbook centred; 'traditional'; framing strong	
Learning			
Risk-taking, exploration, 'ownership'		'Correct answers', strict parameters, 'receivership'	
Assessment			
'Formative' and criteria-referenced, continuous, focus on thinking and reasoning, use of knowledge and understanding, recognising diversity, student and teacher centred, 'competence' based		Summative and normative, 'end-of-course', focus on memorisation and regurgitation of right answers in decontextualised situations, not recognising diversity, student centred, 'performance' based	

Figure 2.1 'Schizophrenia', 'paranoia' and curriculum

Notes

1   This itself is, of course, another contestable proposition, calling to mind John Dewey's question: Why do we hang on so devotedly to the concept of curriculum as though education is incapable of existing without it? Readers will understand, I hope, that, given the title and stated purpose of this book, engagement with that particular question must wait for another time.

2   An alternative way of describing such tensions which readers might find useful (in particular in relation to arguments developed in Chapter 5) is provided by Bruce Kimball (1986) who identifies what he calls 'two traditions of education policy' in the US: the philosophical tradition and the oratorical tradition – each adopting a particular perspective regarding our understandings of truth and knowledge, and each involved in an unending, cyclical battle for supremacy over the other. Within the philosophical tradition, 'truth' is understood as unsettled and elusive, and the search for truth an act of discovery, whereas within the oratorical tradition 'truth' exists (so to speak) and is to be found (to be *recovered*) in the 'great texts' and in traditions. In terms of the curricular orientation of education, the philosophical tradition consequently leads to a more future-oriented curriculum, while the oratorical tradition is more concerned with referencing and drawing on the past. For similar reasons, the pedagogical tradition is more likely to promote process or 'method' (pedagogies enabling students to discuss, to collaborate, to 'discover'), while the oratorical tradition is likely to be weaker on process but stronger on content (the 'knowledge' and its 'truths' that are to be imparted to learners).

3   The English census returns shows a significant difference between statistics from 2001, in which 71.7% of respondents described themselves as 'Christian', to 2011, by which time the figure had dropped to 59.4%: a decrease matched by a parallel increase in respondents describing themselves as having 'no religion' from 14.6% to 24.7% in the same period.

4   For a further illustration of how the terms 'molar' and 'molecular' can be useful in exploring and understanding curriculum theory and design, see Eisner 1979: 36–7.

Chapter 3

What is it? What's it for?

What is a curriculum as we now understand the word? It has changed its meaning as a result of the curriculum movement. It is not a syllabus – a mere list of content to be covered – nor is it even what German speakers would call a *Lehrplan* – a prescription of aims and methods and content. Nor is it our understanding a list of objectives. ...Let me claim that it is a symbolic or meaningful object, like Shakespeare's first folio, not like a lawnmower; like the pieces and board of chess, not like an apple tree. It has physical existence but also a meaning incarnate in words or pictures or sound or games or whatever. [...] Who made it?

(Stenhouse 1983: 155–6)

The question "What should be the aims of school education?" is fundamental to any system. [...] Given that the curriculum is a vehicle, or collection of vehicles, intended to reach a certain set of destinations, we have to begin with the destinations themselves. Once we have these, we have at some point to work out what kind of vehicles are best to help us attain them in particular circumstances.

(White 2004b: 6)

What is it?

The previous chapter highlighted some abiding issues for curriculum theory and policy, along with some of the tensions that might promote or inhibit the development of a curriculum that is continuously and dynamically evolving (or that might undergo a more radical change). Chapter 3 picks up a point concerning the 'contestability' of curriculum as a concept and a set of practices, and offers a partial (in both senses of the word) consideration of some of the main definitions and understandings of curriculum, inviting readers to make their own decisions about which they prefer and which of my own preferences to challenge.

Perhaps the first thing that needs to be said is that as soon as we give something a name – for example, 'curriculum' – we are making a move toward closure. However, we are also creating a space that is contestable. It is not surprising, then, that we may find many different definitions of what we call 'curriculum', which are likely to have some things in common with each other but which will also, often, have significant differences. It would be a mistake, for reasons already introduced, to accept any one existing definition as – 'definitive'. That is not the purpose of this book, or of this chapter. Nor should we necessarily expect different definitions to produce radically different curricula *in practice*;

indeed, an interesting exercise is to identify commonalities within curriculum models that at face value appear to stand somewhat oppositionally to one another.

The important thing to keep in mind is that although we may start with a premise (e.g. that a school curriculum of some kind is necessary and desirable), we need always to remember that alternative curricula are available to us, and that, however eager we are to accept our premise, that premise is itself saturated with all-too-easily ignored questions regarding the forgotten *histories* of school curricula and indeed of the very idea of the curriculum itself, so effectively 'naturalised' has the term and the concept become. As Hamilton (1989: 35) has argued: 'The discourse of schooling is an historical artefact. But its historical responsiveness is not always evident. [...] [T]erms like...curriculum have become universalized – their origins and evolution hidden from both educationalists and historians alike.' In a striking elaboration of this point, Hamilton takes us back to the pre-curriculum world of mediaeval schools, in which there was

> no presumption that every student was "learning" the same passage [...], there was no pedagogical necessity that all students should remain in the teacher's presence throughout the hours of teaching [... and] there was no expectation that students would stay at school after their specific educational goals had been reached.
>
> (ibid.: 38)

Hamilton goes on to suggest that the concept of 'curriculum' itself appears to have only emerged in the late sixteenth and early seventeenth centuries, where it came simply to refer to a *complete course of study* – albeit with a greater emphasis on 'control to both teaching and learning' (ibid.: 45).

In addition to these longer histories, there are shorter ones. The point has already been made that in England, despite a gradual shift of emphasis in curriculum content toward the prioritisation of promoting workplace skills, the structure – we might say, the 'manner' – of the curriculum here (as in many other European countries) has remained remarkably unchanged for over 100 years (indeed, since the very introduction of a universal state education system). We can too easily forget, however, that many countries – both 'large' and 'small' – have a somewhat different curriculum history from that of England, often revealing (at least so it would seem) a rather greater enthusiasm for more radical curriculum change. Some of these – those of Malta, Sri Lanka, China and Japan in particular – will be further examined in Chapter 8.

Curriculum defined

Definitions of curriculum may be both very general and very specific – and there is certainly no shortage of definitions available. I am obliged, given the scope of this book, to be rather selective in this matter, and have consequently opted for the definitions – and those responsible for them – that in my judgement are likely to be of most use to readers, by way of initiating and enriching debate.

Of the many 'curriculum definers' (if one can put it that way), one of the best known and influential, at least in the field of curriculum theory and research, is Lawrence Stenhouse. Stenhouse draws our attention to two understandings of curriculum that persist and continue to co-exist in tension with one another today: the curriculum seen 'as an intention, plan or prescription, an idea about what one would like to happen in schools' and curriculum seen 'as the existing state of affairs in schools, what does in fact happen' (Stenhouse 1975: 2). This distinction has subsequently been refined and developed by McCormick and Murphy (2000: 210) as the 'specified' curriculum (e.g. national curriculum orders, examination syllabuses), the 'enacted' curriculum (what teachers and schools do with the specified curriculum in practice, and how it undergoes change in the process) and the 'experienced' curriculum (how the curriculum is experienced by students, and we might add by teachers).

To anticipate a discussion to be had later on in this chapter concerning what is sometimes known as 'the content-process debate', Stenhouse, and others, have further developed such distinctions, offering, for example (Stenhouse 1975):

- *curriculum as product* (curriculum understood essentially as a body of knowledge, pre-specified and usually norm-tested, linked these days to discourses and practices of performativity and 'standards');
- *curriculum as process* (what actually happens in classrooms – an understanding of curriculum as 'event' rather than 'thing', taking notice of and encouraging school-based curriculum development, seeing curriculum as open to ongoing evaluation, development and change, emphasising meaning-making, thinking and democratic pedagogic conversations);
- *curriculum as praxis* (focusing on teachers exploring and critiquing their own practice, allowing for differing views and perspective);
- *curriculum as context* (reminding us of the curriculum's relationship with and to the 'outside' world, and the extent to which it reflects and perpetuates dominant knowledge and values through its very structures, rules and pedagogic preferences – linked to what is sometimes referred to as the 'hidden curriculum' [Dreeben 1967; Lynch 1989]).

In this current book, there is no room to explore the curriculum as experienced (see, however, Moore 2012) or, in any great detail, the curriculum as enacted other than to encourage us to keep in mind, as each topic is elaborated, Hirst's wise but, sadly, too-often ignored assertion that teachers are able – and indeed should be en-abled – to make 'rationally defensible professional judgements both while they teach and in their planning and evaluation' (Hirst 1979: 16. See also Skilbeck 1984 and Stenhouse 1975, on the virtues of school-based curriculum development). In terms of *understanding* the curriculum, this is an important matter – not least because of a tendency many of us might have to think of curriculum purely as 'a thing' that is, so to speak, manufactured outside the school to be directly transferred inside the school. The fact remains that, despite the persistence of some central governments to ensure the smooth occurrence of such an intended (uni-directional) transference, 'even an external structure such as the [English] National Curriculum has to be interpreted by teachers to become a reality in schools' (Young 1998: 22) – rendering teachers, whether politicians like it or not, *curriculum directors*, and opening up the potential for those curriculum directors to be critical, reflexive, 'transformative intellectuals' (Giroux 1988).

Models and rationales

Stenhouse's invitation to take account of the contexts of education and curriculum is important, not only in relation to our own understandings of curriculum (and indeed our own curriculum work) but also in relation to our readings of curriculum *rationales*.

By 'rationale', I refer to a combination of decisions regarding very broad ideas of what curriculum as a term might mean; what, more precisely, we think it is mainly for; and how best we might model our curriculum to ensure that it will achieve our aims. Invariably, models must 'begin with' or develop from some kind of definition or rationale. However, knowledge of existing models might also impact on the ways in which future curricula are rationalised and defined so that distinctions between these terms – particularly, I think, between 'definitions' ('what it is') and 'models' ('how it is designed, constructed and presented') – can be very slippery. Rather than spend too much time debating what is a definition, what is a model and what is a rationale, I will use the terms in the way I have indicated above, generally preferring 'rationale' to include within it notions of definition and design. There is, unfortunately, no space here to reference in any detail the many curriculum models and rationales available to students of the curriculum – but those interested in exploring these in more depth are recommended to look at my colleague David Scott's (2008) book *Critical Essays on Major Curriculum Theorists*.

One of the better-known rationales for curriculum – which has managed to survive for more than half a century – is implicitly offered by the American scholar Ralph Tyler in a series of 'four fundamental questions' (which effectively amount to a definition of the curriculum as the organisation and monitoring of educational experiences designed to meet specified educational purposes). Tyler's four questions are:

1 What educational purposes should the school seek to attain?
2 What educational experiences can be provided that are likely to attain these purposes?
3 How can these educational experiences be effectively organized?
4 How can we determine whether these purposes are being attained?

(Tyler 1949: 1)

More recently, Alexander, adding emphasis and elaboration to Tyler's references to 'experiences' and 'organisation', has proposed a not dissimilar rationale, describing curriculum as concerning itself with 'the various ways of knowing, understanding, doing, creating, investigating and making sense which it is desirable for children to encounter, and how these are most appropriately translated and structured for teaching' (Alexander 2004: 11). It is interesting to note that neither of these definitions problematises *in itself* issues concerning *by whom and by what means* we arrive at the 'purposes' of education and curriculum (who Tyler's 'we' might be, or what is meant by such apparently contestable terms as 'desirable' and 'appropriate'), although (to flag issues that will be returned to in Chapter 7) Alexander, for whom such matters appear rather more important, reminds us that 'all education is grounded in social and indeed political values of some kind, *and necessarily so*' (ibid.: 8, emphasis added).

In contrast with Tyler, Paddy Walsh, in his excellent book *Education and Meaning: Philosophy in Practice* (1993), asks precisely some of those questions that Tyler eschews. Walsh's own five questions regarding curriculum selection are as relevant as ever:

1 Who (makes the selections, and 'in what ways, at what stages, and to what degree of influence')?
2 Who for?
3 On what basis?
4 From what (e.g. cultural, disciplinary) 'pool'?
5 How do we 'map' culture for the purposes of curriculum selection?

Whether Tyler's questions genuinely imply what I have called a curriculum rationale embedding a particular 'model', or whether they simply offer us another definition, is debatable. My own view is that they do both, and that the rationale (and the model, and the definition), which is a very basic one, has simply become so commonplace as not to be regarded as a rationale at all. It contains and exhibits – or at any rate it leads us toward – what is sometimes known as the *Aims and Objectives Model* of curriculum, not by way of suggesting that curricula *generally* do not have aims and objectives, but in order to distinguish its particular priorities from another cluster of models and rationales proposed by Stenhouse (1975) and others, which are more focused on curriculum as '*process*', or (Blenkin and Kelly 1981) which prioritise *learner development*: each having arguably more capacity to embrace the *idiosyncratic* and the *contingent* in teaching and learning than the model implied (and subsequently elaborated) in Tyler's own approach.

That said, Tyler's first question ('What educational purposes should the school seek to attain?') is the central one that will underpin any curriculum rationale and model we might propose – although, depending on how we understand Tyler's fourth question, the matter of how and when, if at all, those purposes are to be *re-examined* (and perhaps amended) may be seen to remain unrecognised in his account.

Having decided upon our purpose[s], the next steps follow, in Tyler's approach, with a disarming logic:

• we set about establishing the educational experiences, the knowledge and the skills, that are required to satisfy our purposes;
• we 'organise' how this knowledge and these skills are to be taught, how this experience is to be made available (pedagogically and in terms of the structure of the school calendar);
• and we work out the best way to find out how successful our curriculum is proving (through, for example, testing and examining students to gauge how much or how little they have learned, and inspecting schools and teachers to see how effectively they are managing learning, on the assumption that student results alone offer insufficient evidence).

At the time Tyler proffered his four questions we might assume, with some justification, that in many parts of the world his 'we' suggested a set of tasks for teachers, making possible local variations, the co-existence of different curriculum choices, and a relative ease in making curriculum modifications in the light of professional experience. Increasingly, however, that 'we' now refers far more – almost exclusively in some countries – to politicians and policymakers, in whose hands the model becomes not just one of 'Aims and Objectives' but of the *Managed Curriculum*: that is to say, a curriculum, designed by curriculum directors, usually operating outside the experience-space of the school and classroom, for mass consumption, in which the very pattern of defining purposes – selecting skill and knowledge content, structuring pedagogy and the school day, testing and monitoring – reduces both the possibilities of more dynamic, evolving curricula and the opportunities for teachers to engage in curriculum development of their own professionally-informed choosing. It is also a model that struggles to incorporate student-centredness, even in the unlikely event of its seeing this as a good idea. The *(Centrally) Managed Curriculum* is, essentially, an imposed curriculum that seeks closure and completeness; not one that wishes to keep open the fundamental questions that it asks.

But of course, regardless of whether the curriculum is highly 'managed' or not, or whether – to return to an earlier point – it concerns itself principally with inputs or with outputs or equally with both, how we organise curriculum experiences depends in no small part on what we decide those experiences are to be and what weightings we might decide to give them. If, for example, our central purpose is for young people to leave school with their heads full of 'useful knowledge' (whatever that may be), we might design a curriculum differently in some respects than if, say, our main purpose was for them to leave school armed with the desire and the wherewithal to continue their own learning. However, it also depends on how we understand human development and human learning. If, for example, we believe that learning best takes place in bite-sized chunks managed by expert teachers and organised around different kinds of knowledge and skills (a few hours of drawing here, a few hours learning about the Wars of the Roses there, a few hours investigating electricity somewhere else) we might choose to organise our curriculum precisely along the lines most of us are already very familiar with, whether as school students or as schoolteachers or both. If, on the other hand, we were to possess a counter understanding of knowledge and development, that believed in the possibility for and potential benefits of the transferability of knowledge and skills across a range of subject matters and projects, and that learning was fundamentally a social activity, we might organise our curriculum in such a way as to enable students to spend longer periods of time conducting explorations and investigations – some independently, some collaboratively – in ways that break down or reject traditional subject or discipline boundaries, encouraging more eclectic approaches to (for example) problem-solving and knowledge development.

What's it for?

In other publications (e.g. Moore 2012), I have suggested that official policy documentation in the UK and elsewhere (that is to say, Education Acts, National Curriculum Guidelines, government White Papers and so on) tends to highlight a number of *different* curriculum aims and purposes (we might say, different rationales or perhaps 'sub rationales') – all of which the curriculum is required to embody at any given time in its history. To summarise – although each may be given greater or lesser priority at any particular time – these aims tend to be:

- to meet the needs of the national economy and 'business';
- to promote the enrichment and self-fulfilment of the individual;
- preparation for the world of work and for active, appropriate participation in society.

Another way of putting this is offered (again) by Walsh (1993), who identifies four broad purposes of education and the curriculum as: the *instrumental* (related to such matters as the national economy and social cohesion); the *experiential* (related to Dewey's [2009] concept of individual 'growth'); the *ethical*, which (after Peters) comprises an 'initiation into the wise, or at any rate the rational, life' (Walsh ibid.: 111); and the *ecstatic* (related to a love of learning itself and of individual development and enrichment through such love) – while James et al.'s list (2011: 15, para. 2:12) of the 'domains [in all of which] schools are expected to contribute, in a balanced way…in high-performing jurisdictions' comprises:

- [the] Economic (the education of pupils is expected to contribute to their own future economic well-being and that of the nation or region);
- [the] Cultural (the education of pupils is expected to introduce them to the best of their cultural heritage(s), so that they can contribute to its further development;
- [the] Social (the education of pupils is expected to enable them to participate in families, communities and the life of the nation);
- [the] Personal (the education of pupils is expected to promote the intellectual, spiritual, moral and physical development of individuals.

(Taken from James et al. [2011], who add [ibid: 15, para. 2:13]
'many of the jurisdictions that we have considered that have recently
conducted reviews of their curricula have introduced
a high-level reference to sustainability.')

Interestingly, unlike Walsh's list, which sees 'personal' and 'national' interests in potential conflict with one another both practically (over time and resources) and ideologically or philosophically (over whether personal development and fulfilment, usually understood primarily in non-economic terms, is more or less important than the perceived national interest, usually perceived primarily in economic terms), the list provided by James et al. unites each of its four 'domains' (five, if we include sustainability) under the same category of 'the practical and functional contributions that education makes *to national development*' (p. 15, emphasis added) – effectively blurring what might be seen as artificial and unhelpful boundaries between the *individual* good and the *collective* good. This list also – to look ahead to some issues raised in Chapter 8 – highlights what others have seen as ubiquitous omissions from curriculum aims and rationales, as well as offering another reminder of that very important and overlooked question: Who makes these decisions – and on what bases?

Coffield and Williamson, in a fierce critique of recent and current curriculum reform in England, have pointed to the often overlooked or underplayed 'democratic, social and cultural purposes of education' (2011: 9) and of a curriculum approach to *learning* that 'encourages the creativity and risk-taking needed for change, as when citizens use their minds, exercise their human rights, treat others with respect and challenge the status quo' (ibid.). While these aspects may be discreetly embedded in many lists of curriculum aims, they are less often made very explicit, often incorporated within general terms such as 'intellectual, spiritual, moral and physical development' (ibid.) – while the 'Who Decides?' issue remains even more elusive. What are we to make, for example, of the reference in James et al.'s description to 'the best of their [pupils'] cultural heritage'? What is meant by 'best'? Who decides what is 'best'? (Certainly not the students or their families or local communities!) And who is included in this homogenising 'their' anyway? i.e. *Whose* 'cultural heritage' exactly are we talking about – and whose might we be excluding?

Before considering some of the implications of these lists a little further, including the internal compatibility (or otherwise) of the aims and objectives within them, it is also important to recognise that curriculum theory itself and theorists *of* curriculum (that is to say, not just politicians) are likely to bring different emphases to their analyses of curriculum policy and development – these, in turn, often being dependent on or emanating from specific philosophical, political, or ideological preferences. In this regard, Schiro's 'four philosophies' (also referred to by Schiro as 'ideologies') underpinning education theory are potentially very helpful, and indeed may facilitate readers in 'positioning' *themselves* in relation to curriculum theory and practice.

Schiro's four philosophies

Schiro's four philosophies, also called ideologies – which are not necessarily mutually exclusive and are also present in education *policy* – are represented as:

1   the 'scholar academic'
2   the 'social efficiency ideology'
3   the 'learner centred ideology'
4   the 'social reconstruction ideology'

(See also, for comparison, Eisner's 'Five Basic Orientations to the Curriculum' in Eisner 1979: 50–72: these being 'development of cognitive processes'; 'academic rationalism'; 'personal relevance'; social adaptation and social reconstruction'; and 'curriculum as technology'.)

Scholar academics, Schiro advises, 'believe that…[t]he purpose of education is to help children learn the accumulated knowledge of our culture: that of the academic disciplines' (In policy terms, this is a widespread belief that continues to emphasise the identification and sanctification of a body of knowledge, and to adhere to the division of learning into traditional subject disciplines.) (Schiro 2013: 4).

Advocates of the '*social efficiency ideology*', on the other hand (ibid.: 5), 'believe that the purpose of schooling is to efficiently meet the needs of society by training youth to function as future mature contributing members of society'. (An emphasis, that is, on socialisation and economic concerns: on the curriculum as essentially reproductive.)

In contrast with these two rather functional curriculum rationales, Schiro offers the '*learner centred ideology*' and the '*social reconstruction ideology*' (ibid.: 5–6). Supporters of the first of these focus not so much on 'the needs of society or the academic disciplines, but on the needs and concerns of individuals' – as a consequence of which 'schools should be enjoyable places where people develop naturally according to their own innate natures'. Within this ideology, the emphasis is on evolution rather than reproduction: that is to say, the evolution of the individual rather than (necessarily) of the wider society. Here, '[t]he goal of education is the growth of individuals, each in harmony with his or her own unique intellectual, social, emotional and physical attributes'.

Schiro's final philosophy, the '*social reconstruction ideology*', takes evolution a step further, suggesting that curriculum/education has – or perhaps should have – as a central purpose the development of a critically educated citizenry able to engage reflectively and reflexively with the wider society (and indeed the wider social world), opening up greater possibilities for *societal evolution* or more radical societal change:

> Social reconstructionists are conscious of the problems of our society and the injustices done to its members, such as those originating from racial, gender, social, and economic inequalities. They assume that the purpose of education is to facilitate the construction of a new and more just society that offers maximum satisfaction to all of its members.
>
> > (ibid.: 6. See also Kliebard's [2004] emphasis on curriculum's potential as a tool to reform and improve society through the promotion of social justice, and Dewey [2009: 40] on 'the school and social progress')

Interestingly, Schiro describes these four philosophies or 'major curriculum ideologies', each with its own history and its own devout following, as *in conflict* – or 'at war' – with one another in public education in America (ibid: xv) rather than as in a dynamic, dialogic relationship: a conflict which, to hark back to the discussion in Chapter 2, renders 'systematic improvement of the curriculum difficult' and which inevitably produces or supports other conflicts such as that between dominant (conservative and neo-liberal) policy ideologies and ubiquitous (social liberal) teacher ideologies – intruding, often disruptively, into school classrooms, and exercising a draining effect on teachers' energies. Some of the specific battles referenced by Schiro within this wider 'war' will be all too familiar to many readers working in countries other than America:

> Seemingly irresolvable disagreements include the reading controversy over whether it is more important to teach decoding (phonics) or comprehension (whole language), the mathematics disputes over whether it is more important to teach mathematical understanding or mathematical skills, and the history conflicts on whether it is more important to teach knowledge of the past or to build strategies for critically analyzing and reconstructing society in the future. [Such disputes] have recently become so fierce that they have become known as the reading wars, the maths wars and the history wars.
>
> > (ibid.: 1)

Echoing an earlier discussion, we might suggest that such 'wars' are themselves embedded in a larger war: the war between the supporters of the 'reproductive' curriculum and the supporters of the '[r]evolutionary' curriculum.

The 'balanced' curriculum

Whichever list of aims or philosophies or rationales we begin with (and we could find or devise numerous others), the different curriculum purposes they identify are typically presented in the public policy realm as though they are readily compatible, or as though, if they are not already, then schools and teachers will make them so. This sense of the curriculum having many different but wholly compatible elements and functions is certainly implicit in most modern governments' own official statements of curriculum aims and contents, often embedded in a widespread acceptance that the curriculum should be 'balanced': i.e. that each of the different aims and elements should be adequately represented in terms of time and resources, so that no one or no group is allowed to dominate. In the case of England, a statement in the *National Curriculum Handbook for Teachers* (1999, quoted in White 2004b: 2–4), thus advises teachers:

> Education influences and reflects the values of society, and the kind of society we want to be. …Foremost is a belief in education…as a route to the spiritual, moral, social, cultural, physical and mental development, and thus the well-being, of the individual. Education is also a route to equality of opportunity for all, a healthy and just democracy, a productive economy, and sustainable development. Education should reflect the enduring values that contribute to these ends. These include valuing ourselves, our families and other relationships, the wider groups to which we belong, the diversity of our society and the environment in which we live. Education should also reaffirm our commitment to the virtues of truth, justice, honesty, trust and a sense of duty.
>
> *At the same time*, education must enable us to respond positively to the opportunities and challenges of the rapidly changing world in which we live and work. In particular, we need to be prepared to engage as individuals, parents, workers and citizens with economic, social and cultural change, including the continued globalisation of the economy and society, with new work and leisure patterns and with the rapid expansion of communication technologies.
>
> (emphasis added, DEE/QCA 1999: 10)

(Additionally, the curriculum must aim to 'promote an enquiring mind and capacity to think rationally', and 'should enable pupils to think creatively and critically, to solve problems and to make a difference for the better' [ibid.: 12].)

The curriculum here is presented as being both forward looking (preparing for 'globalisation' and rapid change, developing ICT skills and so on) and retrospective or reproductive (preserving traditional values and relationships); it must promote the well-being of the individual as well as the well-being, including the economic well-being, of the nation; it must promote 'mental' and 'physical' development but also 'spiritual', 'moral', 'social' and 'cultural' development – all this in a society which is becoming increasingly multi-faith and multi-cultural. A tall order, it might seem, not simply because of the sheer volume of curriculum content implied in the statement, but because of the unacknowledged tensions that might exist between and among these different content areas. (For instance, the imperative for self-fulfilment and personal enrichment might not always sit comfortably alongside the perceived need for education to respond to the perceived demands of commerce and the national economy.)

Bruner (1996a) and Eisner (1979) are two among many education theorists who have not only cast doubt over this model of the 'balanced', internally compatible curriculum, but have reminded us that although all elements might be present to a degree in the curriculum, they are not always given anything like equal weight. Bruner, for example, not dissimilarly to Schiro, refers to the unproductive tension or what he calls the 'antinomy' between different educational/curricular aims – for instance, between the perceived needs of the national socio-economic community and the curricular needs (and perhaps rights) of the individual:

[O]n the one hand, it is unquestionably the function of education to enable people, individual human beings, to operate at their fullest potential, to equip them with the tools and the sense of opportunity to use their wits, skills, and passions to the fullest sense. The antinomic counterpart of this is that the function of education is to reproduce the culture that supports it – not only reproduce it, but further its economic, political, and cultural ends. For example, the educational system of an industrial society should produce a willing and compliant labor force to keep it going: unskilled and semi-skilled workers, clerical workers, middle-managers, risk-sensitive entrepreneurs, all of whom are convinced that such an industrial society constitutes the right, valid, and only way of living.

(Bruner 1996b: 67)

Highlighting a wider issue concerning what Foucault (see, e.g., Burchell et al. 1991) christened 'governmentality' (i.e. how does a neo-liberal politics both promote individual 'freedom' *and* ensure compliance to existing social norms and mores? Effectively, how does central government seek to reproduce the citizenry it requires for the successful implementation and acceptance of its policies?), Bruner asks:

[C]an schooling be constructed both as the instrument of individual realization and at the same time as a reproductive technique for maintaining or furthering a culture? ...Finding a way within this antinomic pair does not come easily, particularly not in times of rapid change. Indeed, it could never have come easily at any time. But if one does not face it, one risks failing both ideals.

(Bruner: ibid.)

Eisner's concern, in like vein, is that for all the official claims for curriculum to be 'broad and balanced', to address the needs of 'the whole person', to develop a love of learning and so forth, the emphasis in America (but clearly far more widely) is very firmly on national and international economic competition and competitiveness, and that this is reflected not only in curriculum content but in how students' engagement with – their *experience of* – the curriculum is understood and assessed: that is to say, education and the experience of education, so focused on future employment prospects and national economic competitiveness, take place within an 'industrial culture' (Eisner 1979) in which learning is constructed as work and in which work is a necessity rather than a pleasure. To refer back to Bruner's assessment, the ideal of 'individual realisation' may have already been lost to that other ideal of 'maintaining or furthering' the 'culture' (effectively, a triumph for Schiro's 'scholar academic' and 'social efficiency' ideologies) – one of emphasising national and international competition and socio-economic inequalities within the status quo of free-market capitalism bathed in the artificial glow of a widespread belief in and acceptance of the 'organic society'. (See also Ball 2008: 11.)

Not all curriculum theorists speak of such problems, and there are some (though these are often experts writing in and of a different time) who would appear to *subscribe* to the political view of the easy compatibility of different curriculum elements. The celebrated education theorist Franklin Bobbitt, for example (1971), identifies a potential tension between what he sees as 'two levels of educational experience' embedded in curriculum aims and practice – one essentially therapeutic, emphasising the pleasure of learning, learning for learning's sake, personal enrichment and development, the other 'utilitarian', in which educational objectives have to be linked to future careers and/or the national economy and social cohesion (Bobbitt 1971: 3) – but he then rather dismisses it. For example, in answer to his rhetorical question, 'Now, which side is right?', Bobbitt replies: 'Doubtless both are right. It is like asking the question, "Which shall the tree produce, the flower or the fruit?" It must produce both or it will not perform its full function' (ibid.: 6).

Curriculum as product, as content, as process: 'Symphony orchestras' and 'jazz bands'

Bobbitt's identification of the functional and therapeutic aims of formal education, and his suggestion that both can (and indeed must) be accommodated in school curricula, return us to another key debate within Curriculum Studies regarding whether curriculum should be fundamentally aims-and-objectives based or process-and-experience based, more focused on inputs and content or more open and developmental. This is sometimes referred to as the 'content-process' debate, or as the 'product-process' debate, or as the 'objectives-developmental' debate – three constructions which may sound different from one another but which in reality concern the same underpinning difference of opinion between those for whom 'acquisition' (of certain pre-identified knowledge and skills) is key, and those for whom development of the learning process, of learning skills, and of a love of learning are more important.

Before considering (and re-considering) the terms 'content', 'product', 'process', 'objectives' and 'development' themselves – what they might mean, and whether they might be compatible in practice – I want to introduce another curriculum metaphor which I think helps to contextualise the two different emphases within wider philosophical and theoretical perspectives and beliefs regarding how we understand human nature, human development, and indeed the wider purposes of education – and that impels us to revisit from a different angle some of the key curriculum issues we have already considered: issues, for example, around the extent to which curriculum should be centrally mandated or locally devised; how far it should be teacher- and textbook led or student-centred; how 'open' or 'closed' it should be; and whether, in Bernstein's terms, it should be performance- or competence-oriented.

Borrowed from Eugene Holland's account of Deleuze and Guattari's *Anti-Oedipus* (see also Chapter 2) the metaphor I'm using is that of the symphony orchestra and jazz – or the jazz band. It is a metaphor that takes us back, through a different doorway, to the concept of 'Mastery', and to the ways in which different curricula reflect, arise from and support different understandings of *learning* and of *the learner*. Holland introduces the metaphor thus:

> The idea [of jazz] is to take just enough of what is already known – a melody, a chord-sequence, a harmonic mode or tone-system – as a point of departure for the shared production and enjoyment of what is radically new. ...[On the other hand,] symphony orchestras can only hope their performances rise to the genius of the composer whose work they are performing: they hope their content lives up to the pre-existing phrase. ...[J]azz not only presents...an ideal instance of human relations and interpersonal dynamics but actually suggests a social ideal: the use of accumulated wealth as a basis for the shared production and enjoyment of life in

the present rather than the reproduction and reinforcement of power-structures from the past.

(Holland 1999: xi. See also Derrida's account of the relationship between language and discourse as taking place in the field of 'freeplay': 'that is to say, a field of infinite substitutions in the closure of a finite ensemble' [Derrida 1993: 236].)

There is more here perhaps than is normally included in considerations of the content-product-objectives and the process-developmental approaches to curriculum, but not, I would venture to suggest, a lot more, and what little more there might be is implicit in the models. In applying the metaphor to education and specifically to the school curriculum, I'm reminded, indeed, both of Rancière's 'explicator' and of Noddings' quoting of The Professor of Worldly Wisdom from Samuel Butler's *Erehwon* at the start of her Introduction to *Critical Lessons: What Our Schools Should Teach*:

"It is not our business," he said, "to help students to think for themselves. Surely, this is the very last thing which one who wishes them well should encourage them to do. Our duty is to ensure that they shall think as we do, or at any rate, as we hold it expedient to say we do."

The objectives-based approach, subsequently elaborated by Tyler in answer to his own four questions (Tyler, op.cit.), is, thus, closely associated with models of curriculum based primarily on matters of 'hard content' and predetermined 'end products', of the absorption, (potential) interpretation and guided application of pre-existing knowledge – its success demonstrable in and measurable through students' capacities to show or 'evidence' what they have learned and can do (to provide acceptable 'answers' to pre-determined questions) in formal, standardised tests and examinations. The process-based approach, by contrast, while not completely turning its back on the notion of objectives, emphasises knowledge development and creation, and the use of existing knowledge as starting points – its emphasis on the individual learner and its preference for questions and open-ended explorations over approved answers rendering standardised testing less relevant. The notion in jazz of taking 'just enough of what is already known' as a 'point of departure' certainly chimes with Eisner's extended account of issues of process, content and objectives (Eisner 1979), in which the process model is described as establishing the parameters or frameworks within which exploratory learning takes place providing, in Eisner's words, 'the opportunity for ingenuity' (1979: 103).

The two models ('content' and 'process', for short) not only have implications for curriculum design, but also speak of differing understandings of student or worker collaboration. In the symphony orchestra of the objectivist, content approach, each player has a particular job to do, exercising a particular skill or aptitude, so that here collaboration mirrors the notion of the 'organic society' in which different people are allocated (and taught to accept) different roles according to some notions of intrinsic ability or aptitude. In the 'jazz band' of the process model, on the other hand, although different players still contribute using different instruments, they do so creatively, dialogically, often extemporaneously, their collaboration including 'conversations' and acts of co-respondence.

Not without justification, Scott (2008) attributes the development of subject-based, progressional National Curricula to the influence of objectivist and content-based curriculum theorists of the past such as Tyler and Popham, whose own objectives model (e.g. Popham 1972) focused exclusively on what behaviours were to be expected on the part of the student as end product, rather than engaging with pedagogical issues related to teacher development – a rather simple input-output understanding of teaching and learning, rendering the teacher's job as simply working out the best ways of getting students to achieve whatever objectives have been set. This particular difficulty is further elaborated by Stenhouse, in a criticism of the objectives model on the grounds that (among other things) it does not appear to allow for *teacher development* let alone encourage more subtle, reflexive approaches to student learning. As Stenhouse (1975: 96) puts it: 'The objectives model applied to knowledge areas seems to me to concentrate on improving teaching as instruction without increment to the wisdom or scholarship of the teacher.' Stenhouse concludes: 'We do not teach people to jump higher by setting the bar higher, but by enabling them to criticise their present performance' (Stenhouse 1975: 83).

It is Stenhouse himself (1975) who offers one of the most powerfully and cogently-argued critiques of the objectives model, still not bettered since its publication nearly 40 years ago, and who invites us to embrace the 'process' model in its place. He begins his argument, in the same fashion as Bobbitt (ibid.), with a question: 'The issue is: can curriculum and pedagogy be organized satisfactorily by a logic other than that of the means-end model? Can the demands of a curriculum specification...be met without using the concepts of objectives?' (Stenhouse 1975: 84). Stenhouse's response is that there is indeed such an alternative: that is to say, the process model. Unlike the objectives model, which begins by setting out what is to be learned and what is therefore to be included in the curriculum, Stenhouse offers a 'specification of curriculum and the educational process without starting by pre-specifying the anticipated outcomes of that process in the form of objectives' (Stenhouse: ibid.).

Such an approach immediately differentiates itself from objectivist approaches in a number of ways related to how 'knowledge' is understood (epistemological issues) and what it means to be a sentient human being (matters of ontology). Knowledge, for example, is not always 'a thing' to be pre-identified and subsequently absorbed by the learner, but rather a process in itself which involves journeys of discovery on the part of the learner and the teacher – journeys which may well have (though do not have to have) an initial (quite precise or very general) goal, but during which, along the way (we cannot really say 'at the end', for there is no final destination), all manner of surprises are anticipated and found. As Dewey had already argued many years previously, in *Human Nature and Conduct*:

> [E]nds arise as a function within action. They are not, as current theories too often imply, things lying outside activity at which the latter is directed. They are not ends or termini of action at all. They are terminals of deliberation, and so turning points *in* activity. [...] Even the most important among all the consequences of an act is not necessarily its aim.
>
> (Dewey 1922: 223, 227)

Stenhouse additionally points out the issues for *pedagogy and assessment* of the objectives and process models, arguing, for example, that there is something intrinsically contradictory and self-defeating in the former, precisely because of its logical conclusion that the success of the objectives approach must be evidenced in order for it to be validated, and that the only meaningful form of evidence is provided by mass testing – as opposed to a system in which learning is, so to speak, self-validating and, by virtue of its contingent, idiosyncratic nature, resistant to mass assessment. The internal contradiction lies in the fact that, by its very nature, mass testing can never be up to the task of assessing an individual student's internalised knowledge, let alone the uses to which they might put it, so that knowledge itself becomes distorted – either because of the retroactive, limiting influence of the test on how knowledge is perceived and developed, or within the test itself, as students endeavour to squeeze and shape their oceans of learning into the tanks and reservoirs of timed essays.

Not only, says Stenhouse, does the enduringly popular objectives model have this distorting effect on 'the knowledge included in the curriculum' (1975: 86); it also has a very particular – and particularly unhelpful – impact on the way in which the curriculum is taught and how it must therefore understand learning, not least in its total failure to address the subtleties of pedagogy, including that key aspect of the pedagogic *relationship* between the teacher and the learner. As Stenhouse puts it: 'The formulation of a schedule of behavioural objectives helps us little towards the means of attaining them' (1975: 87). The process model, by contrast, precisely because of its emphasis on processes (of learning and of teaching) commands us to address issues of pedagogy – a command that can take us in any number of directions, all characterised by an emphasis on assisting, supporting or even helping to guide the student's development rather than nudging them ever closer to a set of pre-determined and strongly prescribed 'achievements'. To push this a little further, we might say that, unlike the objectives, content-based models of curriculum, the process-based model at least offers the possibility of an open, questioning, exploratory, self-propelling learning experience, with an emphasis on the provisionality of knowledge, within the context of what Deleuze and Guattari (1991, 2004) have called 'the plane of immanence' and the concept of 'becoming'. Thus, in his essay 'The Blindness of Education to the "Untimeliness" of Real Learning', Dennis Atkinson, drawing on Deleuze and Guattari's *What Is Philosophy?* (1991: 35–60) and Stagoll's (2005) analysis of the Deleuzean 'Plane', writes:

> the notion of immanence denotes a flow of becoming which in-itself cannot be conceptualised but out of which emerge crystallisations in the form of concepts and affects that are actualised and provide what we might term holding-forms from which thinking develops. In some ways this can be equated with the constant flow of a river in which eddies form and dissolve, or where intensities form and dissolve whilst at every moment the river around them continues to flow. According to this descriptor becoming is conceived as a constant process of flow with inherent intensities that emerge and subside rather than in terms of more concrete notions of being and subjectivity.
>
> (Atkinson 2013)

'Process' and democracy: 'Nounal' and 'adjectival' curricula

I want to finish this brief account of the objectives and process approaches to curriculum with reference to a particular development of the latter that serves also to remind us of a theme and of an issue which runs across every chapter of *Understanding the School Curriculum*. This concerns the dynamic, which can also be a tension, regarding the extent to which the curriculum (and education in general) can or should be more or less democratic or autocratic, more or less student-centred or adult-led, more or less (r)evolutionary or reproductive.

The development I'm interested in is A.V. Kelly's, which begins with an argument for 'a curriculum based not on common knowledge-content but on common procedural principles' (Kelly 1999: 222). For Kelly, curriculum needs to be founded not so much upon partial selections from existing knowledge and skills but upon notions of what is required of and owing to the citizens of a democratic society, and upon democratic social values. Thus, in an argument that flags up issues of democratic classrooms which I will return to later, Kelly's own version of the process-based curriculum highlights collaborative and lifelong learning for the student and the need to preserve and celebrate teacher professionalism in relation to the classroom practitioner. Kelly's 'appropriate curriculum for a democratic society' would be

> one which allowed for the continuing development of knowledge and understanding, which provided proper opportunities for young people to develop their powers of autonomous thinking and offered them social and intellectual empowerment and which provided teachers with the scope to achieve these goals through the exercise of their own judgement as professionals. ...Democratic education must be recognized as essentially a collaborative rather than a competitive activity. ...The curriculum must be framed, therefore, not primarily in terms of its content but as a set of guidelines delineating the democratic entitlement of every young citizen. ...[D]emocracy is more than a political system; it is also and above all a moral system. It is a political system which is characterised not by particular procedures, such as regular elections of government, but primarily by being based on certain fundamental moral principles.
>
> (Kelly 1999: 223, 225, 219–20)

The fundamental moral principles that Kelly highlights are 'equality, freedom and, binding these together, respect for the rights of the individual' (ibid.).

In a further elaboration of these ideas in their (1998) book *Experience and Education*, Edwards and Kelly put forward the notion of an 'adjectival' curriculum (Edwards and Kelly 1998: Preface): that is to say, 'one which will *de*scribe rather than *pre*scribe the kinds of educational experience to which all young people have an entitlement in a democratic society'. As Edwards and Kelly argue (ibid.: xv):

> [T]he main significance of employing adjectives rather than nouns to delineate the several dimensions of such a curriculum is that they can be seen as describing different aspects of what is essentially a single entity, the developing experience of the individual, rather than as discrete elements to be kept forever apart. An adjectival curriculum, unlike a substantive curriculum, cannot be so readily viewed as an agglomeration of separate entities; it is what they all add up to which constitutes education in the full sense and which also constitutes the entitlement of every individual in such an education. For the entitlement is, or should be, to a coherent

set of experiences, not to a heterogeneous conglomerate whose cohesiveness is left to chance.

> (For a not dissimilar movement of curriculum away from its traditional 'nounal' character – this time toward a 'verbal' conceptualisation – see Pinar's [2004] notion of *currere*.)

Edwards and Kelly's argument is, effectively, one for weaker subject boundaries enabling a more 'cross-curricular', or more appropriately 'whole-curriculum' approach to teaching and learning, and at the same time one which does not, for example, lead to what Michael Young (1998: 75–6) has called a 'divided curriculum' in which (in Young's example) vocational and academic subjects are not simply kept apart but bestowed with differential status. The proposal of 'adjectival' and 'nounal' as metaphoric descriptors of the contrasting 'content based' and 'process based' models of curriculum can help pull together some of the points covered in this chapter, and indeed some of those raised in the preceding chapter. In light of this, Figure 3.1 below suggests what the objectives and process approaches might look like and what their underpinning rationales might be if taken to their extremes, that is to say, if they are permitted to become dominant curriculum *models*. One question for curriculum theory is: can we find a 'middle way' or balance that incorporates elements of both models? And, if we could, would we, in any event, wish to do so? (There are some, of course, who will argue that school curricula already *do* combine content and process in a balanced way, and that they do so inevitably.)

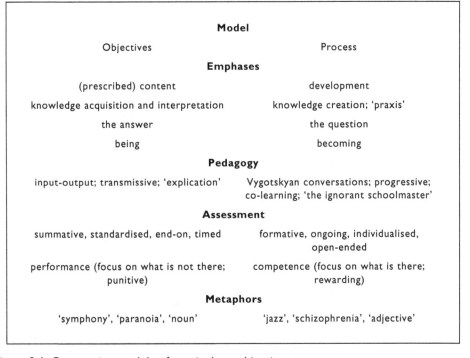

Model	
Objectives	Process
Emphases	
(prescribed) content	development
knowledge acquisition and interpretation	knowledge creation; 'praxis'
the answer	the question
being	becoming
Pedagogy	
input-output; transmissive; 'explication'	Vygotskyan conversations; progressive; co-learning; 'the ignorant schoolmaster'
Assessment	
summative, standardised, end-on, timed	formative, ongoing, individualised, open-ended
performance (focus on what is not there; punitive)	competence (focus on what is there; rewarding)
Metaphors	
'symphony', 'paranoia', 'noun'	'jazz', 'schizophrenia', 'adjective'

Figure 3.1 Contrasting models of curriculum: objectives v. process

Curriculum conspiracy theory

It would be an oversight, I think, to end this discussion of curriculum definitions, rationales and models without giving some attention to the suggestion made by some theorists that formalised curriculum rationales – especially those presented within the 'official recontextualising field' of central policy – are actually faux rationales, expressed in terms that are likely to elicit broad acceptance and compliance, that serve to mask rather less acceptable underpinning or (to anticipate discussions to be had in Chapter 8) 'hidden' rationales. I am referring to such an approach as 'conspiracy theory' not to demean or to mock it (far from it), but simply because the term conspiracy includes within it the kinds of deliberation, secrecy and duplicitousness that its proponents claim, not without good cause, to be at the heart of much public education policy.

Curriculum conspiracy theory begins with one of the key questions or abiding issues we have already considered (and will return to in Chapter 7): If curriculum selections are made by certain groups of people, who are these people? Are they really able or willing to adopt scientific, 'objective' methods in arriving at their selections? And if they are not, then what exactly are their 'vested interests' and what exactly are their intentions? To anticipate some of the 'knowledge questions' to be explored in Chapter 4, if we take the view that *all* knowledge is intrinsically worthwhile, who decides what knowledge is more important than other knowledge, and on what basis?

For some curriculum commentators, the answer is clear. The 'interests' are not those of students – at least, not of all students – but rather of a narrow range of students and their families and of an equally narrow segment of a wider, hierarchised society. In short, a prime function of curriculum is to preserve a social status quo that protects the interests of a ruling élite and teaches others to remember – and, crucially, to accept as both just and natural – their place. Harris argues, for example:

> Education in a class society is a political act having as its basis the protection of the interests of the ruling class. It is a mechanism…for securing the continuation of the existing social relationships, and for reinforcing the attitudes and beliefs that will help ensure that those social relationships will continue to be accepted. Education…is an ideological force of tremendous import…Education is the manipulation of consciousness…and it functions largely without serious opposition of any sort.
>
> (Harris 1979: 140–1)

This view of public education and school curricula – that the hunt for and assertion of universal, self-justifying curriculum objectives and curriculum content is a rhetorical smoke-screen masking an essentially political and ideological set of decisions – suggests that politicians, rather than meaning well but sometimes getting things wrong (or even sometimes getting things wrong because they do not listen attentively or seriously enough to experts in the field) may actually know exactly what they are doing: in short, they are putting into practice and into law what the most privileged members of society, those who benefit most from the prevailing socio-economic system, want them to. As Riley (2011) tactfully puts it, reminding us again of the contested and contestable nature of curriculum and indeed of its vital importance in preserving or challenging or overturning social and economic inequality: 'Public, or government supported schools, since the Enlightenment, first and foremost reflect government aims and goals. *They also reflect special interests and personal agendas of various social groups.*' (Riley in Kysilka 2011a: xi, emphasis added).

Most famously, perhaps, the American sociologists Samuel Bowles and Herbert Gintis (1976) have argued that for all its talk of the intrinsic value of education, of equity and empowerment, public education primarily exists for purely functional, organisational and convenience reasons, to do with social and economic control: keeping young people occupied and off the streets; allowing parents to go to work rather than having to stay at home to care for children; drip-feeding the workforce into employment (or unemployment) in a highly managed and regulated way; reproducing the knowledge and basic skills required of the national economy; and validating, promoting and protecting the interests of some social groups at the expense of others (see also Illich 1973, Ernest 1998, Apple 2004, and Barnes 1986: 85 – who links such a project not only to curriculum content but to publicly favoured pedagogies aimed to 'control', 'select' and 'contain' the working population).

American public schools of 40 or so years ago, Bowles and Gintis argued (though the same charge might be levelled today both at American and at many other national school systems), were essentially nurseries that both mirrored and prepared young people for life in an essentially unaltering, privileging and de-privileging society. They embodied and comprised: 'a bureaucratic order, with hierarchical authority, rule orientation, stratification by "ability" as well as by age, role differentiation by sex...and a system of external incentives (marks, promises of promotion, and threat of failure) much like pay and status in the field of work' (Bowles and Gintis 1972: 87).

Four years later, in an even more vigorous attack on the system, these same critics were to paint a picture of public schooling which could hardly be more different than that most commonly espoused in the rhetoric of much global education policy of today which talks of inclusion, of giving all young people a helping hand up the social ladder, and of learning to take an active part in democracy. American schools in the 1970s, Bowles and Gintis now suggested, 'are destined to legitimate inequality, limit personal development to forms compatible with submission to arbitrary authority, and aid in the process whereby youth are resigned to their fate' (Bowles and Gintis 1976: 266). Bowles and Gintis are by no means the only critics to have suggested that beneath the socially just rhetoric of much education and curriculum policy lies a more devious and far more sinister purpose – a kind of 'hidden curriculum' in the 'ORF' of public policy we might say, to mirror that which other critics have identified in the 'PRF' of school and classroom practice. Harris (1979) has already been cited, while more recently, Apple has argued that schools and school curricula in the USA tend to be organised to reproduce an essentially compliant, obedient, 'quiescent' workforce (Apple 1995), while the British commentator, Alistair Ross has invited us to consider the following summarised account of Ivan Illich's (1973) take on the form and functions of formal education:

Far from having the function of developing a democratic and participatory society, Illich argued that the main tasks of the school were in reality four-fold: they provided custodial care for children, freeing parents' time; they effectively distributed pupils into occupational roles; they transmitted the dominant value system; and they taught pupils to acquire socially approved knowledge and skills.

(Ross 2000: 85)

To anticipate again a discussion to be had in Chapter 7, Ross' own analysis, like Apple's and Bernstein's, takes more account than Bowles and Gintis' of the power of teacher and student *agency*, and their capacity to help bring about changes in schools and schooling that might have a more global change-effect in relation to the wider social system. With an eye to how, in many societies, frequent, high-stakes testing of students shifts curriculum policy away from content that is essentially useful or valuable toward a more instrumental, divisive functionality, Ross does, however, make the point that:

a schooling system which credentializes a particular proportion of the population roughly equivalent to the needs of the division of labour (and de-credentializes the rest) is an almost natural way of maintaining the economic and cultural imbalance on which these societies are built.

(ibid.: 83)

While suggestions such as those of Bowles and Gintis and of Ivan Illich may be easily dismissed (and often are) as 'extreme' or (with a somewhat different inflection from previous usage) 'paranoid', we might argue that they are able to claim legitimacy through reference to some still-available policy statements within the official recontextualising field dating back to a time before politicians had discovered equity and social justice, or at least the need to swear allegiance to some forms of them. In his book *On Being A Teacher*, the American teacher-writer Jonathan Kozol quotes some famous compatriots' published views on the *meaning* of public education and its *rationale* at the point of its introduction in the USA as a universal entitlement. Thus, Horace Mann, in a report to the Massachusetts Board of Education in 1844, had publicly (and without shame or fear of comeback) observed:

in regard to those who possess the largest shares…of worldly goods, could there, in your opinion, be any policy so vigilant and effective, for protection of all the rights of person, property and character, as such a…system of common schools could be made to impart[?] …Would not the payment of a sufficient tax to make such education and training universal, be the cheapest means of self-protection and insurance?'

(cited in Kozol 1993: 5–6)

While the ex-president of the United States, Woodrow Wilson, is quoted as saying: 'We want one class of people to have a liberal education, and we want one class of persons, a very much larger class of persons, of necessity, to forego the privileges of a liberal education and fit into specific manual tasks' (cited in Kozol ibid.: 6. For similar pronouncements by English politicians, see Moore 2012, Chapter 2).

Readers will make up their own minds as to whether things have moved on in the intervening period, or whether current government rhetorics of inclusion, equity and empowerment merely act as a friendly-face behind which lurks the same conservatising rationale. Supporters of curriculum conspiracy theory might well draw strength for their argument from the recent ubiquitous rise of formal *national* curricula, which may be understood either in terms of 'entitlement' or as a means of exercising control to ensure a continuation of an inequitable status quo.

Chapter 4

'Knowledge'

[W]hatever vagaries there have been in the use of the term ['liberal education'], it is the appropriate label for a positive concept, that of an education based fairly and squarely on the nature of knowledge itself, a concept central to the discussion of education at any level.

(Hirst 1998: 246)

"[I]t is the view of the Ministry that a theoretical knowledge will be more than sufficient to get you through the examination, which, after all, is what school is all about. ...As long as you have studied the theory hard enough, there is no reason why you should not be able to perform the spells under carefully controlled examination conditions," said Professor Umbridge dismissively.

"Without ever practising them beforehand?" said Parvati incredulously.

"Are you telling us that the first time we'll get to do the spells will be during the exam?"

"I repeat, as long as you have studied the theory hard enough –"

"And what good's theory going to be in the real world?" said Harry loudly, his fist in the air again.

Professor Umbridge looked up.

"This is school, Mr Potter, not the real world," she said softly. [...] "And now you will kindly continue reading. Page five, 'Basics for Beginners'."

(Rowling 2013: 220)

Knowledge and learning

It has already been noted that one of the main rationales for having a *national* curriculum is that it entitles school students (those in the public sector of education at any rate) to access the same core knowledge and skills as everybody else: that is to say, an *equity and entitlement* rationale. But what do we mean by knowledge and skills? Who (to reprise a question invited by 'conspiracy theory') decides what knowledge and skills people should be 'entitled' to? Where and how do we draw the lines between entitlement and selectivity, between compulsion (which for some students might be another way of understanding and experiencing entitlement) and choice? And do we think that schooling – the curriculum – is *just* about knowledge and skills (albeit of various different kinds, to suit different purposes) – or might it be about other things too? Might it, for example, be about learning more about ourselves as emotional, social beings, or about developing, through experience, the capacity to get along constructively, sympathetically and therapeutically with other human beings, or about developing a sense of responsibility for ourselves, for others and for the planet, or about developing critical skills or personal and collective values? To return to one of the quotations with which this chapter opened: Do we subscribe to the classical view of the 'liberal education', defined by Hirst as 'a process concerned simply and directly with the pursuit of knowledge' (Hirst 1998: 247)? And, if so, do we find the consequent championing of 'an education that frees the mind from error and illusion' (ibid.: 257) helpful, empowering and inclusive or (as some might argue) demeaning, patronising and elitist?

There are many other questions about knowledge that we might feel the need to address, regardless of whether or not our curriculum is to be essentially 'knowledge based' – questions all too easily overlooked within curriculum debates that refine their focus to issues which should perhaps be dealt with later on in the curriculum discussion, such as (to return to matters discussed in Chapter 3) what the 'balance' should be between 'product' and 'process' or (within the context of this current chapter) between 'knowledge' and 'skills'. Do we, for example, understand or construct knowledge – effectively, 'reify knowledge' – as some immutable entity that is 'out there' waiting to be discovered regardless of who we are as individuals? Or do we believe that knowledge is socially and culturally mediated, partial and *produced*? Can knowledge be *both* these things, depending on what 'kind' of knowledge it is? Do we only refer to knowledge as that which is deemed to be irrefutably 'true', either in itself or because human beings have decided it is so (what might be termed 'scientific knowledge' in the first case, and might include much mathematical knowledge in the second)? Or do we include knowledge that might, in some senses, be less 'empirically secure', such as knowledge of causes and effects in the subject discipline of history (as opposed, for instance, to knowledge of dates and official recordings of events)?[1]

Related to these questions, we might consider where our understandings and theories of 'reality', of 'truth', of *learning*, of the human mind itself sit in relation to our identification of curriculum knowledge – or, for that matter, of knowledge in general? What account, for instance, might we (must we) give to McCormick and Murphy's observation that

> [d]ifferent *views of learning* assume distinctly different views of the nature of knowledge (and of achievement) …[and] how we view learning is central to how we…[d]efine knowledge in the specified curriculum[,…] [s]elect activities and establish characteristics of pedagogies to develop that knowledge in the enacted curriculum [and] choose the mechanisms [of both teaching and assessment] that are employed to gain access to the experienced curriculum.
>
> (McCormick and Murphy 2000: 210, emphasis added)

The questioning tone in McCormick and Murphy's analysis raises further, equally important issues:

1   Do we begin curriculum construction with questions *about learning* ('What kinds of learning do we want to encourage, and what sorts of stimuli and pedagogy do we believe will promote such learning?')?

2   Do we start out by identifying our body of 'core knowledge' and (perhaps) skills, and only *then* worry (or not) about the learning?

3   Or do we, perhaps, attempt something that incorporates aspects or elements of both approaches?

The suggestion that we might prioritise learning – and learning how to learn – in curriculum planning and design, placing knowledge *at the service of learning* rather than the other way round, is not a new one, nor perhaps as radical as it may sometimes appear. Hirst, for example (1998: 249), cites the *Harvard Committee Report* of 1946 in its identification of 'the elements of knowledge' as 'the means for developing…the cultivation of certain aptitudes and attitudes of mind', and in suggesting replacing the traditional 'body of knowledge' approach to education with what might be described today as a more skills-based and values-based curriculum, focusing on the ability 'to think effectively, to communicate thought, to make judgments, [and] to discriminate among values' (1946: 64–5).

As I write, the *Harvard Report* and the Review on which it was based is nearly 70 years old. However, the argument as to which has priority (if either) – 'knowledge' or 'learning' (akin to 'content' or 'process' in Chapter 3) – is as relevant and as fiercely contested today as ever it was. I'd venture to suggest that the general answer to this 'Which comes first?' question, in the case of a good many state-managed curricula, is that (in contrast with the *Harvard Report*'s recommendations) the curriculum in *terms of knowledge content* is perceived as the priority, and teaching and learning are understood to be in service *to* that content. In the case of curricula which are particularly specific in identifying the knowledge and skills that are to be taught and learned (see, for instance, 'objectives' curriculum models, above), this is likely to be accentuated, whereas a more 'open', exploratory orientation to learning, perhaps along the lines of the Ancient Greek notion of 'askesis', comprising the continuous exercise and practice of *enquiry*, is likely to place significantly less of an emphasis on *what* is to be learned, being at least as interested in learning itself and in promoting the skills required for learning to most effectively take place.[2]

Such a view might not always be evident in official national curriculum *orders* (though is far more so in some than in others), but remains widespread in curriculum *theorising and research*, including in the UK where, for example, the Teaching and Learning Research Programme (TLRP) emphasises that effective pedagogy promotes the *active engagement of students as learners*, and suggests that one of the main aims of 'higher learning' should be the promotion of learners' independence and autonomy (see, for example, Hofkins 2008). This involves engaging students actively *in* their own learning, and ensuring that they acquire a repertoire of learning strategies and practices, develop positive learning dispositions, and build the confidence to become agents in their own learning.

One of the implications of choosing learn-*ing* rather than *what-is-to-be learned* as the founding principle of a curriculum (the latter broadly, if not exclusively, following on from the former, rather than vice-versa), is that, rather than beginning by itemising the specific topics, skills and so forth to be covered within various pre-determined *subject areas* (unless we take the view that each subject area in any event represents or 'promotes' a very specific kind or kinds of learning), our curriculum might be organised in such a way that the traditional 'disciplines of knowledge' are replaced by teaching and activities around various learning skills and study skills – leading to the role of the disciplines being changed, if they are kept at all, to that of servicing the requirements of learning or providing meaningful fora and contexts for active learning development. In such a curriculum model (and there are already some in existence in both the public and private sectors of education, as we shall see a little later on), instead of insisting that young learners should (for example) sequentially/chronologically be taught key facts in relation to History or Science, the teachers' imperative is to ensure that students are (inter alia):

- developing skills in collaborative problem-solving;
- exploring current social or political issues by using library and electronic resources;
- forming balanced and informed judgements;
- and listening to and synthesising the views of others

– in short, that students are *making use of knowledge*, and that they understand that different kinds of knowledge might be required for different kinds of enquiry.

To anticipate an issue that I will return to in Chapter 8, such an approach might allow for something of a more central role to that much-maligned, increasingly marginalised set of skills and understandings and knowledge related to what is sometimes referred to as 'critical literacy': i.e. a 'learning that'/'learning how' programme, which threatens 'established systems of privilege and resource distribution because it reduces the potency of indoctrination and disinformation', enabling learners to 'read between the lines, to look skeptically at apparently benign and plausible surface structures, to analyze claims in relation to empirical data, and to question whose interests are served by particular forms of communication' (Cummins 1996: 219).

All of this is not, let it be added, to say that no school student should ever study in depth certain events and developments in their national history or about the science of radiation or tectonic plates, for example, or how to be literate and numerate (indeed, Cummins' account *expands* arguably limited conceptualisations of what literacy and numeracy mean, so that in the case of numeracy confusions disappear between what it is to be 'numerate' and what it is to be able to think mathematically). Rather, it is to seek to bring together 'knowledge that', 'knowledge of' and 'knowledge how' in a partnership in which the one is not perpetually subordinated to the other(s) and in which power relations in the learning process swing back from the unquestionable authority of the 'Master' (whether this is the teacher, the curriculum, the syllabus, the examiner or the textbook) to the investigative authority of the learner. We might say that, rather than beginning with a *what knowledge* question (too easily elided to a *what information/what facts* question, and leading to curriculum as a list of skills and knowledge to be 'taught and acquired'), a learning-based curriculum concerns itself more with a set of questions around what learning is and how learning is developed – underpinned by a desire to help students develop as active, social and independent learn*ers* for whom education is not exclusively located in the school itself but rather understood as infusing 'every sector [of society], linking together individuals, communities and institutions through diverse, overlapping networks of learning relationships' (Bentley 1998: 187).

Categorising knowledge: Hirst and Peters

The idea implicit in much of what has been discussed thus far – that 'knowledge' might be understood not so much as a homogenous entity (whether perceived as existing-in-itself or as 'constructed') but rather as 'knowledges' – is common. One of the more influential attempts to disaggregate knowledge (so to speak) by identifying different types or categories is provided by Paul Hirst and R.S. Peters, both in their individual work and via their collaborations with one another. Hirst (1965), for example, famously identified three 'forms of knowledge', still widely referenced in education theory and debate, all of which are important in our understandings of knowledge and curriculum:

- Propositional knowledge: i.e. 'knowledge that' (essentially, factual knowledge).
- Procedural or practical knowledge: i.e. know-how (riding a bike, making a magazine rack).
- Knowledge by acquaintance, or knowledge with a direct object – where what is known is an object like a person, a place or a work of art.
      (See Hirst and Peters 1970, Hirst and White 1998; and Walsh 1993: 131 for a fuller summary.)

Elsewhere, Hirst has offered a more detailed elaboration of seven 'domains' of knowledge, described as: logico-mathematical, empirical, interpersonal, moral, aesthetic, religious and philosophical (Hirst 1974; see also Hirst and Peters 1970, and, for interesting points of comparison, Gardner's [1983, 1993] 'multiple intelligences'; Lawton's [1975, 1989] 'cross-cultural dimensions', and the 'areas of experience' proposed by Her Majesty's Inspectors of schools in the UK [DES 1977, 1984]).

An interesting feature of these subsequent modified disaggregations of knowledge is that although propositional, procedural and 'by acquaintance' knowledge can be readily mapped on to the different 'domains' of knowledge, any effort to do so suggests that most of the 'domains' are likely to incorporate all three kinds or categories of knowledge to one degree or another, and that any one of the three kinds can find a home of sorts in any or all *of* the domains. Consequently, rather than supporting the traditional subject-discipline based curriculum, with a certain kind or kinds of knowledge located within each one, this twin disaggregation into kinds of knowledge and domains of knowledge might equally be deployed in support of a curriculum that is based not on existing subject disciplines at all, so much as on the range of knowledge – or 'knowledges' – that we want our students to develop, whether through cross-curricular work within traditional subject-based frameworks (whereby the subjects would retain a supportive or structural role), or by scrapping traditional subject frameworks altogether. Hirst himself did not suggest that his different 'forms of knowledge' offered a 'pattern for curriculum units', so that, while certain kinds of knowledge might be linked to certain subjects or disciplines, cross-curricular teaching and learning – effectively, a matter of the *organisation* of knowledge – were not ruled out. Perhaps in response to this possible confusion or over-interpretation of the 'domains' and 'forms', Hirst was subsequently to re-cast forms of knowledge into two broad types:

1   *Distinct disciplines* or forms of knowledge (subdivisible): mathematics, physical sciences, human sciences, history, religion, literature and the fine arts, philosophy.

2   *Fields of knowledge*: theoretical, practical (these may or may not include elements of moral knowledge).

(emphasis added, Hirst 1998: 260)

Regardless of curriculum organisation, in terms of curriculum selections themselves (see also Chapter 7), i.e., which knowledge and which knowledges to include in and to exclude from the curriculum, Hirst and Peters would appear to see such selection as a matter of self-justification: that is to say, it is demonstrably and scientifically possible to identify certain different kinds of knowledge (mathematical, linguistic, scientific, and so forth, and thus certain knowledge 'disciplines'), and within those different kinds of knowledge to identify certain specific items of knowledge that are essential to the different roles and functions that a fully active citizen might expect and wish to play in adult society. The fact that, historically and geographically, the same forms and domains of knowledge appear, reappear and survive challenges to their dominance in the realm of public and private education is invoked in support of such a view.

There is, indeed, much that is attractive in this proposition, including for subject specialist teachers within disciplines like history and geography who are able to reference the theory in support of the distinctiveness of their disciplinary practice and therefore its ongoing necessity *in* the curriculum.[3] Furthermore, to look forward again to the discussion of curriculum selection in Chapter 7, the theory suggests an approach to curriculum construction which is, so to speak, value free, able to rise above the vagaries and dangers of human prejudice and partiality, constructing itself on what Hirst calls 'more objective ground' – 'based on the nature and significance of knowledge itself, and not just on the predilections of pupils, the demands of society, or the whims of politicians' (Hirst 1998: 248). However, it is a theory and an approach that is not without its critics, even among those who might be broadly supportive of it. Not long after the publication of Hirst's *Liberal Education and the Nature of Knowledge* (1965) and Hirst and Peters' *The Logic of Education* (1970), for example, the sociologist and philosopher of education Michael Young observed that Hirst's view seemed to be based on an '*absolutist* conception of a set of distinct forms of knowledge which correspond closely to the traditional areas of the academic curriculum and thus justify, rather than examine, what are no more than the socio-historical products of a particular time' (Young 1971: 23). Others have taken issue more fundamentally with such theories of knowledge, challenging not just the choice of forms and domains but the very idea of knowledge itself as commonly conceived. (Foucault, for instance, in his critique of the dominance of rationality in post-Enlightenment theory, has gone so far as to describe knowledge as 'an "invention" behind which lies something completely different from itself: a play of instincts, impulses, desires, fear, a will to appropriate. It is on the stage where these elements battle one another that knowledge is produced' [Foucault in Miller 1994: 214] – while McCormick and Murphy, in their argument for 'situated cognition', talk of knowledge understood as 'social, related to action, and not a "mirror of reality"' [McCormick and Murphy 2000: 211]).

The issue of whether knowledge naturally presents itself in certain forms (and perhaps priorities) or whether we merely impose such forms upon it certainly qualifies as 'abiding', and will inevitably be returned to in the pages that follow. For now, I am more concerned with the partially-concealed value judgements inherent in Hirst's account (and, later, in that of Peters and – earlier – that of Bloom et al. [below]), and in the capacity of such accounts not simply to establish what we might see as a false or simplistic distinction between knowledge and *skills* but also a somewhat demeaning view of the latter, which has previously served to underscore various forms of educational *apartheid* (in England, for example, the splitting of secondary education into 'grammar schools' for students deemed more worthy of following a mainly academic curriculum, and 'secondary modern' or 'technical' schools for students deemed more worthy of following a mainly practical curriculum).

Demonising the practical

For a particularly powerful elaboration of this issue (the academic–practical 'divide' and hierarchisation), readers can do a lot worse than refer to Michael Young's book *The Curriculum of the Future* (Young 1998: 75–6, 79) or to John Dewey's account of the history of such a divide in his classic text *The Quest for Certainty: A Study of the Relation of Knowledge and Action* (1960).

Tracing Young's 'divide' back to a time when manual work, experienced as laborious, was associated with the poorer classes in society, Dewey suggests that such an association has a habit of living on in culture and in the collective conscience, so that 'action' continues to be 'disparaged', and the implementation of thinking into *doing* as 'inferior' and 'menial' (Dewey 1960: see also 'Useful and powerful knowledge', below). 'Work', Dewey suggests:

> has been done under compulsion and the pressure of necessity, while intellectual activity is associated with leisure. On account of the unpleasantness of practical activity, as much of it as possible has been put upon slaves and serfs. Thus the social dishonour in which the [working] class was held was extended to the work they do.
>
> (ibid.: 4–5)

Such 'deprecation' of the manual, Dewey argues, extends to knowledge and understandings related to practical activity, so that 'The disrepute which has attended the thought of material things in comparison with immaterial thought has been transferred to *everything associated with practice*' (ibid.: 5, emphasis added). Speculating on why such divisions – especially that between knowledge and skill – persists to this day (Dewey's 'this day', of course, being nearly 100 years ago, though the issue continues to be relevant today!), Dewey poses a number of pertinent questions:

> What is the cause and the import of the sharp division between theory and practice? Why should the latter be disesteemed along with matter and the body? …How has the separation of intellect from action affected the theory of knowledge? …What would the effect be if the divorce were annulled, and knowing and doing were brought into intrinsic connection with one another? …What modifications would ensue in the disciplines which are concerned with the various phases of human activity?
>
> (ibid.: 5–6)

There is not sufficient space here to explore these questions in any depth. Dewey does, however, go on to make one very interesting suggestion which has particular relevance to an argument that will be explored later on in *Understanding the School Curriculum*, and indeed later on in this chapter. That suggestion is that in our endlessly uncertain individual and collective lives knowledge is (conservatively) associated with 'certainty' – suggesting the possibility of replicability and universality – whereas action is more typically understood as provisional, contingent, risky, associated not with fixety but with change:

> Practical activity deals with individualized and unique situations which are never exactly duplicable and about which, accordingly, no complete assurance is possible. All activity, moreover, involves change. The intellect, however, according to traditional doctrine, may grasp universal being, and Being which is universal is fixed and immutable. Wherever there is practical activity we human beings are involved as partakers in the issue. All the fear, disesteem and lack of confidence which gather about the thought of ourselves, cluster also about the thought of the actions in which we are partners. Man's distrust *of himself* has caused him to desire to get beyond and above himself; in pure knowledge he has thought he could attain this self-transcendence.
>
> (ibid.: 6–7, emphasis added)

Humanity's attempted 'escape from peril' (i.e. the dangers and uncertainties of life) has, Dewey suggests, led to the 'quest for certainty' (ibid.) that knowledge may aspire to and that has underpinned the continuing elevation of theory over practice and of factual knowledge over knowledge-infused action in schooling as in society. To flag issues that will be returned to in subsequent chapters, Dewey indicates that in fact we should be less insecure and fearful of action (and perhaps less precious about 'pure' as opposed to applied knowledge), and that instead of continuing our quest 'for absolute certainty' by cognitive means as a way to escape from peril, we might seek to 'search for *security* by practical means' (ibid.: 24–5, emphasis added). To push the argument a little further than some might wish, and to resurrect a metaphor from Chapter 2, we might say that the emphasis on theoretical knowledge over practical activity in curricula is symptomatic of a 'paranoid' approach to curriculum, whereby theoretical knowledge achieves its superior status not so much because of any intrinsic value as because it often represents the safer option.

When is a skill not a skill? 'Knowledge' – and how to use it

Whatever we may think of Dewey's philosophical account of the relationship between conceptualisations of knowledge and skill, theory and practice, in Hirst's account, so-called 'propositional' knowledge (which we might associate with academic study) certainly appears to be assigned a higher status over 'procedural' knowledge – reflecting, perhaps, a hegemonic hierarchisation in the wider society in which 'being clever' is very often contrasted with and afforded a higher status than being 'sporty' or being 'good with your hands'. Peters is perhaps more direct about it:

> Curriculum activities…such as science, history, geography, literary appreciation, and poetry are "serious" in that they illuminate other areas of life and contribute much to the quality of living. They have, secondly, a wide-ranging cognitive content which distinguishes them from games. Skills, for instance, do not have a wide-ranging cognitive content. There is very little to know about riding bicycles, swimming, or

golf. It is largely a matter of "knowing how" rather than "knowing that", of knack rather than of understanding. Furthermore what there is to know throws very little light on much else. In history, science, or literature, on the other hand, there is an immense amount to know, and if it is properly assimilated, it constantly throws light on, widens and deepens one's view of countless other things.

(Peters 1966: 159)[4]

While the idea of knowledge, of the curriculum, acting in an illuminating way whose effects carry on outside the classroom both synchronically and diachronically may be appealing, Peters' conceptualisation of (effectively) the distinction between knowledge and skills is a little more problematic, and one whose difficulties quickly become apparent as soon as we begin to consider specific examples.

Let's take, for instance, two of Peters' own examples of riding a bicycle and of playing golf. We could all agree, I imagine, that to an extent we learn to ride a bicycle by learning to ride a bicycle! More precisely, we learn to ride a bicycle through a process of trial and error, by becoming better, more effective, at the activity through practical experience, by tacitly and informally acquiring knowledge (along the lines of Bernstein's 'competence' model) about such important matters as balance or how to reduce one's speed gradually to effect a comfortable stop. But we might equally argue that even such a fundamentally practical activity as bike-riding demands a considerable amount of what might be called factual, propositional knowledge that can be, and often is, learned in more formal situations and that might have wider applicability. For example, although bike-riding ability might appear to be purely instinctive, we might argue that we need, first, to know various things *about* bikes and bike-riding, and indeed about *ourselves*: about how the pedals make the wheels go round; how the brakes work; which side of the road to ride on and what traffic lights are for; how to achieve or restore balance when we are in danger of losing it rather than just hoping our instincts will kick in; the things we are already accomplished in that might help us; the 'personality traits' we have identified in ourselves that might, if unmanaged, hinder us, and so on. Golf, similarly, might demand of us a great deal of propositional or technical knowledge if we are to become as good at it as we can be: for example, knowledge to do with trajectory and swing, weight of club in relation to distance to be covered, the effects of the wind on fairways, or the borrow on greens.

Unlike bike-riding and golf (which do not normally feature in school curricula), carpentry is a subject which very often does, albeit, as Bernstein (2000) notes, under the 'recontextualising' term woodwork. The 'skill' of the carpenter tends to be defined *as* skill by virtue of its practical, perhaps creative nature, and by the fact that we associate it with usage and with processes (specifically, of manufacturing). But of course when carpenters set about their work they, too, are making use of what we have already called knowledge: in this case, the knowledge, for example, of design, of how different tools interact with different woods, of what end product might be suitable in specific settings, perhaps even knowledge of fashion and taste, or of how to interpret the requests of potential clients. The carpenter may thus possess certain physical abilities or talents, linked to hand–eye coordination, manual strength and dexterity, an 'eye' for each job, all developed and refined over a period of time through repetition and experience; however, without the required knowledge, the practice of these skills would be of limited use. Indeed, we might say that skill in this case is at least partly a matter of *knowledge-enactment*.

The very examples of 'skills' provided by Hirst and Peters – which often appear to locate skills almost exclusively within 'games' – highlights an additional difficulty, both with reference to Hirst and Peters' categorisations of knowledge and in relation to distinctions and possible *relationships and inter-dependences* between knowledge and skills – overlooking or marginalising, for example, the ('transferable') 'thinking skills' and 'learning skills' that we hear so much about in curriculum development these days: skills which enable learners to (among other things) make selective *use* of knowledge to decide on the best choice of action in accordance with the uniqueness of whatever situation they are in and whatever problem they are being asked to deal with (that is to say, combining the general and the generic with the personal and the contingent): skills, in short, which, like Peters' account of curriculum knowledge, can also 'constantly throw light on, widen and deepen one's view of countless other things'. Partly because of this partial omission, the definitions of knowledge provided by Hirst and Peters run the risk of placing a metaphorical wall between knowledge and skills, effectively limiting the definitions of both. It also, however, to return to a point already made, appears to *downgrade* skills, placing them below knowledge in the cognitive pecking order – not very helpful for those wishing to widen the notion of what counts as achievement in compulsory education, and not entirely supported either by research or other evidence. There is an additional worry, too, which will be returned to in considering the concepts 'useful knowledge' and 'powerful knowledge' below. It lies in an apparent assumption in Peters' account that knowledge 'itself' will act to 'illuminate', to 'widen one's view' and so forth, as though this is some intrinsic quality of knowledge. If we believe this, then there will be no need in our curriculum to help our students *to develop the skills needed to make use of the knowledge they have*, not just while they are still at school but in that substantially larger part of their life that in all probability awaits them once they have left.

The assumption that the curriculum's job is done when knowledge has, so to speak, been 'absorbed' is a highly questionable one, as is the notion that knowledge without the skills – and the 'meta-knowledge' – required to make use of it can result in its becoming 'powerful' in anything like a 'constant' way.

To be fair to Hirst and Peters (and it would be churlish to appear dismissive of what remains some of the most important, thoughtful and influential education theory of recent times), the role of knowledge-related skills is not entirely overlooked in their analysis. Hirst, for example (1998: 253), argues that 'each form of knowledge, if it is to be acquired beyond a general and superficial level, involves the development of creative imagination, judgment, thinking, communicative skills, etc., in ways that are peculiar to itself as a way of understanding experience' (1998: 253). Their curriculum emphasis, however, was clearly very strongly in favour of – and more explicit about – knowledge itself than the skills required for the bearers of knowledge to make best use of it, and even these skills themselves must apparently be determined by and in service to the particular form of knowledge with which they are linked.

Bloom's taxonomy

As has already been noted, Hirst and Peters are not the only commentators seeking to identify different kinds of knowledge, areas of knowledge, or different ways of knowing – an activity, indeed, which has its roots in the philosophy of the Ancient Greeks. Another relatively recent, very well-known and still influential attempt exists in what is commonly known as 'Bloom's Taxonomy' (a taxonomy that also exists in a 'revised' form in Anderson and Krathwoll 2001).

Bearing a not insignificant similarity to Hirst's three 'forms of knowledge' (propositional-factual, procedural-practical, and 'knowledge by acquaintance'), in 1956, Bloom and a team of colleagues had already published a 'taxonomy of educational objectives', and 'classification of educational goals' (see Bloom et al. 1956) in which they had identified three learning 'domains' of their own: that is to say:

1   the 'cognitive' (mental skills, factual knowledge);
2   the 'affective' (feelings, attitudes, self-knowledge and understanding); and
3   the 'psychometric' (manual, physical *skills*).

Within each of these domains, a series of sub-divisions was proposed, so that the cognitive domain, for example, could be broken down to include knowledge, comprehension, application, analysis, synthesis, and evaluation.

It will be immediately obvious that in spite of any similarities there is at least one fundamental differences between Bloom's taxonomy and Hirst and Peters' forms or domains of knowledge: while Hirst and Peters address knowledge specifically, Bloom's approach is to identify educational 'objectives' which include from the start a mixture of knowledge, skills and – significantly – experiences and *feelings*. In relation to issues regarding what I have already suggested is a tricky distinction between two slippery concepts – knowledge and skill(s) – Bloom's taxonomy is particularly interesting, however, in the way it almost accidentally introduces a distinction (taken up and developed, as we have seen, by Hirst) between two different *kinds* of skill – one associated with academic learning, and one with more practical activity: that is to say, 'mental' skills (such as the 'learning skills' and 'transferable skills' which are so popular in national curricula and education programmes today) and 'physical' skills such as those described by Peters (ibid.). Thus, we must assume that, in the sub-divisions of cognition, we are likely to find and to require specific 'skills' related to the application of our learning, to analysis, to evaluation and to comprehension. Quite how such skills as these differ qualitatively from 'knowledge' is not entirely clear, nor how we are to understand and position skills in the 'affective' domain – leading me to suggest again that the distinction between knowledge and skills might not be either as easy or as 'real' as some might have us believe, and that we need to think very carefully when we are considering such matters as that of curriculum 'balance' between the two. (What exactly *do* we mean when we talk of 'skill(s)'? And how *are* these different from knowledge?)

By way of illustrating the potential blurring of the boundaries between what we mean by knowledge and what we mean by skill in our everyday discussions of curriculum content (I use 'content' here to include everything that is planned and undertaken within a curriculum, be it cast as knowledge *or* as skill), we might consider the case of group work. It is fair to say, I think, that group work is still typically understood and practised in classrooms as in an auxiliary role to knowledge: that is to say, as a means or a strategy to support knowledge acquisition and development. However, this is not always the case – nor does it have to be. In some national curricula (see, for instance, the case of Malta, described in Moore 2012), group work itself is given the status of a curriculum element or *requirement* rather than a mere supporting role: that is to say, its inclusion, promotion and development is, itself, included as a mandatory curriculum element – a curriculum policy that certainly seems to challenge Peters' claim (op.cit.) that 'Skills...do not have a wide-ranging cognitive content', at the same time, as I have already suggested, as seeming to conform to his definition of 'serious' curriculum elements in its potential to 'illuminate other areas of life', to 'contribute much to the quality of living' and to have 'a wide-ranging cognitive content which distinguishes [it] from games'.

In such cases, although group work may be understood as an important *skill*, it is also understood as, in itself, requiring of participants both a set of *sub*-skills and a certain knowledge base. This knowledge base is not the knowledge of 'facts' and 'pseudo-facts',[5] of being able to recall the square root of 16, or recite sequentially a list of the nation's kings and queens, or list the main events of the Second World War, or draw a diagram of a simple electric circuit or plan and draw elevation representations of a three-dimensional object, but it is knowledge nevertheless: the kind of inter-personal and intra-personal knowledge referenced, for instance, in Gardner's 'multiple intelligences' (1983, 1993) that is (again) not so much knowledge *that* as knowledge *of* or *about*: knowledge, for instance, of how people are likely to respond differently according to how one makes a suggestion or asks a question; or knowledge about one's own learning and ability or inability to work with new ideas and challenge existing ones. (We might say, examples of Hirst's 'knowledge by acquaintance'.)

In summary, the knowledge-skill developed in and required of group work has an enduring quality in that it is likely to be carried on and made use of in adult life. Within group work, the 'sub-skill' of negotiation, for instance, requires participants to have and make use of knowledge about how groups function best, about how to self-present and how to present an argument, about the nature, problems and possibilities of compromise, and a sophisticated, perhaps independently-found-out knowledge of what it is that is being negotiated. The examples of group work and negotiation lead us once again to the idea of skill as knowledge-in-action: i.e. both knowing something *and* knowing how to make more effective use of that initial knowing.

In the end, perhaps a more helpful distinction than that between knowledge and skill, or indeed between 'knowledge that', 'knowledge how' and 'knowledge about', without denying that knowledge itself might come in any number of different forms, is between *knowledge* and *knowing* – the former within this pairing being sometimes conceived in terms of 'reification', and thence lending itself to processes of 'commodification'[6] whereby demonstrations of its ownership can, in themselves, be used to obtain financial and social rewards, and whereby, via fetishisations that endow a value in certain knowledge in excess of its 'intrinsic' value, profit can be turned by 'selling' pre-identified, pre-valued knowledge to willing customers in accessible packages.

McCormick and Murphy (2000), referencing Sfard (1998), propose two metaphors that are useful here, underlying contrasting theories of learning and how they relate to epistemology, and suggesting that both need to be included in school curricula. These, which I have referenced briefly in connection with Dewey's contrast between 'acquisitiveness' and 'inquisitiveness', are the 'acquisition' metaphor and the 'participation' metaphor.

McCormick and Murphy's acquisition metaphor references thinking about knowledge as a commodity or as an object that can be developed, constructed or transmitted, that can, so to speak, be 'accumulated'. The participation metaphor, on the other hand, replaces 'knowledge' with 'knowing', and 'having knowledge' with 'doing', and (appositely, given our example of group work) is linked to being a member of a community or group of learner-doers rather than an isolated or privatised learner storing up knowledge-capital for one's own exclusive use and benefit. Along with Lave and Wenger (1991), McCormick and Murphy propose a difference between on the one hand knowledge that is 'acquired' *out of context*, and on the other hand learning that is 'situated' (see, e.g., McCormick and Murphy 2000: 213).

The concept and importance of situated knowledge itself can be traced back, as so much else in progressive educational theory, to the pioneering work of John Dewey and, in particular, to his short work *My Pedagogic Creed* (Flinders and Thornton 2009) which, though written over 100 years ago, references many of the issues for curriculum theory and design that continue to tax us today. Speaking of a curriculum (and therefore a pedagogy) that takes full and proper account of the young learner's existing experiential knowledge rather than (as is often the case) acting as if this did not exist, Dewey argues:

> One of the greatest difficulties in the present teaching of science is that the material is presented in a purely objective form, or is treated as a new peculiar kind of experience which the child can add to that which he [sic] has already had. In reality, *science is of value because it gives the ability to interpret and control the experience already had.* It should be introduced, not as so much new subject matter, but as showing the factors already involved in previous experience and as furnishing tools by which that experience can be more easily and effectively regulated.
>
> (ibid.: 38, emphasis added)

Interestingly, this view, which stands in stark contrast to the notion that knowledge exists independently, 'out there', waiting to be discovered, is apparently supported by Bobbitt, who has also argued (1971: 34): 'Educational experiences must take place where they can be normal. Frequently this is not at the schools.' (Bobbitt's own observation is, however, followed by the rather unfortunate example of 'the training of girls in sewing' followed by the example of girls' 'cooking' [ibid.].)

'Useful' and 'powerful' knowledge

The difference between 'having knowledge' and using knowledge – or having the *opportunity*, perhaps, to use knowledge – inevitably raises questions about what 'useful knowledge' means when we use the term as a justification for curriculum inclusion. We might argue that *all* knowledge is potentially useful – but only potentially so, until such point as it is put to some (therapeutic or practical) use, just as all knowledge is potentially (from any individual's point of view) use-less. Not only might we be constrained or enabled by our specific socio-economic, cultural and socio-psychological circumstances to turn potentially useful knowledge into actually useful knowledge (knowledge-in-use); there is also the tricky question, particularly important in the rapidly changing times in which we currently live, of gauging the 'shelf life' of those specific 'items' of knowledge which we may feel are more contingent than universal and timeless. As the Director of Singapore's National Institute of Education, Lee Sing Kong, has recently suggested, looking ahead to current school students' job prospects and the demands of the national economy: 'It is estimated that knowledge will double every two and a half years. ... Employers are telling us that they cannot predict what kind of jobs will be available in five years' time.' (Reported by William Stewart in *TES News* 2013.)

Some knowledge, as well as being described as 'useful', is often described as 'powerful' (see, e.g., James et al. 2011: 11). 'Powerful', of course, has a different inflection from 'useful', and seems to speak of a different education project. 'Useful' sounds rather functional, pragmatic, and easily conscriptable to the cause of an education for the national economy or as preparation for the world of work. 'Powerful', on the other hand, suggests emancipation and empower*ment* – and is perhaps more easily conscriptable by curriculum theory and design that prioritises individual opportunity in a broader sense than simply employment opportunity, or perhaps even of collective critical action: the empowerment of the dis-empowered, we might say. But how 'powerful' *is* curriculum knowledge? How 'powerful' *can* it be? And to what extent does its perceived and intended 'powerfulness' depend – like that of 'useful knowledge' – on context and contingency? As with 'useful' knowledge's capacity for useful-ness, so we might argue that no knowledge achieves powerful-ness until and unless its potential is at the very least achievable. As White (2004c: 22) says: 'Making one's own way in life depends on *the existence of options* among competing ways of life, activities, belief systems, careers' (emphasis added) – a suggestion which reminds us that the empowering possibilities of knowledge may turn out to be of limited value when inserted into essentially disempowering contexts in which 'options' themselves are overly limited (and limited much more for some than for others). Knowledge and skills related to money management for example, are unlikely to be of very much use if one does not have very much money to manage; and indeed, the perceived likelihood of such a circumstance on the part of the learner prior to entering adult life might well make such learning appear 'use-less' at the time of its teaching.

The above is perhaps a crude example; however, there is a very important point here. It is that at their most successful, knowledge and skills acquired and developed in the school setting may indeed be made use of idiosyncratically by the learner in any one of a range of circumstances or contingencies in future life – or at any rate retain their *potential* for such use – *but*, as Bruner has very persuasively argued, a circumstance *like* poverty is likely to have a considerable, typically negative impact both on the uses available to someone of whatever skills and knowledge they may have acquired at school, and on the way in which they perceive, experience and respond to the curriculum during the course of their formal education. As Bruner wrote, not so long ago, of the situation in the USA:

> We are witnessing, particularly in the United States, a sharpened polarization between those who live in poverty, often segregated in ghetto-like neighbourhoods and housing developments, for whom schooling no longer seems like a "way out", and those who (however insecure their long-term outlook) feel securely enough established in national and class identity to aspire for their children.
>
> (Bruner 1996b: 81)

A not unconnected difficulty takes us back both to the hierarchised division between academic and non-academic curricula (or of programmes of study *within* curricula), and to the impact of Dewey's 'quest for certainty' in relation to modes of educational assessment. As Atkinson (2013) points out, politicians these days tend to be very keen on stressing the importance of every young person receiving a good education – of having access to the same 'useful' and 'powerful' knowledge – regardless of their socio-economic background. However, such a desire is set within, and somewhat negated by, *assessment systems* which themselves are aimed at stratifying students against constructed academic and vocational 'norms':

> The notions of "every child matters" or "no child left behind", though aspirational, become perverse if education equates to examination success and academic competition, because within such systems as they currently function there are many who plainly in the end do *not* matter or *are* left behind. In such systems these aspirational discourses become no more than empty rhetoric giving the false appearance of equity.
>
> (Atkinson 2013: 17–18)

Atkinson's argument is echoed by Burbules, who (prophetically) suggests, reminding us again of Bernstein's performance-competence dichotomy:

> [worthwhile] knowledge is being defined in terms of what standardized tests can measure. If tests cannot measure something, then it is not regarded as an essential part of the curriculum …[T]ests are made to be failed. If a test were designed on which the vast majority of people could score highly, then it would be judged insufficiently difficult, and would be made harder, until only a relative few could do well at it.
>
> (Burbules 2004: 8)

If knowledge has the potential to be *powerful*, we need – as with the notion of 'useful' – to be clear about what we mean by it; and the fact that the term has enjoyed popularity in both left-wing and right-wing, progressive and traditional policy thinking suggests that it can mean very different things to different people. For example, it can speak *either* of empowering people to do well – or as well as the wider system allows them to do – within an essentially unchanging socio-economic context, *or* empowering people to recognise and seek to work, with others, to remedy perceived inequities and injustices within the existing socio-economic context, perhaps by way of creating more and better life opportunities for themselves and for others whom they may perceive as receiving unfair treatment.

Among the most vociferous proponents of powerful knowledge – more precisely, perhaps, of the *power of knowledge* – on the political left have been Marxist social commentators such as Antonio Gramsci and Louis Althusser. In *Problèmes Étudiants*, for example, Althusser (1964, cited in Ross 1991: xvi) sees formal education as having the potential to *empower* workers and their children, providing them with knowledge which will give them both the tools (e.g. literacy and a critical knowledge of how the wider socio-economic system works) and the self-belief to challenge the socio-economic status quo: that is to say, a *revolutionary* function. Thus: 'The function of teaching is to transmit a determinate knowledge to subjects who do not possess this knowledge' (Althusser: ibid.). To be fair to Althusser, his preferred version of mass education was not simply about 'transmitting knowledge' to the previously ignorant, but also about encouraging such newly-empowered citizens to conduct their own *research* into the effects of the wider social system in future years, and about raising their 'consciousness' in order that they might re-configure social inequalities presented as 'natural' as socially-constructed problems that might be solvable. Althusser's language, however – the option of a 'transmissive', behaviourist language of pedagogy in which (Rancière, op.cit.) the task of the 'knowing' teacher is to pass on or 'explicate' knowledge to the uninformed learner, and the apparent identification of knowledge as 'reified', 'out there', pre-selected and somewhat 'fixed' – remains interesting. While the message speaks of empowerment and revolution, of education as a project aimed at overturning a hierarchised status quo, the means by which this is to be carried out appear to be anything but revolutionary, and certainly not democratic – and we might be forgiven for thinking they reveal a very poor understanding of how teaching and learning take place.

Effectively, and perhaps surprisingly given that they might appear to be essentially on the same educational 'side', Althusser's approach seems oppositional to Dewey's, tending, as others on both the left and the right of education theory and policy have done, to dismiss progressivism not just as the practice of woolly-minded, well-meaning but essentially misguided middle-class liberals, but also as actively harmful to the interests of students from less privileged backgrounds. As Ross has pointed out, Althusser's approach is not unreminiscent of that expounded by the (left wing) French linguist Jean-Claude Milner (or for that matter the current *right-wing* Head of the Office for Standards in Education in England), who saw fit to involve himself in French education debates in the 1980s – taking what many saw as an 'anti-pedagogy', pro-transmissive stance to mass education. For Milner:

> The unequal relation between teacher and student was not to be dismantled but rather celebrated, for in its inequality, as in that of psychoanalyst and patient, lay the key to success. Inequality produced in the student the desire to know. True equality in schooling meant transmitting the same knowledge to each student.
>
> (Ross 1991: xiv)

Others on the Left have taken an approach to empowerment which finds some common ground with these other commentators, but which also stands distinctly apart from them. One notion of empowerment that has become particularly popular among such thinkers, for instance (see, e.g., the work of Chris Watkins and his colleagues [Watkins 2005; Watkins, Carnell and Lodge 2007]), embraces the notion of students 'owning' their learning, developing as autonomous, critical, lifelong learners – the emphasis here being on encouraging the skills of active, critical enquiry alongside the acquisition of knowledge, so that the emphasis is on the ongoing development in school of important knowledge, and so that empowerment – as an attitude of mind – begins, as part of the curriculum project, long before school is left behind. Another approach is that of the already-mentioned 'critical literacy', which is also aimed at educating critical citizens willing and able to recognise and challenge social injustice – recognising and embracing the importance of basic literacy and knowledge 'about' (about, for example, how socio-economic systems 'really work'), but doing so within more fundamentally democratic, student-centred pedagogies.

As far as the (educational) Right is concerned, knowledge may also be presented as 'powerful'; however, it is clearly a different knowledge that is in mind here, often linked to a transmissive pedagogy and therefore to a more 'out there' view of knowledge in general. Critics of Rightist curriculum policy, and indeed of a broader Rightist association with politically 'neutral', knowledge-based curricula in general (see, e.g., Ball 2013; Pollard 2012) have argued that, far from having a liberating and equalising effect, an obsession with 'knowledge' and its 'acquisition' can be *dis*empowering, undermining the individual learner's capacity and licence for independent, creative thinking and doing. Pollard (2012), in a critique of what he sees as an over-emphasis on knowledge acquisition in the proposed revised school curriculum for primary school students in England, talks, thus, of '[t]he constraining effects on the primary curriculum as a whole', suggesting that 'the preservation of breadth, balance and quality of experience [in the revised curriculum] will test even the most committed of teachers', while Ball (2013) endorses Pollard's view that the revised curriculum proposals in England owe more to an uncritical acceptance of the ideas underpinning Hirsch's 'Core Knowledge Foundation' in the United States than (as claimed) research into the curriculum approaches in a range of other countries. Hirsch himself (1987), in a fierce critique of progressivism and multi-cultural approaches to curriculum, assessment and pedagogy in public education in the USA, espouses a return to the 'virtues' of verbal instruction and repetitive practice, in the service of the transmission of a body of 'solid' knowledge. To quote Ball's excellent summary of Hirsch's position, reminding us both of Bobbitt's objectivism and of the distinction drawn above between 'national' and 'nationalist' curricula and between curricular fundamentalism and curricular evolution:

> [Hirsch] argues that the public school curriculum [in the USA] is incoherent and that "local" knowledge and multicultural knowledge have replaced "valued content". For him, education is a cognitive-technical process, the consumption of traditional subject matter and a "shared" national culture, which is beyond politics. He also sees this approach to the curriculum and teaching and learning as the means of addressing the knowledge deficiencies, the "famished minds", of children from culturally impoverished homes, and thus a way of addressing and redressing social inequalities.
> (Ball 2013: 23)

This appeal and (rather dubious) justification of the 'core knowledge' approach, i.e. that – unlike 'progressive' 'multicultural' approaches – it will most benefit the less socially, culturally and economically privileged members of the school student body, finds its echo in recent (equally dubious) claims by the Secretary of State for Education in the UK that pen-and-paper, end-of-course examining of knowledge acquisition will most benefit students from poorer income families. For an interesting and persuasive critique of the current re-emphasis on examinations and testing in England and America (the 'mania', as he calls it), linking the move to developments in global capitalism and, specifically, to capitalism's need to maintain rather than to eliminate social and economic differentials, readers are encouraged to seek out Bertell Ollman's essay 'Why So Many Exams? A Marxist Response' (Ollman, n.d.).

And (last but not least) 'Cultural Knowledge'

Thus far, this chapter has chiefly concerned itself with knowledge 'that' and knowledge 'for': that is to say, to return to Hirst's three 'forms of knowledge', propositional (factual) knowledge and procedural (practical) knowledge. However, I want to round the chapter off by saying something more about 'knowledge about': about the more specifically 'cultural' aspects of the school curriculum, including what might be called 'cultural knowledge' – and to remind ourselves that empirical knowledge and associated learning skills are by no means the be-all and end-all of formal education. There is, of course, a great deal that can be said about this kind of knowledge. However, as I have written at length about it elsewhere (e.g. Moore 2012), I will, for the sake of avoiding repetition, keep my observations here relatively brief.

What we mean by the 'cultural aspects' of curriculum always needs a word or two of explanation. Lawton's observation that a school curriculum is 'essentially a selection from the culture of a society' (Lawton 1975: 7) reminds us not only that knowledge itself – all knowledge – has a cultural aspect, but that (in contradiction of the 'objective', 'scientific' approach to curriculum theory and design) cultural preferences are always at work when choices are made regarding what knowledge to include in the curriculum and (Chapter 8) what knowledge to exclude. When it comes to what James et al. (op.cit.) have specifically called 'the Cultural' in school curricula – that is, the introduction of students to 'the best of their cultural heritage(s), so that they can contribute to its further development' – decisions regarding what is and is not included will be touched by this cultural bias in just the same way as any other major curriculum element.

There are two broad aspects of 'the Cultural' as identified by James et al. One concerns the development of familiarity with – and, it is to be hoped, some considerable measure of pleasure and enjoyment from – existing cultural artefacts: items drawn from music, art, literature, dance, drama and so forth (what we might call *knowledge about* or, after Hirst [1965] 'knowledge by acquaintance'). The other concerns students' own development as expressive, creative communicators and producers (that is to say, *producers* of their own literature, music, art, and so forth) ('knowledge to', or the development of expressive, creative, productive *skills*). The knowledge selections related to 'the Cultural' therefore come informed by two aims:

1   A therapeutic, developmental aspect, based on a view that engagement with certain cultural artefacts will bring its own rewards, helping young people to have potentially more fulfilling, satisfying lives and become more rounded individuals – an *entitlement*, we might say, to the same potential sources of happiness and intellectual stimulation as any other person might experience.

2   An exemplary aspect: that is to say, the way in which exposure to and engagement with existing works of literature, art and music exists as a support for – and a set of possible models for – students' own development as communicative creative, productive and sensitised citizens.

So far, so relatively uncontentious. There are problems, however, concerning such selections, precisely because they are themselves inevitably infused with cultural preferences and biases, even though they may often be presented as though they are not, as though, in Bobbitt's terms, they have been 'scientifically' or 'objectively' arrived at: self-justifying, unbiased curriculum inclusions based in the intrinsic, undisputable value and superiority of some artefacts over others, rather than indicative of the specific *tastes* of a particular social group (very often, a social élite) with particular cultural interests. Whether or not it is possible to identify works of music, literature and art that are indeed intrinsically superior to others (rather than having been *invested* with superiority by the individual reader, listener or viewer) is a moot point. Many politicians and policymakers – not to mention university-based examining boards – clearly believe that it is possible, as is witnessed by the ubiquitousness of certain 'standard' inclusions in, for example, the texts that students are required to study for mother-tongue literature examinations. The current Secretary of State for Education for the UK clearly subscribes to such a view, as indicated in the following extract from a recent speech given at the University of Cambridge:

> I am unapologetic in arguing that all children have a right to the best. *And there is such as thing as the best.* Richard Wagner is an artist of sublime genius and his work is incomparably more rewarding – intellectually, sensually and emotionally – than, say, the Arctic Monkeys. Yet it takes effort to prise open the door to his world. That effort is rewarded a thousandfold. The unfulfilled yearning of the Tristan chord, the battle between power and love in the Ring, the sublimity of sacrifice in Parsifal, all these creations of one mind can, today, move and affect the minds of millions with a profundity almost no other work of man can achieve.
>
> (emphasis added, Michael Gove to Cambridge University, 24 Nov 2011.)

This politician's belief that, because his own life has been enriched and rewarded by his 'persistence' in 'discovering' Wagner, that same experience should not be denied to other people (specifically, young people from disadvantaged backgrounds), that it should be seen as an 'entitlement', and that enrichment such as Mr Gove has found can and indeed must be discovered by any young person via their own and their teachers' persistence and hard work (and by turning their back on the false gods of so-called popular culture), is a not uncommon one within both Rightist and Leftist education policy thinking, often attaching itself to appealing discourses of inclusion, equity, and even some form of (symbolic) social justice. Such an approach, often heart-felt, will argue that (for example) not teaching Shakespeare in 'traditional' ways to Black and minority ethnic students (instead, making the plays more accessible to some such students by using rap or by 'translating' speeches or scenes into 'non-standard' dialects or by using role play) is insulting to these students and their families, implying an incapacity on their part to achieve the kind of rewards described by Gove via their own intelligence and perseverance.

It is only when we *challenge* this notion of intrinsic superiority (of some cultural artefacts and preferences over others), when we suggest that appreciation of the Arts is largely a matter of taste, and that similar rewards can be experienced by different people engaging with different material (we might politely enquire whether Mr Gove has ever listened to the work of the Arctic Monkeys, let alone given it the same 'persistence' as he has afforded Wagner), that we run into difficulties. What if we reject the notion that Wagner's work is intrinsically 'sublime', for example (as indeed many opera-lovers do)? Or if we accept that, however much we may personally love Shakespeare's plays or Wagner's operas, we should not force others to love them if they can achieve similar loves elsewhere?

Apart from making comments such as those of Mr Gove appear essentialist and exclusive rather than inclusive and caring[7] (espousing equity, yet doing so via a missionary-like claim that the existing cultural preferences of some sections of society are superior to those of others, who must be taught to change their preferences by whatever means it takes), such questions raise other very important issues for curriculum philosophy and design: most notably, if developing a love of Wagner or Shakespeare is such hard work, and if it doesn't pay off for large numbers of students (as those of us who have taught English literature in state schools will know to be the case, for all our best efforts), on what basis are we not only including it in the curriculum, but perhaps even making it a compulsory – and testable – curriculum item? Are we genuinely seeking to 'entitle' our students to spiritual and aesthetic 'enrichment'? Or are we simply attempting the impossible project of persuading them to be like and feel like 'us'?

Notes

1   I am conscious that writing a chapter on 'knowledge' (as opposed to a book or a series of books) is a somewhat dangerous exercise, only to be undertaken after a good deal of consideration and in recognition of the fact that it can very easily become a hostage to fortune. There is a lot about knowledge – theories of knowledge, including those coming out of and characterising the discipline of philosophy, for example – that I simply have not had the room to include in these few pages: theories concerning hierarchies of knowing, or the relationships and distinctions between knowledge and knowing, or between knowing and thinking, or more recent feminist theories of knowledge and knowing, or the nature of rationality – and much, much more. These theories are all inevitably present in one way or another in the discussions that inform and follow this chapter, albeit often implicitly or in partial 'hiding'. However, I have chosen to approach the subject of knowledge in this particular book essentially from the perspective of a teacher: attempting to focus on the knowledge issues that I think most impact on our practice as teachers, on how we might approach learning theory and curriculum design in relation to *praxis*, and indeed on the knowledge questions that are most frequently put to us (explicitly and implicitly) *by our students* – and to try to do so in a way that facilitates the connections we might wish to make *between* theory and practice. More detailed considerations of knowledge, including several which also specifically link issues and theory to practice, can be found elsewhere. Readers interested in further exploring knowledge issues are likely to find Blake et al.'s book *Philosophy of Education* (2003) a more than helpful staring-point.
2   See the discussion of 'acquisition' and 'participation' metaphors, later on in this chapter; also, Dewey (1933) on the curriculum of 'acquisition' versus the curriculum based on enquiry and *inquisitiveness*.
3   I am grateful to my colleague Chris Edwards for reminding me of this fact.
4   Perhaps it is unkind to ascribe too much power and durability to the impact of class consciousness on 'objective decision-making'. However, Hirst's examples of the kinds or 'forms' of knowledge that are required for 'effective thinking' to have any value are worth noting: 'The development of effective thinking is of no value until this is explicated in terms of the forms of knowledge which give it meaning: for example in terms of *the solving of problems in Euclidean geometry or coming to understand the poems of John Donne*' (emphasis added, Hirst 1998: 253).
5   In what might be called the 'Pub Quiz Curriculum', facts predominate to an excessive degree, and the value of the facts selected tends to be self-referential (i.e. they are of value insofar as they enable us to answer specific questions requiring only factual answers). By pseudo-facts, I mean, within such curricula, opinions and interpretations which are presented *as if they are facts*. The 'causes of the First World War', for example, might be presented as facts to be learned, remembered and repeated at some future date (that is to say, treated *and experienced* as facts): however, in reality they will inevitably comprise partial selections from a range of possible causes and a range of possible interpretations.
6   For a fuller account of the commodification of knowledge, see, especially, Lyotard (1984), and, for a helpful summary and thoughts on the applicability of the concept in post-compulsory education, Roberts (1998). Elsewhere, Hellström and Sujatha (2001) provide a useful counter analysis, reminding us that the concept of 'knowledge commodification' can itself become a marketable commodity which, as a kind of knowledge itself ('knowledge about knowledge'), is also not immune to the commodification process.
7   Observations such as this call to mind the opening lines of Martin Scorsese's 2006 film *The Departed*, spoken by Jack Nicholson's psychopathic gangster Frank Costello: 'I don't want to be a product of my environment. I want my environment to be a product of me'. In relation to curriculum policy, not only must the curriculum embedded within such a philosophy reflect

the particular interests and self-perceived qualities of the curriculum maker at the same time (misrecognised or misrepresented in this case as *universal* interests and qualities); it also implicitly models the curriculum 'client' (that is to say, the student) as agentive in a very specific, entrepreneurial, ultimately conservative way (one which, in effect, mimics the character and agency of the curriculum maker at the same time as it contributes to the perpetuation of economic and social divisions and hierarchies). The 'culture of self' implicit in such an approach is close to what many people in the UK still describe as 'Thatcherism'.

Chapter 5

Learning in and out of the classroom

The impact (or otherwise) of digital technologies

> If we look at learners' experiences of using ICT at the beginning of the twenty-first century [...] the most startling fact to emerge is the difference between those experiences at home and at school. Many young people have access to state-of-the-art computers and broadband connectivity at home, as well as peripherals such as speakers, camcorders and digital cameras; their access to ICT, including the internet, is often unrestricted both in terms of time and screening filters.
>
> (Somekh 2006: 121)

Some 'newer' issues

This and the following chapter will consider some specific issues which, although they provide sites of discussion and practice relating to the 'abiding issues' and debates about knowledge and learning discussed in previous chapters, nevertheless have a distinctive 'newness' about them, suggesting that they also offer curriculum – and curriculum theory and policy – a fresh set of challenges leading perhaps to a fresh set of approaches and policies. These are:

- the actual and potential impact on curriculum of rapid advances and the widespread, global use of digital technologies;
- globalisation, in its various guises;
- the *pace* of social, political, technological and environmental change that we are currently experiencing (and contributing to) in the world today, which some have suggested renders our present particularly fragile and our future particularly unpredictable and uncertain.

An exploration of these issues will not focus in detail on the historical development of ICT or 'internationalisation' within various national curriculum specifications, but will rather attempt to identify some of the broader curricular and pedagogic implications of such developments in the wider world. I will suggest, sometimes more implicitly than explicitly, that while each development provides yet another site for more familiar educational debates and disagreements, each is significant in offering curriculum policy what I want to call *the clarity of radical choice*: on the one hand, the choice of breaking with traditional, time-honoured theories and consequent practices of curriculum, of pedagogy, and of public education generally; on the other hand, the option of incorporating such developments into a curriculum, a pedagogy and a public education that remain essentially *un*-changed (what, after Deleuze and Guattari [1977], we might call a 'reterritorialization' process, or, after Bernstein, a manifestation of the 'prospective pedagogic identity'). The context for this 'choice issue', if we can call it that, was introduced in the second part of Chapter 2, in its consideration of some of the complementary and oppositional forces at work in the wider socio-economic (and, we might add, the psychic) world, that either encourage debate, dialogue and contestation (central or local, collective or individual) in curriculum design and practice, or else impede it.

'Charlie don't surf': Repressive classrooms

> [B]y the time we got to the fifth paragraph the teacher asked us about the scenery and objects that were described in the text. Because we said the wrong thing the teacher got very angry with us and we felt terrified. Ever since then when the teacher asks us questions none of us dare to answer. Even if we have thought of the right answer we will not dare to speak because we are afraid of saying something wrong and that we will once again be criticized…
>
> (Sixth Grade Student in school in Gansu, China, recorded in 2004, quoted in Adams and Sargent 2012: 3)

There is a work by the Italian artist Maurizio Catellan called (after a famous line in the film *Apocalypse Now*) *Charlie Don't Surf*. It comprises a mannequin: a student, apparently quite young, seated upright at a school desk. The student's feet are off the floor, the seat being too high for their legs, and their hands are resting palm-down on the desk top. There are no books in sight. Instead, the student's attention is focused on some point directly in front of them, their expression a vacant stare as though their brain has been emptied. They are unable to leave the desk, as their hands have been fixed to it by having had two pencils drilled through them like nails, holding the subject in the 'study position' whilst at the same time preventing any creative use of the writing implements themselves. The title of the piece, which is deliberately ambiguous, can be read as a commentary, as an instruction, as a warning, or even (as in *Apocalypse Now*) as a spurious justification. It is, in essence, a representation of the artist's own very unhappy school experiences as a child, during which his creativity and alternativity – we might say, his 'difference' – rather than attracting interest and praise were construed at best as eccentricity and at worst as a brand of wilful, maliciously-motivated and not-to-be-tolerated rebelliousness.

Whatever reading of Catellan's title we choose (commentary, instruction, warning, faux justification) – not limiting ourselves, perhaps, to any one single option – *Charlie Don't Surf* serves as a powerful metaphor for everything that so many teachers, and indeed a significant number of politicians and policymakers, have struggled on a daily basis to prevent or to resist over the years, often in the face of very powerful opposition. The metaphor represents what much public education in England looked like – and was experienced as – in Victorian England, and experience suggests that it remains as an ideal of public education in the minds of many of our more conservative politicians and draconian school inspectors, albeit often conceived and celebrated within those same discourses of equity and inclusion that announced the introduction of our first national curriculum in the 1980s. 'Education' of this variety is experienced by the student (and potentially by the teacher too, who may also feel 'nailed to the present', forced into coping with an imposed here-and-now, their creativity stifled under the perceived demands of 'business' and 'market values') as a punishment, as a trial, and as a stressful, high-stakes competition in obedience, collusion and regurgitation. The writing implements, which could be used to create and to explore (in modern parlance, and with a nod to the meat of this chapter, to 'surf'), have been conscripted to a form of punitive control, pinning the student to a particular place and time and rendering them 'captive', introspective, isolated and immobile. This student, neither able nor expected to engage in open-ended, exploratory, interactive, adventurous or risk-taking learning, is enforced into passivity and absorption – the 'receiver' of whatever is 'transmitted': the servant, the underling, the subject constructed as, first and foremost, in need of being controlled and managed, caught in a hideously lopsided power relationship with whomever – or whatever – has drilled those pencils through their hands: just one among many of 'the docile bodies sitting at their desks waiting to be directed by their teacher' (Keck 2012: 184).

In such an education, the curriculum, and its attendant modes of implementation and surveillance (essentially, its testing and examination regimes and its controlling pedagogies), is the principal means or instrument by which discipline and control are established and maintained in relation to both students and teachers – and it is not too fanciful to read *Charlie Don't Surf* as a metaphor not just for the student experience, but for the school curriculum too, as it has been widely designed and practised in the past and is still widely designed and practised today: a curriculum characterised by fixety, by individualisation, by an obsession with answers (however misleading they might be), and by processes of normatisation; to return to the ideas explored in Chapters 2 and 3, a curriculum that is both backward-looking and constraining; a curriculum underpinned by an understanding of learning and teaching that is at its core both behaviourist and facile.

Taken as this 'dual-purpose' metaphor, we might, see in Catellan's mannequin both sides of Marcuse's oppression–repression dualism: an 'educated subject' exposed to and controlled by a curriculum that is always the imposition of someone or some group's selections and choices on everybody else and that, precisely because of its selectivity, inevitably represses, through exclusion, certain other knowledge, skills, characteristics and experiences that learners might bring with them into the formal learning situation (Bourdieu and Passseron's [1977] 'symbolic violence'). While neither oppression nor repression *in itself* might necessarily be seen as undesirable or bad (and in fact might be said to have very important functions in the field of mass education and in sustaining social relations in the wider world), the problem for Charlie lies in an education and in a curriculum that are *overly and obstructively* oppressive, and whose imposition simultaneously produces and relies on the *over*-repression of the individual(ised) learner.

I must be quick to add – because I hear cries of protest already – that a critique of such an education and such a curriculum does not equate to an argument for exclusively open-ended teaching and learning, or indeed the abandonment of a formal, pre-set curriculum altogether. The identification of certain core curricular skills and knowledge may be seen as both an inevitability and a desirability if we are to provide successful, equitable and inclusive compulsory education freely available to all young people. It also needs to be acknowledged that for very many students and teachers (though not for all) times have changed, and the curricular and pedagogical excesses exhibited in Catellan's piece apply, if at all, only in a 'watered down' or increasingly symbolic (though, we might argue, still unacceptable) form. In England, for example, not only have so-called traditional, transmissive models of pedagogy been supplemented by others promoting student-centredness, open-endedness, risk-taking and the co-construction of knowledge, but we might argue that, to an extent at least, the old relations of power have changed too, as middle- and upper-class domination and control of the working classes has evolved into slightly more conciliatory, dialogic (we might say, more subtle) forms in the wider society. In the field of formal education, such changes have manifested themselves in developments such as 'parent power' and 'pupil power' – including, for some at least, an element of choice over which schools to send one's children to, and increased opportunities for students to make successful complaints against schools and teachers in their new identification as 'customers', 'clients' and 'consumers'.

However, something else is happening too. In the world outside the classroom, young people in particular are increasingly embracing the new digital technologies, access to which (at least in the so-called developed world) is becoming increasingly affordable and easy – forging their own local, national and global social and learning communities in ways that are significantly different from how things continue to work in most schools and classrooms, often developing more 'powerful knowledge' (op.cit.) than many of their teachers can lay claim to, and helping to widen a growing gulf between learning as understood and approached in the traditional school curriculum, and learning as understood and approached via the 'information superhighway'. As Bennett et al. have observed in their account of the 'technical age of teaching', albeit in relation to young adult learners, large numbers of students have been immersed in technology all of their lives, 'imbuing them with sophisticated technical skills and learning preferences for which education is unprepared' (Bennett et al. 2008: 775).

Learning in and out of school

The notion that there is a gulf between what and how students learn in school and what and how they learn outside school is an old one. Lev Vygotsky, for example, drew a clear, if not entirely convincing, distinction between informal, contingent learning that may take place outside school and the formal, organised learning of the classroom (Vygotsky 1962), while as long ago as 1970 Ivan Illich, considering the possibilities of a formal education that *drew on* existing informal learning rather than demeaning it, argued (in what some may see as an unknowing anticipation of the future existence and learning possibilities of the worldwide web) for 'a new kind of formal education and agencies which, though quite different from schools, would be specifically educational...called learning networks or "webs". These would be voluntary rather than compulsory [and] provide access to resources rather than "pre-packaged" criteria' (Walsh 1993: 85–6). Bruner, too, has famously contrasted life in schools and classrooms with life outside, concentrating this time on *cultural* mismatches between typical formal educational cultures and those embraced and experienced by many students at home and in local communities, going so far as to suggest that (in spite of any rhetoric to the contrary) schools as communities, in which students effectively compete with one another over the symbolic capital materialised in marks, grades and teacher reporting and in which students from poorer backgrounds have little faith in the power of educational qualifications to lift their economic and social prospects, have had the bizarre effect of undermining the qualities and attitudes that are more widely required of community life:

[S]chooling may even be at odds with a culture's way of inducting the young into the requirements of communal living. Our changing times are marked by deep conjectures about what schools should be expected to "do" for those who choose to or are compelled to attend them – or for that matter, what school *can* do, given the force of other circumstances.

(emphasis added, Bruner 1996a: ix)

More recently, John White, conscious of the changing nature of the wider social world and the resistance of some school curricula to be appropriately responsive to that change, has been very critical of school curricula that remain locked in 'the grip of custom', reminding us that 'life beyond the school gates in the twenty-first century is a universe away from what it was in the nineteenth' (2004d: 179) – a re-statement of Raymond Williams' lament some years previously regarding the *English* school curriculum as 'essentially created in the nineteenth century' and, in terms of its basic forms, structures and rationales, having changed very little since (Williams 1961: 188).

The idea that curriculum might *learn from* changes that are occurring in the wider world (rather than simply responding to or ignoring them) – in particular, those such as the rapid development and increasingly ready availability of access to the internet and the worldwide web (which might involve, for example, a heightened emphasis on independent, exploratory learning and *research*) has been taken up by Coffield and Williamson in their argument for formal approaches to education which they characterise as 'communities of discovery': 'Open, unconstrained communication is one of the key ingredients of a community of discovery. The possibilities that have been opened up by the internet are beyond anything that could have been imagined two decades ago, and new uses for digital democracy are being discovered on a daily basis' (Coffield and Williamson 2011: 57). Coffield and Williamson go on to cite the work of Victoria Carrington, who, in emphasising the importance of wanting and knowing how to access knowledge and information, and the enabling possibilities in this regard of the new technologies, argues for curricula which are less prescriptive in terms of the precise identification of bodies of knowledge and that, to reiterate Coffield and Williamson's own account, 'democratise' education and learning, effectively pursuing the competence approach to formal education put forward by Bernstein (2000, op.cit.):

> The new technologies make possible new, open curricula that in principle can be made available all over the world. New learners are no longer just receivers of information, but can become active players in its production and dissemination. In Victoria Carrington's words, we should be "celebrating the ability, or more importantly the right [of students] to produce, disseminate and comment on information" [Carrington 2008: 162].
>
> (Coffield and Williamson: ibid.)

The circumstance identified by these commentators questions the extent to which existent, 'fixed', knowledge-based curricula can – or perhaps should – survive in a social world in which the manipulation, 'creation' and informed access to information and knowledge appears to be becoming at least as important as the information and the knowledge itself. Certainly, the internet speaks of very different modes of learning than those suggested by traditional books. Unlike a book, which can take months or even years to write – or, indeed, to read – information and knowledge on the internet can circulate almost as soon as it is thought (and indeed, in the experience of very many regular users, *does so*, via blogs and tweets). Unlike the fixed, book-based curriculum, with its body of facts, knowledge and skills (to reprise Dewey, its response to the 'quest for certainty'), the internet may be experienced as flexible, responsive, provisional, ever changing, and quickly and easily accessed; sometimes purposively, sometimes more randomly, even whimsically. Furthermore, when its use does relate to looking for answers, these are typically answers to questions brought *by the would-be learner* rather than by an authoritative textbook or teacher or examination syllabus – and not necessarily just one answer either, but a whole range of possible answers and opinions to be weighed and compared to one another.

'New kinds of learning': ICT and constructivism

In his essay 'Learning and Curriculum: agency, ethics and aesthetics in an era of instability' Gunther Kress (2006) adds some flesh to the specific ways in which the kinds of 'external' ICT-based learning undertaken by young school-students in countries like the UK, where access to ICT is relatively widespread and straightforward, (a) differs from the more traditional, formalised approaches to teaching and learning still to be found in most countries, (b) presents both opportunities and challenges for these traditional approaches, (c) has important implications for *social relationships* both at school and in the wider world.

Kress addresses these issues by comparing and contrasting the content, layout and underpinning pedagogic relationships manifested in a traditional school textbook and pages that are available on the internet. The traditional textbook, Kress suggests, had an air of appropriateness at a time when relations of 'authority' in society at large were reflected and replicated in the treatment of learning and knowledge in the curriculum, and where, unlike today (when students, on leaving the school gates, may enter a world of communication and information-exchange that remains both hidden from and beyond the experience of a great many of their teachers), schools' and teachers' knowledge of students' life experience might be much more easily and securely estimated or obtained:

> [T]he directionality of authority [in earlier times] was clear: state power supported the school, the school had clear purposes, its links with state, society and economy were clear and in some ways worked with some benefit for most, even with huge differentials, and so its values, principles, resources, among them its curricula, were clear and legitimate…There was a unidirectionality of power and authority, and there was a unidirectionality of the problems the school was there to solve. The school knew the constitution of the life-worlds of its students, and its curricula promised and provided the resources for their solution…But that relation of authority was homologous with that of society at large; it was there in all forms of communication around authoritative knowledge, with the same directionality.
>
> (Kress 2006: 163–4)

The 'forms of representation and content' in the traditional school textbook, Kress continues, fitted 'exactly' a ubiquitous pedagogic task, which was one of transmitting (we might add 'in the manner of Rancière's Master explicator') suitably presented knowledge in an ordered, incremental and highly controlled way to receptive, 'acquisitive' learners.

However, the 'contemporary world of representation shows a situation which is entirely different' (ibid.: 164). Taking as his example the 'homepage' of his own academic institution, Kress observes:

> The homepage offers neither 'knowledge' nor an order in which it should be read. Where the traditional page had one 'entry point' – in the case of an English-language text, the top left hand corner – and a set reading path, this "page" has twelve or thirteen entry points. What it offers is "information", as does the rest of the website. If the author of the traditional page…knew [their] audience – a myth, though a potent one – the authors/designers of this page do not…[T]he homepage is organised according to the assumed interests of the visitors who might come to the site. These visitors will navigate the site in accordance with their interests and the facilities offered by the site.
>
> (ibid.: 164–6)

Simultaneously identifying the taxing challenges and the new opportunities for formal education of these new modes of representation and learning provided by the internet (reminding us, perhaps, of Bernstein's account of that other great change, discussed in Chapter 2, in which schools and teachers may be impelled to – or may endeavour to – embed a 'prospective management culture' into a fundamentally traditional, conservative, 'retrospective' pedagogic relationship), Kress concludes:

> This is an example of the shift from the power/authority of the author (and the institution) to the power/agency and interest of the reader, as of the child/student. Children in school are users of these media, they have become subjects [whose 'habitus' in terms of their power/authority relationship to knowledge and interest is] shaped by that use…This provides an apt and essential metaphor for (re)thinking school, curriculum and learners, and their relation. Equally, it indicates the *habitus* with which children now come to school, only to meet there an entirely different model of the relationship. This poses the problem that the school faces in sharp relief: that of the power of institutional authority versus the interest of the learners, and the need for their consent, in a world where, ideologically at least, the directionality of power, authority and knowledge to learner and life-world has been inverted.
>
> (ibid.: 167)

Kress is by no means alone in his identification – and advocacy – of the new modes of learning made available by advances in digital technology, or of their implications for school curricula and pedagogy. The simultaneous connectivity with/qualitative difference between informal e-learning and formal school learning has led Bridget Somekh (2006), for example, to suggest that the study of young people's interactions with digital technologies might offer a more fruitful and realistic avenue into developing and renovating school curricula in the twenty-first century than the more common practice of simply (re-)deciding what items to include within a list of fairly static 'subject areas' or disciplines.

Somekh offers a particularly persuasive argument that in the world of today we need to ask very serious questions about the relevance of knowledge- and facts-based curricula, suggesting that developments in and the increasingly widespread use and availability of

ICT encourages – perhaps even necessitates – a curriculum shift to constructivist-based approaches, which promote the kinds of 'situated learning' described by (for example) Brown et al. (1989) and Lave and Wenger (1991). Effectively, this involves a change both in the student's experience of schooling and in the role of teachers – but also a radical change in central curriculum policy: one which allows and encourages a move away from the traditional 'teaching curriculum' (McCormick and Murphy 2000: 229) which is *constructed for* newcomers and mediates the meaning of what is learned through the external view of the teacher' (ibid.), toward Lave and Wenger's *'learning curriculum'* which comprises 'situated opportunities…for the improvisational development of new practice' (Lave and Wenger 1991: 97).

Such a curriculum is guided by overarching education principles and the identification of desired learning *experiences* more than by an insistence on universally available facts and knowledge, so that knowledge is as often invoked in support of practice and experience as the other way round, and the relationships between teachers and learners, and indeed between teachers, learners and curriculum, undergo a radical change in which learner and teacher 'identities' themselves become blurred within a set of joint learning ventures. As Somekh puts it, curriculum policy would then be promoting

> *an open knowledge framework for collaborative learning*, enacted by the interactions of teachers, pupils and a wide range of tools, in an environment which is inherently supportive of the kind of transformative learning that ICT makes possible [– a situation in which] teachers' and learners' roles are interchangeable, and pedagogical practices [are adopted] *in which learners play an active part in structuring their own curriculum.*
>
> (emphases added, Somekh 2006: 128)

As Somekh's account suggests, such a curriculum has inevitable implications not just for pedagogy but for assessment too – not least because of its focus on knowledge-in-use rather than on knowledge 'stored'. It is hard to see, for example, what space or obvious place there might be in the kinds of learning environment described by Somekh for summative, writing-based tests – certainly, not as the *dominant* mode of student assessment, in any event. It may remain important to have a clear sense of what children have learned and of what they know, in order to offer them future life guidance and to ensure that, as adults, people are doing work that they both enjoy and are good at. However, in the more open, exploratory classroom described by Somekh, with its 'flatter structures', 'more open access to knowledge', 'interchangeable roles' and learners 'taking control of their own learning', assessment *for* learning (sometimes known as 'formative assessment') achieves at least an equal – and arguably a greater – degree of importance as assessment 'of' learning. Through assessment *for* learning, teachers and students together, in the 'flatter structure' described by Somekh, would expect to make sophisticated, informed judgements regarding the student's capacity to operate in a range of settings and in response to a range of challenges, both independently and collaboratively. Assessment *of* learning then takes on the added function of providing teachers with the information they need *about* a student's learning in order to help them to learn more – or to learn more effectively: that is, a first step in a process that focuses on learning itself rather than on internalised knowledge. Unlike most current arrangements for summative assessment, whereby student performance is often linked rather crudely and bluntly to teachers' abilities, assessment *for* learning in this context would feed directly and voluntarily back into modifications to the *teacher*'s approach, in order for the teacher to be able to offer more effective ongoing support for the student's learning but also to use the information to develop their own professional practice. It is, thus, not just the learner who is given more control over the shape and direction of their own learning; it is the teacher too.

Some examples in practice

It has to be acknowledged that the changes to curriculum, pedagogy and assessment proposed by Kress and Somekh are unlikely to take place overnight (if at all, though some might see an inevitability about them) and are more likely to occur in stages, over time, in the manner of a longer term, almost unnoticed cultural 'revolution'. There are signs, however, that such a revolution may already be starting, and it is worth briefly considering a couple of these before moving on, if only to indicate that the theory in Kress' and Somekh's arguments has viability (and is embraced with some enthusiasm) in the 'official' practical world of schools and classrooms.

One of the difficulties of incorporating any innovation into time-honoured, culturally established social systems and practices is that if the system does not close its borders to the bearers of radical change it is likely to seek to incorporate them in ways of its own choosing that modify their nature and that require little or no change to its original character. Thus, while it is true that the internet and the worldwide web are increasingly and perhaps inevitably entering the daily life of the school classroom, they are very often doing so in ways in which they find themselves conscripted in the pursuit of more traditional understandings of and approaches to curriculum and learning (Moore et al. 2003). There is evidence, however, that some individual schools – and indeed the politicians and policymakers of some nations – are beginning to recognise the potential value and impact of forms of learning that many of their students are increasingly engaging with outside the school classroom, and are looking for creative ways to incorporate these into the curriculum offer and experience. (As has often been the case in my own search for examples of innovative curriculum practice, I have been obliged, somewhat disappointingly, to look beyond state education in England, both toward our own private sector and toward initiatives in other countries. Even more disappointingly, I have been obliged to look beyond the education systems of poorer countries, in which curriculum choices are severely limited by a lack of resources, and in which the affordances of regular access to the new technologies remain out of the reach of millions of young learners and their families.)

One example of the incorporation of 'outside' into 'inside' learning, and of open, individual, research-based 'e-learning' into the formal, group-based learning of the traditional school, is that of so-called 'flipped learning', which involves students bringing their own guided but independent web-based research into the classroom as an entry-point into more formal classroom-based, teacher-facilitated learning (rather than, say, as a piece of developmental homework arising exclusively out of a pre-set classroom lesson). Flipped learning is already being introduced formally into a small number of national curricula (for instance, that of Singapore). However, it can also be found in practice in a number of individual schools around the globe, including the famous Eton College public school in England, whose Principal, Tony Little, has recently offered the following helpful account and rationale of the practice:

> The notion of a school is that you turn up to the lesson, the teacher explains a lot of things in your 40 minutes and you go away and do homework to show you've understood. A flipped lesson turns it the other way round. The information you would need to have is available online, you're set all this in advance and what the lesson then becomes is seeing if you have understood the information and can develop it or manipulate it in creative ways. It's not a question of every lesson suddenly becoming a flipped lesson. But what's really good for students is seeing there's different ways of going about things. That, I find rather exciting. We're developing a whole range of different ways of students learning – a lot of which enables them to take greater control for themselves, more independent learning.
>
> (cited in Harris 2013)

Lest we are encouraged to think that 'flipped learning' is another new idea only made possible by developments in information and communication technologies, it is worth remembering that, as with so many other 'new ideas' in education, John Dewey was advocating something very similar more than 100 years ago in his short work *My Pedagogic Creed* (re-published in Flinders and Thornton 2009). In presenting the school student as 'an inheritor of the funded capital of civilization', Dewey was at pains at the same time to promote the idea of learners as active meaning-makers, as best able to learn in the local contexts in which they find themselves, and as being allowed to bring curriculum *to* the classroom (so to speak) rather than just being exposed to a curriculum that enforces learning as 'a pressure from without' (2009: 17). Rather than developments in ICT being *responsible* for this particular approach to learning, we might, therefore, say that such developments have, rather, *facilitated* such an approach, making it more possible within the large teaching groups of typical school classrooms, and that perhaps it has encouraged more educators to appreciate the potential value of the approach. It is also worth adding that politicians concerned with equity and entitlement might need to extend their concerns about making curriculum elements available to all students to include such practices as flipped learning (which are underpinned by a certain trust in and respect for students as independent learners), rather than simply on 'teaching them' the same pre-selected facts and how to appreciate [sic] the same pre-selected cultural artefacts.

'The tyranny of The Answer'

> The goal of instruction should be to allow students to deal sensibly with problems that often involve evidence, quantitative consideration, logical arguments, and uncertainty; without the ability to think critically and independently, citizens are easy prey to dogmatists, flimflam artists, and purveyors of simple solutions to complex problems.
>
> *American Association for the Advancement of Science 1989*

The kinds of learning – indeed, the kind of *education* – proposed in Somekh's account of the potential affordances of digital technologies do not only affect matters of pedagogy and assessment, or understandings of linguistic and cognitive development. They also (to hark back to issues discussed in Chapter 4) offer a challenge to the dominance of canonical 'knowledge' in curriculum design, and to the ideals and influences that might be said to underpin it.

Eisner (1979: 15) has argued that the 'dominance of scientific epistemology in education…has all but excluded any other view of the way in which inquiry in education can legitimately be pursued' – a view echoing that of Carr (1995: 87), that Enlightenment ideals, in their belief in and pursuit of reasoned 'truth', have prioritised 'knowledge over experience, certainty over contingency, and stability over change' (ibid.: 87). Within this world-view, the physical and social world are there to be *known*, to be described, to be understood: everything in the physical world is knowable, and knowledge is freedom – freedom from ignorance and, ultimately, freedom from the chains of poverty and injustice. There is, somewhere, an answer – a 'right answer' – to every question.

I want to suggest, after Somekh, that whatever dangers and caveats we might bring to the relationship between ICT and (formal or informal) learning (more of which below), the former would appear to offer at least an opportunity to begin to envision an education and a curriculum that does not remain locked in Enlightenment ideals, that *makes use of* knowledge (and helps students learn how best to do so) rather than valuing it in its own right, that embraces change, and that treats 'certainty' for the imposter it is. Above all (perhaps) it replaces curricula that are overly dominated by 'answers' with the possibility of curricula (more in line with Dewey's 'inquisitive' curricula) that focus predominantly on asking *questions*: that is, on placing challenging questions *before* students, perhaps giving them more responsibility for accessing some of the knowledge they might need in order to respond to them, but also on encouraging students to ask and to explore *questions of their own* – both in school and in the 'world outside' – recognising, in so doing, that it is the endless cycle of questioning and answering that drives us forward intellectually and therapeutically both as individuals and as a species.

To elaborate a little further, what is being suggested here (and, I think, by the kinds of learning identified by Kress and Somekh, by Dewey, Eisner and Carr) is not an *abandonment* of answers (which would be foolish even if it were possible), but rather a recalibration within the curriculum of the *relationship between* answers and questions – a relationship in which every answer is treated as provisional and contingent, its brief satisfaction leading us to ask further questions rather than dropping us off in a comfort zone beyond which there appears to be no need of further enquiry: a relationship, perhaps, which does not refute Dewey's account of the 'quest for certainty' but that might re-frame the problem so that it becomes a virtue – emphasising the 'quest' itself, while recognising the 'certainty' as a necessary illusion. The problem, thus conceived, is not with answers themselves, therefore; it is, rather, that answers, which should be our friends rather than our enemies, should not be allowed (as is so often the case) to become *The Answer* – that is, when answers and quests for answers are allowed to coagulate into a single, dominant, fascinating feature in the educational landscape, becoming at once an ideology and the ultimate rationale for what we learn in school and how we learn it.

The Answer in such cases is *tyrannical* not just in its un-negotiated imposition of a sacrosanct, pre-determined body of knowledge, but also in its insistence on students' obedience to it through testing regimes which themselves require the sacrificial offering of 'right answers' rather than a capacity to ask informed and pertinent questions. In such situations, rather than representing that which brings about excitement and *wonder* (we do, after all, inhabit a pretty wonderful and staggeringly fascinating universe!). The Answer engenders anxiety and the mundane. Rather than supporting our ongoing learning, The Answer seeks to scribble an impenetrable chalk line under it. To borrow from Dewey again, in place of a curriculum of 'acquisition' (of answers, of 'knowledge', of facts and of the other acquisitions related to these acquisitions – 'certification, credentials, money, possessions, jobs, and so much more') the recalibration of the question–answer relationship that I think is implicit particularly in Somekh's argument, and which an appropriately welcoming, formalised incorporation of 'e-learning' can promote and facilitate, suggests instead a curriculum of 'inquisitiveness' (Lopez Schubert and Schubert 2011: 109; Dewey 1933). It is a curriculum which, to introduce another distinction I want to offer, prioritises *problem-solving* over *solving problems*: that is to say, unlike the traditional subject- and knowledge-based curriculum, which focuses on students' providing – or demonstrating a grasp of – answers or solutions to 'problems' which are not only determined by others but whose solution is also pre-determined, waiting to be found, a curriculum which focuses on the cognitive, linguistic and social *skills and processes* demanded by creative, intellectual activity at least as much as on rightness or otherwise of the solution itself. As Eisner puts it: '[T]he solution to the problem in problem-solving objectives is not definite. …The solutions individual students or groups of students reach may be just as much a surprise for the teacher as they are for the students who created them. … *The opportunity to use ingenuity breeds interest*' (emphasis added, Eisner 1979: 102–3).

Problem-solving thus represents the acquisition and use of a set of transferable skills that can be applied when addressing all manner of problems – both those 'presented' to us or created by others, and those concerning our own personal choices and the contingencies of our own individual lives – either alone or in collaboration with others, either during our school days or later on into adult life. To reprise some earlier metaphors, problem-solving is more jazz band than symphony orchestra (Holland 1999), more schizophrenia than paranoia (Deleuze and Guattari 1977) – resonant perhaps with Carse's (1986) notion of 'infinite' as opposed to 'finite' games, where the latter applies to relationships and actions within social structures and organisations that have winners and losers, beginnings and ends, specific, inflexible rules of engagement, and the former to actions and relationships which are unscripted and unpredictable, less easily controlled, ultimately more rewarding and liberating.[1] Resistant to a widespread requirement in public education that 'demands everyone to get to the point' (Britzman 1998: 37), problem-solving demands, in line with Somekh's proposals, not only a radically different curriculum, but a radically different pedagogy – one that reflects within the individual classroom and the individual teacher–learner relationship Michael Oakeshott's (1962: 198–9) celebrated account of the 'conversational' narrative of human history and development:[2]

> As civilised human beings, we are the inheritors, neither of an inquiry about ourselves and the world, nor of an accumulating body of information, but of a conversation, begun in the primeval forests and extended and made more articulate in the course of centuries. It is a conversation which goes on both in public and within each of ourselves. Of course there is argument and enquiry and information, but wherever these are profitable they are to be recognized as passages in this conversation, and perhaps they are not the most captivating of the passages. …Conversation is not an enterprise designed to yield an extrinsic profit, a contest where a winner gets a prize, nor is it an activity of exegesis; it is an unrehearsed intellectual adventure. … Education, properly speaking, is an initiation into the skill and partnership of this conversation in which we learn to recognize the voices, to distinguish the proper occasions of utterance, and in which we acquire the intellectual and moral habits

appropriate to conversation. And it is this conversation which, in the end, gives place and character to every human utterance.

Some caveats

Whatever we may think of Somekh's vision – including those of us who find it exciting – there are, not surprisingly perhaps, difficulties and tensions that schools, teachers, parents and theorists will need to address if it is ever to replace or to offer a serious challenge to existing orthodoxy.

Somekh (like Kress) focuses, very helpfully, on the potential *affordances* of ICT, both in relation to the individual learner and in relation to the ways in which, through its offer of '*an open knowledge framework for collaborative learning*' (ibid.) it can promote more collaborative, 'democratic' classrooms (a far cry, indeed, from the model illustrated in *Charlie Don't Surf!*). Arguing for what is, by and large, a particular *process model* (op.cit.) of curriculum, the *sine qua non* here as that rather than treating ICT as if it presents some kind of threat that needs to be domesticated, or introducing it into curricula as 'just another subject area', curricula need to take advantage of the new learning possibilities that ICT has made available, and construct the curriculum around these possibilities: possibilities which (and here let us think of Dewey again) promote 'the kind of learning [which was always] perceived to be ideal, but [which the previously] available tools – e.g. school libraries, exercise books, textbooks and work sheets – did not support...well' (Somekh 2006: 128).

What, however (lest we get too easily carried away), are the arguments *against* looking toward developments in digital technologies as a beacon for radical curriculum reform? For one thing, it has to be said that although the internet and the worldwide web may indeed offer unique opportunities for teachers and students to explore the physical, social and cultural world and to develop their own knowledge and understandings in new and exciting ways, in the end (to anticipate a discussion to be had in Chapter 7) the internet is a market-led phenomenon underpinned by 'market values': indeed, it is a market *place* – of ideas as well as of products – and, as Somekh (ibid.) herself points out, a largely uncontrolled, perhaps even, to a considerable extent, uncontrollable one at that. It is a virtual 'place' or 'space' where knowledge can be posted without censorship and accessed by whomever has the relatively modest means to do so, be they adults or children. It is a place where products can be bought and sold, and where ideas and ideologies can be discovered, discussed and exchanged: a market that is very weakly (and very often reactively) regulated, even by current standards, and which itself provides a screen for and makes possible the existence of a completely unregulated 'hidden market'. In addition to more 'neutral' forms of information and knowledge, it promulgates propaganda of all varieties, offering access to right wing, left wing, centrist and militant movements, as well as to various forms of self help, to petitions, to interest-groups, but also to organisations promoting hatred, intolerance and terrorism. It is a place where people – including and perhaps predominantly – young people can come together to 'network' socially to inclusive, constructive ends, but also to ex-clusive, destructive ones.

While this e-marketplace is hardly values-free, we might argue that it is not guided, shaped and managed by an *overall* set of values, and it is in this respect, not only in its mode of information exchange that it stands in stark contrast to the standard, fixed, book and examination led curriculum that we are all used to: a site of information- and knowledge-exchange that, to return to the metaphors of Deleuze and Guattari (1977, 2004, op.cit.), is as 'schizophrenic' as the formal school curriculum is 'paranoid' – with all the potential positives and negatives, affordances and dangers inherent in such a nature. Whatever we may think of a school curriculum's underlying values – and I have often criticised those that underpin the national curriculum in my own country – we need to recognise, perhaps, that the traditional curriculum has always had the capacity (and sometimes the will, too) to promote values which stand in opposition to what many of us see as the less acceptable values of the marketplace and which, as a society, we might wish to see endure: values such as promoting collective rather than individual work and achievement; the common good rather than self interest; the quality of life rather than stark materialism.

This is not to say that the kinds of learning made possible by the internet, with the internet itself at the very centre *of* learning, cannot also be allied within formal educational settings to such values. However, to do so, given the emphasis on very high levels of student empowerment within such a reshaped curriculum clearly represents, as Kress (op. cit.) has pointed out, one of the major challenges for public education – a challenge that needs to be set alongside a parallel and not unrelated one, which is to ensure that, rather than challenging outdated, top-down curricula that simply seek to preserve the social status quo, ICT does not become conscripted to that same essentially conservative cause. As the ever-wise William Pinar cautions:

> If only we place computers in every classroom, if only school children stare at screens (rather than at teachers. Evidently) they can "learn", become "competitive" in the "new millennium". Information is not knowledge, of course, and *without ethical and intellectual judgment* – which cannot be programmed into a machine – the Age of information is the Age of Ignorance.
>
> (emphasis added, Pinar 2004: xiii)

Pinar's words of warning, which focus less on the learning opportunities afforded by ICT more (in stark contrast to Somekh's 'open knowledge framework for collaborative learning') on the potentially isolating effects on learners and the possible ousting of 'knowledge' by 'information' (itself having the potential to become an internally contradictory term) is supported by a not unrelated concern, that the greater inclusion of ICT as a subject and as a learning tool into national school curricula might come with a pragmatic, neo-liberal rationale rather than with a pedagogic, genuinely empowering and 'democratic' one. Tseng, for example (2013: 60), regarding the case of curriculum development in England (and implying, perhaps, a deliberate policy conflation of 'knowledge' and 'information' that might be used to *undermine* objections such as Pinar's) argues that, as a result of central government concerns and reforms in the 1980s and 1990s, '[s]chooling was placed very much at the centre of building a knowledge-based economy, in which information technology and knowledge were seen to be the primary assets to create wealth and further maintain the dominance of a nation state in a global competitive environment'. Tseng's suggestion might well help to explain attempts in centrally mandated education policy – not just in England – to introduce a new subject, 'ICT', into the curriculum, whether as a separate discipline, as a cross-curricular skill, or as a bit of both. But it also, I think, draws us toward another regrettable possibility – one that returns us to that awkward alliance suggested in Chapter 2 between conservatism and neo-liberalism in much public (education) policy. It is that although ICT might *appear* to promote freer, more open, discovery learning, promoting greater learner choice and control, this might all prove to be something of an illusion – a constructed neutrality of information and facts that conceals its own choices, preferences and purposes, and that, however different it might appear on the outside, is a mere repackaging or re-formulation of existing dominant conceptualisations of and intentions for learning. According to such a view, in our (now illusory) voyages of discovery, we (and our young students) are being just as much 'led' and controlled, albeit in different, perhaps more subtle and insidious ways and in slightly different and potentially even less empowering directions, as in our more traditional school-based learning within its constructed and (either tightly or loosely) bounded curriculum: this time, not by the overt conservative and neo-liberal ideologies and policies of central government, but by the more covert intentions and desires of the designers and manufacturers of search engines and computers.

Another way of putting this is to conceptualise ICT-based learning as a specific form of what Bernstein (2000: 78) calls 'segmented' pedagogy being incorporated into 'institutional pedagogy' while retaining its segmented characteristics – and indeed having viral potential to infect institutional pedagogy. To quote Bernstein:

> *Institutional pedagogy* is carried out in official sites (state, religious, communal), usually with accredited providers, and where acquirers are concentrated voluntarily or involuntarily as a group or social category. *Segmented pedagogy* is carried out usually in the face-to-face relations of everyday experience and practice by informal providers. This pedagogy may be tacitly or explicitly transmitted *and* the provider may not be aware a transmission has taken place. Unlike institutional pedagogy the pedagogic process may be no longer than the context or segment in which it is enacted. Segmental, that is, *unrelated* competences result from such pedagogic action. For example, a child learning to dress, tie up shoes, count change in a supermarket, are competences acquired through segmental pedagogies which may vary in their explicitness and in their code of realisation. Learning to be a patient, waiting room behaviour, doctor/patient conduct and report [are examples of] a tacit mode of a segmental pedagogy where the provider(s) *may* be unaware that they are providers. What is of interest is the interactional consequences of the relation between institutional and segmental pedagogies.

Before concluding, I want to draw attention to two points in Bernstein's account that I think are of particular relevance to our current considerations. The first is his suggestion that in 'segmented' learning, which takes place outside the 'Pedagogic Recontextualising Field' of schools and classrooms (Bernstein 2000), not only is pedagogy more tacitly experienced by the learner than in more formal 'institutional' learning situations, but the 'provider' might not always be aware of it: in the case of ICT, for example, those working within the ICT industry might genuinely believe *themselves* that they are producing a revolutionary yet contextually neutral 'information superhighway' along which (despite the contradiction implicit in the metaphor) the 'user' can travel in any direction for as long or as little as they choose. The affordances of ICT then become false affordances: not *replacing* previous power relations in teaching and learning, in which choices are radically shifted from the 'master' (teacher, textbook, curriculum, examination syllabus) to the student, but merely re-presented in fancy dress. To return to Pinar's concerns, such a reading of the potential role and impact of ICT on students' learning in relation to their development from the 'recipients' of knowledge and wisdom to becoming their own researchers becomes seriously undermined, i.e. unless they are particularly adept at seeking out 'alternative' sites, the 'researcher student' might simply be 'finding out' what dominant groups (consciously or unconsciously) *intend* them to find out – an e-version, perhaps, of the traditional classroom techniques described by Edwards and Mercer (1987) to ensure that the curriculum experience is delimited or constrained in a disguised fashion so that students arrive at 'right answers' within a convincing pedagogic illusion of open, exploratory, student-centred learning.

The second issue that I think is of particular interest concerns the essential *unrelated* or *disconnected* nature of 'segmented' learning – the fact that it reaches the learner from a range of unconnected sources and therefore lacks the coherent inter-connectedness that institutional learning can provide (although we might argue that it very often does not). To return to Pinar's concerns, while ICT undoubtedly does offer students and teachers the potentially emancipatory learning opportunities described by Somekh, there is also the danger that instead of expanding our knowledge and our capacity to make use of that knowledge, it might actually – by substituting the seemingly endless availability of unconnected facts and items of information *for* knowledge – contribute to a dilution of genuine thinking and learning in which facts and information contribute to knowledge development, and its replacement either with vast repositories of disconnected data or with easy, often quickly forgotten answers to a range of similarly disconnected questions.

This is an important challenge that can be connected to the argument put forward earlier in this chapter concerning the virtue of 'problem-solving' over 'solving problems' – a virtue and indeed a distinction which are by no means shared by all commentators, for some of whom the apparently positive, student-centred, progressive inflection that I have ascribed to problem-solving merely disguises how it functions (and perhaps what, in the end, it *is*) in reality: that is to say, a means of perpetuating a traditional, dis-empowering, repressive curriculum regime *of solving problems*. As Popkewitz (2009: 304) argues, referencing 'official' descriptions of problem-solving (that is, those to be found in official curriculum documentation) rather than my own (though it might equally be applied to my own):

> problem-solving embodies salvation themes about the future; the child's problem-solving is to enable successful living in the future "learning" or "information" society as the cosmopolitan citizen, with self-realization and self-fulfilment. The salvation themes function in the curriculum as cultural theses about how one should live as a particular kind of "modern" person. The kinds of problem-solving person being offered brings together, assembles, and connects different principles about who the child is and should be. These principles entail, for example, notions of agency in which the individual calculates, orders, and directs actions, conceptions of time that bring actions into a flow of development and growth that enables planning for the future, and the taming of change so that the uncertainties of life can be problem-solved, that is put into a regulated practice. To develop curricula and undertake research on problem-solving is to theorize, regularize and rationalize processes to change people. The insertion of problem-solving into the curriculum is an inscription

device to order and classify conduct. The cultural theses of the problem-solver are not only about what a child is. *They are also practices of governing what a child should become.*

Problem-solving thus described, while not wedded to The Answer in quite the way I have described, is nevertheless seen as wedded to and supportive of another conservatising force discussed in Chapter 2: that of neo-liberalism. It is not, despite much rhetoric to the contrary, an approach which embraces change or promotes independent, exploratory learning, but rather one which, ultimately, seeks to *control* change and to *manage* the individual whilst at the same time creating an *illusion* of giving them freedom and respecting their right to choose. Perhaps, in the grammar of Foucault, it is an approach that encourages in learners the internalisation of a *misrecognition* of freedom and creativity that actually masks *from* the individual an agreement to comply. It hardly needs pointing out how this particular understanding of problem-solving might relate negatively to the kinds of ICT-connected learning espoused by Somekh. To return to an issue already raised, though from a slightly different starting point: Does engagement with ICT itself promote independent, creative learning? Or does it merely create the *illusion* of doing so, clandestinely shaping the web-user in ways that are as powerful as they are 'invisible'? To refer again to Rancière's teacher-explicator, is there a danger that, in the relationship between ICT and the ICT-user ICT itself, holding all the answers, becomes simultaneously constructed and misrecognised by the user as the all-knowing Master of the un-learned apprentice?

This issue of 'who is in control here?' has become particularly pertinent in recent months, reminding us that it might not only be the forces and values of 'the Market' that are guiding and refining our selections and choices for us, but that (with Foucauldian potential!) our apparently free-ranging internet journeys and discoveries and conversations might also fall under the perhaps even more sinister and worrying gaze, even within self-styled democracies, of the State as the potentially empowering, [r]evolutionary possibilities of the internet come to be experienced and re-constructed as a threat by certain interests – an issue raised by none other than the designer of the worldwide web himself, Tim Berners-Lee:

> The web and social media are increasingly spurring people to organise, to take action and try to expose wrongdoing in every region of the world. But some governments are threatened by this. A growing tide of surveillance and censorship now threatens the future of democracy. Bold steps are needed to protect our fundamental rights to privacy and freedom of opinion on line.
>
> (Tim Berners-Lee, Smith 2013, www.bbc.co.uk/news/technology-25033577.)

Far from taking us away from the pedagogic relationship summarised in *Charlie Don't Surf*, the danger here is that the same relationship returns in a different, perhaps less brutal but equally 'watching' and controlling way. All of which might suggest the 'real task' for education and curriculum: to bring formal teaching and learning experiences more closely into line with the teaching and learning experiences of students outside the formal learning situation in ways that are reciprocal and mutually beneficial (perhaps 'flipped learning', described above, offers one example of how such a relationship might be achieved), but which do not rely upon or revolve around the internet itself – making use of computers in schools to promote and support 'new' kinds of learning but avoiding the mere transference of 'pedagogic authority' (Bourdieu and Passeron 1977) from schools and teachers to the worldwide web.

Notes

1   The traditional school curriculum might also be understood in terms of a 'finite game', characterised by pre-ordained solutions to pre-ordained problems, winners and losers, specific, inflexible rules of engagement, and the introduction of 'judges' to oversee rules and rule changes, to determine who wins and who loses, and so on.
2   Oakeshott's account is quoted at length by Hirst (1998). I do likewise in the hope that such a repetition does not lead readers to assume wholehearted support for Hirst's argument, or indeed for some of his own and his colleagues' more negative views on student-centred education.

Chapter 6

Internationalising the curriculum

We must not delay. Upon the speedy provision of elementary education depends our industrial prosperity. It is of no use trying to give technical teaching to our artisans without elementary education; uneducated labourers – and many of our labourers are utterly uneducated – are, for the most part, unskilled labourers, and if we leave our workfolk any longer unskilled, notwithstanding their strong sinews and determined energy, they will become over-matched in the competition of the world...If we are to hold our position among men of our own race or among the nations of the world we must make up the smallness of our numbers by increasing the intellectual force of the individual.

(William Forster, introducing the first great Education Bill on 17 February 1870: Hansard, 17 Feb 1870, quoted in *English Historical Documents XII [1]* ed. Young and Handcock 1954: 914)

Over the past ten years, the pressure to "be international" and to "internationalize" has dramatically intensified in all aspects of education. Spurred on by the contested processes of globalization...international education – until recently a relatively marginalized term – has moved closer to the center of educational research throughout the world.

(Dolby and Rahman 2008: 676)

(Global) learning communities

The concerns raised at the end of the previous chapter regarding the potential negative effects of ICT on learning – and how learners construct themselves as learners – need to be taken seriously. However, it is equally important not to use them as a reason for rejecting the transformative possibilities suggested in Somekh's argument. Rather, I would suggest they serve as an important reminder of the central role that teachers, schools and politicians have to play in ensuring that ICT promotes and enhances 'institutional' learning, with perhaps a knock-on benefit within informal, out-of-school learning – that its potential benefits are put to the best use and its potential negative effects are identified and (always as far as is possible) dealt with. It is for this reason that, in introducing this new chapter, I want to return to the more positive note on which the previous chapter began.

I have already drawn attention to the potential 'learner insularity' that ICT can engender or reproduce, and to its capacity to be used for coordinated personal attacks and other practices that I imagine the vast majority of us would condemn. Others, however, have preferred to focus on its capacity to bring people together in friendship and in collective endeavour, and thereby to have the capacity to make the world not only a more knowledgeable, 'switched-on' place but also a more harmonious and, thereby, a safer one. As Gardner and Walsh (2000: 80) have observed, in a passage reminiscent again of Somekh's 'open knowledge framework':

> Whether between individuals or groups, the communication-related dimensions of technology have the potential to break down the physical and cultural barriers that currently separate the peoples of the world. More so than either television or telephony alone, it truly opens up the world and its citizens to the concept of "large group consciousness", enabling dialogue in a manner that simply was not possible before.

Suggestions such as this take us significantly further than considerations of the individual classroom and the individual school. They remind us of ICT's capacity for promoting easy and affordable connectedness, and possibilities for knowledge- and experience-sharing, between people in general but most importantly, in relation to our current considerations, between young students from different geographical and cultural backgrounds and of different ages – both within their own nation state and, even more importantly, perhaps, between different nation states: that is to say, the possibility not only of students sharing ideas and experiences with one another, but of teachers similarly engaging with one another in ways that do not demand long-distance travel or the relative ponderousness and lack of immediacy of the written word. We might even suggest that ICT makes more possible some kind of *inter*-national minimum curriculum if so desired: either one which, in the fullness of time, results in common curriculum elements across all or some of the nations of the world, or (as is perhaps both more likely and more desirable, given comments that have already been made about balancing sameness and difference) one in which individual national curricula take on much more of a global or international *perspective* – perhaps embracing the promotion not just of national but of global *citizenship*.

It is to this second new issue, of some of the effects, implications and educational affordances of (a particular manifestation of) globalisation and of the 'internationalisation' of curricula that I now want to turn. However, before I do so, it is important to note how I am using these terms. When I speak of 'internationalisation' it is in relation to the curriculum itself. 'Globalisation', on the other hand – not so much 'economic globalisation' as forms of globalisation related to changes in communications technologies of various kinds – is used in relation to the circumstances or contexts within which curriculum internationalisation might be promoted and developed. Broadly, 'internationalisation' is thus taken to mean the incorporation of global or international strands, dimensions or principles *into* national curricula, while 'global curriculum' refers to a curriculum which both takes a fundamental global perspective in some of its aspects *and* in which those aspects are formally incorporated at some level of specificity in the curricula of subscribing nations around the globe. In everyday discussion, of course, the terms 'global' and 'international/ised' are often used interchangeably, as also, as will become evident in the later stages of this chapter, in much of the theory and literature on this topic.

Globalisation, internationalisation and nationalism

As the quote from William Forster used at the start of this chapter suggests, a central rationale for introducing state education *in the UK* nearly a century and a half ago was essentially an economic argument, connected to fears that Britain would not be able to remain economically competitive in the context of global trade (this at a time when Britain still ruled over a substantial global empire) – and it is, arguably, a rationale which sustains its dominance to this day, often finding itself having to share the curriculum agenda with incomers like 'fostering a love of learning', 'producing well rounded individuals' or 'promoting values and morals', but seldom in danger of losing its status as the principal reason for sending young people off to school. (For a little more on the history of public education in Britain in this regard, see Moore 2012: 47–54.) Nowadays, this concern about economic competitiveness extends its reach beyond what is actually *done* in the workplace (and how it is done) – i.e. modes of working, 'quality control', inter-worker and inter-company competition – to what is done in the classroom, both in encouraged practice and via international tables of measured achievement in numeracy, literacy and so forth, as if each nation needs to 'sell' to other nations not only its goods and services but also notions of its *productive potential*: 'Invest in us; work with us: our future is bright!'

It is easy to see why such concerns continue to predominate, and hard to argue that they should not. However, international competitiveness has changed somewhat since Forster's day, and so have some of the problems and possibilities facing not just individual nations but the world as a whole: those problems, for example, referenced in Chapter 1, related to climate change and the natural environment, or to creaking inadequacies in dominant global forms of political-economic organisation; but also opportunities afforded by high-speed travel and the internet, which have made the world seem a much smaller place and have – at least potentially – the capacity to promote relatively rapid, relatively collective international and intercultural communication, decision-making and understanding. There is also, perhaps born of this combination of a recognition of shared problems and communicative possibilities (not to mention the power of shared technologies in *addressing* problems and *creating* possibilities), a sneaking, growing, if at times reluctant awareness that some of the global problems facing us might be better dealt with on a global, cooperative basis: a kind of 'global politics' emerging from Gardner and Walsh's 'large group consciousness' (op.cit.). Related to such an awareness within the political domain is a growing acceptance that some more specifically 'national' or 'local' problems (extreme poverty, starvation, infant mortality, sectarian violence, warfare) might also not just be solvable through such joint enterprise, but that their solution might be of benefit to all.

In a speech given at the Progressive Governance Conference in London in February 2010, the then Prime Minister of Great Britain and Northern Ireland, Gordon Brown, suggested such an argument. The speech both promoted global 'progressive' politics and underlined one of the major difficulties in bringing it about: i.e. politicians' and their constituents' primary concern with what happens *in their own country*:

> It is clear and understandable that national politics is still first and foremost in the minds of political leaders. Politics remains a local and national affair. And yet the challenges everyone faces have huge global components [all of which] require

international cooperation... [P]eople today know that no one country can solve terrorism or conflict or poverty or climate change on their own, that there is no firm line separating what happens "over there" from what happens "over here".

(Brown 2010: 9)

At this same conference, Jean-Francois Rischard, the former vice-president of the World Bank, asked why it was that international cooperation and collaboration in solving such global concerns as climate change had hitherto proved so very difficult:

> The list of pressing global problems – those that can *only* be addressed through international cooperation – is growing longer. ...We now have no less than 20 such global problems on our hands ranging from dangerous climate change, the prevention of further financial crises...and tackling terrorism. Many of these problems, most notably climate change, must be resolved within the next 20 years or less; otherwise it may be too late to reverse the effects. At the same time, technically feasible, financially viable and politically manageable solutions exist for all these problems. Yet none of them are being solved. Why is this the case?

(Rischard 2010: 38)

Answering his own question, Rischard developed Brown's argument concerning the prioritisation of national needs, pointing an accusing finger toward rampant nationalism and the problem for politicians in democratic countries of securing their own or their own country's political interests rather than addressing those of the planet:

> [The] root cause [of the problem] is the lethal clash between the territorial and short-term electoral perspectives of the nation-states and their politicians, and the non-territorial, long-term solutions necessary to address global problems: for example, politicians running for election every four years may hesitate to embrace a global 100-year plan to reduce carbon emissions.

(ibid.: 38)

It would not be hard to apply a cynical reading to such arguments: in this case, they are born less of the social, humanitarian, altruistic concerns we have touched on above, more of a selfish determination to maintain the prosperity and economic advantage of already well-off nations (or to sustain the already-wealthy, including the heads of multi-national companies, in their wealth regardless of their nationality or country of residence), and to maintain and to protect and extend a dominant free-market capitalist system, i.e. not only do global problems need to be addressed in order that the global free market can continue to thrive free of the threats that such problems might pose, but the global effort itself can create new markets, new consumers, and more – and cheaper – producers of the 'right stuff'. (For a well argued account of such an interpretation, see Weber 2004.)

Such a reading lurks just below the surface of many such arguments within the field of global politics, emerging tentatively from time to time in a variety of official sources. DFID (the UK Department for International Development), for example, urging global solutions to local poverty and famine, appears to do so at least partly on the basis that what happens 'over there' is not so much an effect of what happens 'over here' as a potential threat to the quality of life 'over here' – an idea also present in the UK DfES (Department for Education and Skills) paper *Developing the Global Dimension in the School Curriculum*, which acknowledges:

> The actions of all people impact on others throughout the world. For example, the direct and indirect effects of environmental damage such as land degradation and greenhouse gas emissions do not stop at national boundaries. Equally, economies around the world are more interdependent than ever, reliant on both trade with, and investment from, other countries. What a consumer in one country chooses to buy affects a producer in another country. The solutions to many global problems, whether climate change or inequality, are more likely to be realised through genuine understanding of our mutual interdependence, and of that between humans and the natural world.
>
> (DfES March 2005: 5. See also, coming from a different perspective, Ahmad's [2010: 107] observation that '[t]he world has reached a unique epoch of mutual interdependency, in which states can no longer expect that the effects of their actions in some distant part of the world, or amongst the global community, will not at some level come back to affect them; and where regional instability can lead to global insecurity.')

Be this as it may, there does appear to be a growing alliance of politicians from a range of parties (though perhaps in the main those positioning themselves publicly as 'left of centre') urging international cooperation and collaboration to solve (or perhaps 'address' more accurately, since in a case such as poverty any genuine solution is likely to result in a more radical reassessment of global capitalism than most politicians appear prepared to countenance) certain major world problems. Inevitably, this invites the question: What might this mean for education? And particularly, what might it mean during times when nation states are busy producing *national curricula*, along with citizenship education programmes which are, in the main, introspectively focused on perceived 'national interests' in a 'competitive world'?

This last matter is of no little importance. While Dolby and Rahman, in their comprehensive review of literature and research into 'global education' published in 2008 (a passage from which has helped open this chapter) were broadly positive in relation to the weight of education *theory* supporting 'global' or 'international' curricula, they were somewhat less enthusiastic when it came to assessing the actual *impact on practice* of such theory, describing it as very variable – a finding which echoes the report of Tye (2003) in a separate study of 52 countries carried out some years earlier, that, despite a growing recognition of the importance of internationalising curricula, many nations were still focusing on building 'national loyalties'. Studies like Tye's suggest that while internationalism is (or at least was at the time) thriving in the curricula of some countries, such as New Zealand and Japan, in others – for example, the USA – global education is (ironically) becoming increasingly ethnocentric, showing a far greater interest in *managing* the rest of the world and the nation's position and immediate economic interests within it than in promoting concepts around our shared humanity. (As Connell et al. [1982: 208] observe: 'Education has fundamental *connections* to the idea of human emancipation, *though it is constantly in danger of being captured for other interests*'! emphasis added.)

These research findings – along with Rischard's political analysis of the situation – to a considerable extent mirror those of other researchers in the field, indicating a long-term difficulty in promoting the internationalising of curricula that appears particularly resistant to change: one in which globalisation is first and foremost responded to in terms of international *competition* rather than international collaboration and understanding. Thus, Kysilka (2011b: 285), writing in response to an American education reform report from the 1980s *A Nation At Risk* (National Commission on Excellence in Education 1983), observes:

> This report indicated that the United States' worldwide leadership in commerce, industry, science and technology was threatened by and weakened as a result of increased world-wide competition. Students in our schools, according to the report, had lower SAT and international achievement scores than in previous years while business and the military were complaining about the poor performance of students in the work environment, thus leading to the conclusion that the "educational foundations of our society are presently being eroded by a rising tide of mediocrity that threatens our very future as a Nation and people" [NCEE: 5].
>
> (Kysilka 2011b: 285)

Towards the end of the last century, Green was to link education policy more widely to specific national economic issues, suggesting that politicians were much more convinced of the capacity for education to contribute positively to such demands than to perform 'other developmental functions such as the cultivation of social solidarity [or] democratic citizenship and national identity' (Green 1997: 30). Even where public policy rhetoric and policy do appear to encourage a more internationalised curriculum, what is actually encouraged may not *challenge* the global inequities produced and supported within current global politics so much as support them via an educational policy of promoting charitable giving, an interest in and tolerance of the 'exotic' cultural practices of global others, and a sense of personal guilt. As Hunt has recently observed of developments in global education in the UK:

> [Primary] schools tend to promote a "soft", non-threatening global learning' [emphasising] awareness of other cultures and diversity and developing learners as socially-aware, responsible global citizens [so that for most children] active engagement in global learning seems to relate to their interactions with link schools overseas, fundraising activities and making small-scale life changes.
>
> (Hunt 2012: 9–10)

Such commentaries invite more questions than, inevitably, they are able to provide answers:

1   Is there any mileage in seeking to develop national curricula that are also, in part (but in substantial part) *inter*-national?
2   What are the chances of national politicians, particularly those in wealthier nations, risking (as they might see it) the electoral and economic consequences of an immediate 'hit' in terms of national competitiveness, against the possibility of a more secure, more socially just global future?
3   To return to a possibility introduced at the beginning of this chapter: How desirable and feasible might it be for countries to sign up to some form of common core

curriculum and an agreed set of values? What might these be? How might a culture of self-interest in the wealthier parts of the globe shift to one of global cooperation, collaboration and shared interest?

4   And is it too much, in any event, to ask of formal education that it might make a major contribution toward creating the social, ethical climate within which the global cooperation mooted by Brown and Rischard might take place – and perhaps become itself less 'political', less economy-driven, and more humanitarian in nature?

Globalisation...and globalisation

There are many education theorists who clearly do believe that education has a key role to play, not just in promoting forms of internationalised curricula but of resisting what threatens to be an overdominant impact of *economic* globalisation and its values in public education (see, for example, Lauder et al. 2006; Spring 2009). Of course, in tightly state-controlled education systems this is easier said than done, requiring a rather large political move on the part of central government than is perhaps generally the case. The move toward a more global *politics*, for example, does not only involve reallocating resources toward problems identified *as* global, however 'local' their immediate effects might appear to be; it also, in the field of education, needs to ensure an increased focus on making students knowledgably aware of such issues, as well as understanding what they might do as individuals and in groups to help alleviate them – leading, perhaps, to a redefinition of what we mean by 'patriotism' and how we promote it within our schools and classrooms. After Bobbitt (1971: 122–3) we might, indeed, be led to consider the possibility of a choice between 'two kinds of patriotism': one concerned exclusively with the national interest, the other linked to 'intra-group' obligations and service that might begin 'at home' in the classroom, through the curriculum, within the nation state, but that easily lends itself to global expansion, to 'globalisation' of quite another kind than the one we associate with markets and 'big business'. As Bobbitt demands of us (ibid.: 123):

> Men take great pride in self-sacrifice, and are willing to lay down even life itself to promote the welfare of their people, so long as it is the anti-alien type of social service. Why should there not be equal willingness for self-sacrifice in the service of those same people when the service is social? And why should not the intra-group service be equally honoured?

Bruner (1996b: 83) makes a not dissimilar point, linking the notion of patriotism, though he avoids using the term, more to social justice than to the success of competition with other nations or to asserting (on the flimsiest of grounds) national superiority – arguing, in the process, for nothing less than a change of culture:

> If the broader culture took on the challenge of becoming a mutual community, perhaps our boasts about our future prowess might be accompanied by the guarantee that making the country richer by working hard in school would not just make the rich richer and the poor poorer, but would result in a new pattern of distributing the national wealth more equitably.

Given the individualistic, competitive, nation-focused curricula that continue to predominate in many (perhaps most?) nations around the world, such a development evidently requires, as Bruner goes on to suggest, something of a major change of culture – and, some might say, a change of culture that itself is global in scope rather than remaining localised within certain isolated national curricula that rarely speak to one another in any meaningful way: perhaps, as the American historian Allan Wood suggests in relation to his own country, a move beyond national declarations of 'independence' to an international 'Declaration of *Inter*-Dependence – that realigns our national and global priorities to respond to our present array of challenges' (Wood 2008: 32: original emphasis).

In the case of England, such a development seems a long way off given current central government policy on education. The UK government's most recent proposals for revisions to the school curricula for citizenship and geography in England, for example (subject areas which might be expected to take the lead in developing a global culture of the kind we are discussing), make a point of reducing almost to the point of elimination requirements for students to study global and environmental issues, rendering it far more difficult for schools to help foster the attitudes (or often, as has been suggested, to foster the *change* of attitudes) necessary for young citizens to grow up both understanding global issues and having the determination to do something positive in response to them. This current policy shift is particularly noticeable, and some might say particularly unfortunate, in that it appears to reverse previous policy, not simply to promote young students' knowledge of events in the wider global community (indeed, to help them to understand that there might be such a thing as, and that they might have membership of, a global community) but also promoting a sense of national and personal responsibility in relation *to* that community. In 2003, for example, Gough (2003: 151) was able to argue, writing of national curriculum developments in England: 'Global issues and concerns have long functioned as topics or themes in specific learning areas such as history and geography, and efforts to give more emphasis to global perspectives in school curricula are well-documented.' (Gough cites, by way of example, various curricular initiatives from the 1980s: *Living in a Global Environment* [Fien 1989]; *Educating for Global Responsibility* [Reardon 1988]; *Global Teacher, Global Learner* [Pike and Selby 1987]; *Making Global Connections* [Hicks and Steiner 1989]; and the World Wide Fund for Nature's [WWF's] Global Environmental Education Programme [Huckle 1988].)

More than ten years earlier, the UK government, too, had appeared to be very supportive of developing a more inter-national curriculum, albeit with an emphasis on 'Europeanization'. Following the passing of an ECC resolution in 1988 to include a 'European dimension' in national education programmes, for example (Resolution 88/C177/02), the UK Department of Education and Science had published its own statement *The European Dimension in Education* (DES 1991), supportively quoting in a subsequent publication (DES 1992) another resolution, instructing that education should: 'help make the younger generation conscious of their common European identity without losing sight of their global responsibilities or their national, regional and local roots.' (Resolution 1 of the 17th Session of the Standing Conference of European Ministers of Education, October 1991: 'The European Dimension of Education: teaching and curriculum content' quoted in DES 1992: 2.) Even as recently as 2005, the UK Department for Education and Skills (DfES) was exhibiting arguably its most radical commitment to internationalising the school curriculum, advising teachers in its guidance on *Developing the global dimension in the school curriculum*:

> Education plays a vital role in helping children and young people recognise their contribution and responsibilities as citizens of this global community and equipping them with the skills to make informed decisions and take responsible actions. Including the global dimension in teaching means that links can be made between local and global issues. It also means that young people are given opportunities to: critically examine their own values and attitudes; appreciate the similarities between peoples everywhere, and value diversity; understand the global context of their local lives; and develop skills that will enable them to combat injustice, prejudice and discrimination. Such knowledge, skills and understanding enables young people to make informed decisions about playing an active role in the global community.
>
> (DfES 2005: 5)

It is fortunate, perhaps, that what happens in England, where this earlier commitment to cultural change regarding the internationalisation of the school curriculum appears to have foundered, is not necessarily reflected elsewhere in the world – and there is evidence in both educational theory and educational policy of many educators feeling that *attitudinal* change, linked to particular forms of 'powerful knowledge', not only can but must be achieved through *material* changes in the taught school curriculum: a taught curriculum, it should be added, that turns its back on reproducing the existing socio-economic order, in favour of encouraging the evolution of both the individual nation state and (it is hoped without the precondition of a global apocalypse!) of what one commentator ('RE', 2013) has called 'homo collaboratus'.

By way of example of the determination and strength of feeling among many educators committed to internationalising school curricula both within the context of and in a critical stance toward 'globalisation' as most broadly understood, we might briefly consider the following recent call for papers for the 33rd Annual Bergamo Conference on Curriculum Theory and Classroom Practice in the USA: a conference specifically designed for 'teachers, students, scholars, theorists, administrators and cultural workers'. The call begins with the following battle-cry:

> The present realities of global imperialism, standardization, corporate take-over, and the ever-growing, unending assaults on public education, working people, and equity are persistent. We are increasingly interconnected during this moment when the few benefit at the expense of many. A sense of interdependence and commitment to activism, occupation and advocacy are more important now than arguably ever before. Manufactured educational crises, political wrangling, and deliberate efforts to end social support services designed to serve the most vulnerable are destroying civil liberties, freedom, and participatory action in the United States and around the world.
>
> (2012 Call for Papers: 33rd Annual Bergamo Conference on Curriculum Theory and Classroom Practice: 'Crisis, Compassion, and Curriculum of Global Imagination: Toward Inter/Trans/National Activism, Occupation and Advocacy')

The call continues with the following questions for curriculum theory and design:

> In what ways do we enact *opposition, activism and advocacy* in Curriculum Studies? What are alternative visions for moving toward beyond current established and enduring popular imaginations limited by the constraints of past and current realities? How do we look inward and look outward to enact a curriculum of global imagination that transforms the nature of relational dynamics into the direction of embracing international connectedness and relationships within, between, and among the local, the national, and the global?
>
> (ibid.)

The revolutionary tone struck by the Bergamo call – which focuses less on the specific economic and environmental issues identified by Brown and Rischard (see the discussion in Chapter 6 above) and more on a political project aimed at promoting social justice via organised international collaboration and militancy – is mirrored elsewhere in much of the literature on international curricula, which positions such curricula within social/improvement agendas rather than within economic/reproductive ones – that is to say, agendas concentrating on the project of helping to bring about a more equitable global society rather than simply preparing its young people to operate effectively and competitively *within* such an environment. Bates, for example, argues:

> Globalization then, amorphous concept that it is, is the context for our conception of curriculum. But that is not to say that the curriculum can be derived directly from the character of globalization as it is currently presented to us. There is a strong political tendency to see globalization as a solely economic process – one driven by the logic of markets. Indeed, under such a conception many argue that the purpose of the curriculum is the enhancement of the capacity for successful national and individual competition in a ruthlessly competitive international market. The survival of individuals and societies, we are told, depends upon it.
>
> (Bates 2005: 102)

For Bates, the global education project is an unambiguously political one, underscored by a 'need to rescue society from the ravages of global markets through education' (ibid.: 95), rather than to assist in the perpetuation of such ravages, i.e. an education characterised by criticality rather than by familiarity. (See also Michael Ruskin's suggestion in *The Guardian*, Wed. 29 October 2008, that: 'A more radical programme could now be gathered together as globalisation's other imperative, as the construction of the new global democratic institutions and actions which are needed if the destructiveness of markets is to be contained and their potential for good realised.') This is clearly an ambitious project, which might involve a public education that could only be achieved – to refer back to issues raised in previous chapters – by revisiting what 'counts as knowledge', in order to include, for example, what Foucault has called 'subjugated knowledge': knowledge about how, for instance, social injustices came – and come – about, or how to 'de-naturalise' such phenomena as national and global poverty so that they are understood as socially constructed and 'permitted' (and therefore rectifiable through human action), rather than as simply unfortunate facts of life.

It's true that not all commentators adopt quite such a revolutionary tone as Bates or as the Bergamo Conference call; however, there is a growing argument (an agreement, perhaps) that global education needs to dissociate itself from a straightforward identification with globalisation as understood and practised in economic, market terms, and that, at its heart, there should be what is elsewhere referred to as critical education (see again DfES 2005: 5, above). This might begin by drawing a distinction between what we are invited to regard as the acceptable and unacceptable faces of globalisation. As Ikeda puts it:

> The great wave of globalization sweeping contemporary society, in areas such as information and communications, science and technology, and the market economy, is a contrast of light and dark. The positive potentials are democratization and the spread of awareness of human rights; the negative aspects are war and conflict, rising economic disparities, the obliteration of distinctive cultures, and the destruction of the global ecology.
>
> (Ikeda 2005: ix)

In relation to education specifically, Ikeda continues: 'Education, *in the genuine sense of the word*, holds the key to resolving these problems' (emphasis added, ibid.) – while, in not dissimilar vein, Nussbaum links the addressing of global issues with the promotion of *democracy and critical thinking* in formal curricula, suggesting that:

> cultivated capacities for critical thinking and reflection are crucial in keeping democracies alive and wide awake. The ability to think well about a wide range of cultures, groups, and nations in the context of the global economy and of the history of many national and group interactions is crucial in order to deal responsibly with the problems we currently face as members of an interdependent world.
>
> (Nussbaum 2010: 18)

Nussbaum's call for 'critical education' as a prerequisite for and key characteristic of global education echoes Ikeda's emphasis on an education that is 'genuine'. A 'genuine' education thus understood is a fundamentally political project that also renders students political: that encourages students not necessarily to be 'party political' but to be interested in and to have the capacity to engage with local, national and international issues; to be true democrats in the sense of wanting to be actively involved in democratic processes; and to develop as citizens who understand how the world works, rather than simply being inducted into a national culture or becoming literate and numerate or existing as the collective repository of (often rarely referenced) facts. To quote Ahmad (2010: 107) again (in a language that will be very challenging to many of the architects of national curricula), politicians, teachers and students en bloc will need, in this approach, to forge far stronger links between what is learned and discussed in school and what takes place in the wider world: 'To embrace the shift towards a more integrated globalised world in a progressive fashion, a new generation of global citizens is needed, who will act with, and seek to change society through, a sense of global moral responsibility.'

Internationalising curricula and 'global' curricula: From theory toward practice

As many readers will know, there are already in existence some educational programmes (often described as 'transnational') that are common to and impact on school curricula across a range of countries. Sadly (for those of us committed to the ongoing development of high-quality, freely available *state* education), such programmes tend to flourish outside the domain of mainstream educational provision (in independent international schools, for example), where, additionally, they are often focused on thinking and learning skills themselves rather than on the social and political uses to which such skills might be put. Two relatively well-known examples of this are the Future Problem Solving Programme International (FPSPI) and the International Baccalaureate, whose 'internationalism' lies essentially in the fact that they are followed by and common to students and schools in a variety of nations, rather than having a specifically 'global' or 'international' emphasis in terms of values or knowledge. Where globalism or internationalism does appear in *national* curricula, it typically does so as an unexamined (and consequently perceived as 'low status') element or topic or strand, and though there may be some commonalities across nations as to what to include in such elements ('sustainability' is a particularly popular item for inclusion), such commonalities tend to be fortuitous rather than planned.

Noddings points out that in relation to the possibility of promoting global *citizenship* within existing education systems (that is, forms of citizenship which do not just have a 'global dimension' but in which the citizen identifies with, and assumes some responsibility for, the world and its peoples as a whole), the same sort of difficulty identified by Brown and Rischard in the wider political world replicates itself in education policy and practice. This raises a number of very difficult questions once we move beyond initial attempts (if we even progress this far) to agree 'trans-nationally' on a core body of useful knowledge and/or key skills:

> There is no global government to which we as individuals owe allegiance, and there are no international laws that bind us unless our national government accepts them. [...] We must ask whether global citizenship...is compatible with national citizenship. Should we put the concerns of globe or nation first, or is this a bad question? Should our choice depend on the particular concern under consideration? Is there an inherent conflict between patriotism and global citizenship? [And with a nod, perhaps, to Bobbitt:] Can patriotism be redefined in a way that removes the conflict?
>
> (Noddings 2005: 2, 4)

The key to answering this last question for Noddings would seem to lie in the implication in Ikeda's and Nussbaum's analyses, that:

- what is good for the globe is – sooner or later – good for the nation (see also Ahmad, op.cit.);
- there is (or could be) a humanitarian imperative that overrides national economic concerns;
- and there need be no conflict between patriotism and internationalism: i.e. curricula can be simultaneously national and international – not necessarily dependent on

there being some kind of joined-up thinking across nations, but more likely to be effective if there is.

As with Bobbitt, patriotism in this understanding might be defined in terms of a love of and pride in one's country, co-existent with a love of and pride in humanity, that does not exclude *criticisms* of one's own nation's institutions, customs and practices and that takes an interest in learning *from* the institutions, customs and practices of other nations – rather, that is, than seeking to impose its own ways of doing things on others or to believe, and to encourage its own citizens to believe, that *its* ways are the only right ways. (This latter approach is what I have previously called national*ism*, which I am defining as somewhat different from patriotism. It is the kind of nationalism often inscribed within neo-conservatism, as discussed in Chapter 2.)

Bates (2005) identifies similar problems for those who would promote some form of – or elements of – a shared global school curriculum, echoing Noddings in pointing out that '[t]he broader framework of international law, economic policy, health and the redress of poverty is beyond our capacities as educators' – albeit adding: 'though we might well have something to say about what is required' (Bates 2005: 104). Bates further suggests that it is not only an enduring emphasis on the interests of the nation state – promoted by its politicians and internalised by its people – that stands in the way of developing more global curricula, but also powerful, widespread neo-liberal and neo-conservative discourses that emphasise and hegemonically normalise many of the values and practices that a global curriculum would need and seek to work against. In a perceived battle against the gravitational forces of both neo-liberalism and neo-conservatism, Bates thus identifies not just uncontrolled market forces as a threat to social and educational globalisation but all those who would 'enclose us in the unchanging traditions of particular communities, be they religious, ethnic, geographic or whatever else' (ibid.: 106).

The way Bates puts the argument to us as educators is perhaps even more challenging than that in Noddings' approach, in that it recognises that, as potential *global educators*, we might not simply need to challenge the curriculum itself; we might also, partly as a prerequisite, need to challenge our own educational identities (never an easy project!) – engaging in a difficult but necessary 'break with our past'. While my own experience suggests that the kind of globalised curriculum envisioned by Bates, Noddings and others would be very warmly welcomed by large numbers of teachers (more so, one suspects, than by students or their parents), there is, nevertheless, likely to be a considerable pedagogic difficulty for many practitioners, not least in encouraging changes in student behaviour from that traditionally promoted within school curricula, promoting a critical literacy that might turn itself against some traditional aspects of school life, and in the rejection of clear-cut answers that such a curriculum might demand:

> If the condition of our times is a form of globalization based upon the untrammelled operations of markets with the consequent de-socialization of production and the relations of production, and the attendant breakdown of personality, what could our response be? It is not difficult to see that as educators with a traditional responsibility for socialization and the development of personal identity, these changed conditions undermine the very foundations of our profession. How can we respond?
>
> (Bates 2005: 103)

How – to reference a central theme for curriculum theory, policy and practice – do we square a circle that seeks to combine 'socialisation *into* society' with a reasoned critique *of* society? How do we combine or balance 'reproduction' with '[r]evolution'?

Despite their articulations of some of the difficulties confronting a global education project – whether this be the internationalising of individual national curricula or efforts to seek common, globally-responsive elements across national curricula – neither Noddings nor Bates is deterred from making suggestions as to where such a project might take us, or what, in its broadest terms, a more global or internationalised curriculum might look like and what role educators in schools and classrooms might have in moving it forward. Noddings thus calls for curricula constructed around 'economic and social justice', 'protecting the earth', 'social and cultural diversity' and 'educating for peace' (2005: 5ff), while elsewhere Thornton cites 'peacekeeping, economics, and the environment…as particularly important topics for internationalism' (2005: 81). Conscious of what teachers, schools and academics can and cannot achieve, Bates (2005: 104) answers his own tricky question (ibid.) as follows:

> Our territory [that of public educators] is the territory of socialization, culture and identity and it is on this terrain that we might seek to construct a global curriculum. This is a challenging agenda, for we have not yet succeeded in constructing national curricula that redress problems of exclusion, hierarchy and misrepresentation. However, the pursuit of a global curriculum might well offer us some insights into better strategies at a national level.

In a suggestion of the parameters within which we might work as educators committed to some form of educational globalisation, Bates goes on to propose the following 'twin foundations of our global curriculum':

> Firstly, the foundation of intercultural communication and understanding upon which, in the recognition of the Other, we can form a democratic social structure that celebrates human rather than market values. Secondly, the building of… capabilities that [can serve as] as a foundation for participating in social development in ways that enhance individual freedom to live a valued way of life.
>
> (ibid.: 106)

The first of these foundations or 'principles' leads Bates to suggest that 'our global curriculum must be based around [an] *understanding* [of] rather than simply…a description of the Other: of other cultures and their ways of life, values, artefacts and histories' (emphasis added, ibid.) – a move which effectively seeks to replace incipient, often unrecognised xenophobia with a genuine recognition of ourselves 'in the Other' (for example, understanding that people in other parts of the world may live very different lifestyles from our own but are, nevertheless, fundamentally no different as human beings) and, relatedly, understandings of how economic and social inequities are *produced* and how those of us in economically and socially advantaged positions are implicit in their production.[1] Without creating what might be called a 'curriculum of guilt', or forgetting that education should also be a celebration of each person's uniqueness and of the world's and the universe's richness, such a curriculum might take 'real and observable inequalities as its starting point, and [make] an active attempt to compensate for them' (Touraine

2000: 270). It might also, therefore, mean that 'those of us living in privileged societies take some responsibility for the educational disadvantage of those living in third world conditions. What is it that *we* could contribute to *their* learning?' (emphasis added, Bates 2005: 106–7).

If the first of Bates' principles concerns itself fundamentally with a different kind of *knowledge*, the second is more concerned with the development of 'capabilities' that are fundamental 'not only to economic development, but to the development of freedom itself', and to a new kind of wised-up, inclusive, resilient and critical citizenry. These 'capabilities' refer to:

> the economic, political, social, transparency and security capabilities that constitute both institutional structures and personal agency. So our curriculum must be concerned with both the social and the personal: indeed the purpose of our global curriculum is precisely to reassert the place of the personal and social and their integration in the face of the disintegrating function of untrammelled market forces.
> (ibid.: 107)

It has to be said that while curriculum theorists such as Bates and Noddings have developed the argument for globalising or internationalising school curricula at some length, policymakers and politicians, for all their rhetorical approval, have been slower to support the incorporation of some of these perspectives into curriculum content and design (to reprise an earlier observation, slower and more resistant in some countries than in others), both by actively excluding them from the mandated curriculum, and by reducing the amount of room and time available to develop such perspectives once the mandated curriculum has been implemented.

Some policy initiatives

I will end this chapter with a brief look at the ways in which some texts in the 'official recontextualising field' of public policy (as opposed to the 'pedagogic recontextualising field' of educational theory and pedagogic practice) regard the importance and possible nature of globalising or internationalising school curricula, followed by a brief counter-argument to developing global or internationalised education.[2]

After what I have already said about the situation in England, it seems most appropriate to start with policy initiatives there, in a return to the DfES document of 2005 *Developing the Global Dimension in the School Curriculum* – noting, in passing, (a) its reference to a 'dimension' rather than to a more 'root and branch' overhaul, (b) the already-mentioned fact that more recently, the current UK Secretary of State for Education appears to have indicated a desire for a reduction in the global elements of key subject areas such as geography and citizenship education.

This particular document (the residue, perhaps, of a briefly more enlightened period of UK education policy reform), which was intended for 'headteachers, senior managers, governors, local education authorities, teachers and early years practitioners' (and afforded the status 'recommended'), advises:

> Global issues are part of children and young people's lives in ways unfamiliar to previous generations. Television, the internet, international sport and increased

opportunities for travel all bring the wider world into everyone's daily life. UK society today is enhanced by peoples, cultures, languages, religions, art, technologies, music and literature originating in many different parts of the world. This provides a tremendous range of opportunities to broaden children and young people's experience and knowledge. However, although economic advances have meant huge improvements that have changed the lives of millions of people, one in five of the world's population still live in extreme poverty. They lack access to basic healthcare, education and clean water, with little opportunity to improve their condition. Global poverty impacts negatively on us all.

(DfES 2005: 5)

This document clearly highlights most of the key aspects of 'global education' (that is, to return to an earlier definition of these terms, an internationalised curriculum that gives a considerably enhanced presence to issues of global rather than merely national or local significance) found in the more strictly academic and theoretical literature, drawing our attention to:

- environmental damage
- inequality
- social justice
- mutual interdependence

and promoting:

- informed decisions
- making links between local and global issues
- developing a critique of one's own values and attitudes and a pluralistic orientation to the values of others
- taking an active part as global citizens.

From such a broad base, the document identifies eight 'key concepts' to be addressed across the curriculum:

- global citizenship
- conflict resolution
- diversity
- human rights
- interdependence
- social justice
- sustainable development
- values and perceptions.

(ibid.: 8–9)

These sentiments expressed in the UK documentation reflect others to be found in a range of national curricula around the globe, also finding support in the education policy recommendations of the United Nations. From Australia (Commonwealth of Australia

2012), for example, comes a set of 'global perspectives' in education that bears a marked similarity to those listed in the DfES documentation, that is to say:

- **Interdependence and globalisation** – an understanding of the complex social, economic and political links between people and the impact that changes have on each other
- **Identity and cultural diversity** – an understanding of self and one's own culture, and being open to the culture of others
- **Social justice and human rights** – an understanding of the impact of inequality and discrimination, the importance of standing up for our own rights and our responsibility to respect the rights of others
- **Peace building and conflict resolution** – an understanding of the importance of building and maintaining positive and trusting relationships, and ways conflict can be prevented or peacefully resolved
- **Sustainable futures** – an understanding of the ways in which we can meet our current needs without diminishing the quality of the environment or reducing the capacity of future generations to meet their own needs.

(Commonwealth of Australia 2012)

The Australian documentation continues with the following advice for curriculum content.

A global perspective offers students and teachers:

- an approach which takes into account the whole of human society and the environments in which people live;
- an emphasis on the future, the dynamic nature of human society, and each person's capacity to choose and shape preferred futures;
- an opportunity to explore important themes such as change, interdependence, identity and diversity, rights and responsibilities, peace building, poverty and wealth, sustainability and global justice;
- a focus on cooperative learning and action, and shared responsibility;
- an emphasis on critical thinking and communication.

(www.globaleducation.edu.au/global-education/what-is-global-ed.html)

Elsewhere, the United Nations, as part of a 'global education' project of its own that has a somewhat different emphasis ('global education' centrally construed, here, in *entitlement* terms, as every child in the globe's right to an education), argues in its *Global Education First Initiative* ('Priority #3 Foster Global Citizenship'):

The world faces global challenges, which require global solutions. These interconnected global challenges call for far-reaching changes in how we think and act for the dignity of fellow human beings. *It is not enough for education to produce individuals who can read, write and count. Education must be transformative and bring shared values to life. It must cultivate an active care for the world and for those with whom we share it.* Education must also be relevant in answering the big questions of the day. Technological solutions, political regulation or financial instruments alone cannot achieve sustainable development. It requires transforming the way people think and act. Education must fully assume its central role in helping people to forge more just, peaceful, tolerant and inclusive societies. *It must give people the understanding, skills and values they need to cooperate in resolving the interconnected challenges of the 21st century.*

(emphasis added, www.globaleducationfirst.org/220.htm)

Importantly, the UN documentation is quick to recognise the difficulties in implementing such an initiative, and the likely resistances to it: resistances which come both from the wider socio-economic system itself, dominated, as has already been suggested, by an alliance of neo-liberal and (neo-)conservative thinking and ideology, by the anxieties of parents bringing children up in that neo-liberal/(neo-)conservative world, by the power of educational tradition itself, and by a related reluctance to re-allocate national educational resources. In its own list of barriers and threats to the development of more global or internationalised school curricula, the UN's programme (ibid.) cites:

- legacy of the current education system
- outmoded curricula and learning materials
- lack of teacher capacity
- inadequate focus on values
- lack of leadership on global citizenship.

The development of one of these threats and obstacles – 'Legacy of the current education system' – which has particular relevance to many of the broader curriculum issues discussed in *Understanding the School Curriculum* (not least those related to ICT in the previous chapter) and might be of particular interest to any Ministers or Secretaries of State for Education who happen (unlikely though this is) to be reading it, continues as follows:

> Schools have traditionally prepared people to pass exams, proceed to the next level and graduate into the workplace. We now face the much greater challenge of raising global citizens. Promoting respect and responsibility across cultures, countries and regions has not been at the centre of education. Global citizenship is just taking root, and changing traditional ways of doing things always brings about resistance. This entails changing the way education is organized – making content more relevant to contemporary life and global challenges, introducing innovative and participatory teaching and learning styles. *We must rethink the purpose of education and prepare students for life, not exams alone.*

(emphasis added, ibid.)

'Against globalising the curriculum'

I am very aware that, particularly in such a brief overview as this, it is all too easy to oversimplify issues – especially when, as here, issues concerning globalised or internationalised curricula can only be referenced alongside several other competing curriculum issues. Indeed, all that can be attempted here is an introduction to what I have understood as some key ideas.

Readers interested in learning more could do a lot worse than trawl the excellent International *Journal of Development Education and Global Learning* (JDEGL), or to read the regular reports produced by the Institute of Education University of London (UK)'s *Development Education Research Centre* (DERC). Some important features to emerge from such publications are that:

- There is 'considerable variation' in the ways in which the term 'global dimension' is perceived and articulated in schools (Bourn and Hunt 2011: 5).
- Often (Miller et al. 2012; see also Smith 2004), 'development education' is funded by NGOs, with a particular bias and within a particular discourse. (To return to an earlier discussion, such education may be prompted by economic, neo-liberal concerns rather than by more humanitarian, altruistic, social liberal ones – with clear implications for curriculum content and for the parameters within which global education is constructed and confined.)
- Much work in schools focuses on/limits itself to counteracting stereotyping (e.g. of Africa and its peoples) and promoting diversity and awareness of other cultures (e.g. Hunt 2012: 9).

The debates and findings reported in JDEGL and by DERC return us to a number of important questions and areas of contention concerning globalised/internationalised curricula: for example, How 'political' is/should it be? Can it indeed avoid being political? What are the implications if such sub-categories as development education are embedded within dominant discourses and ideologies of neo-liberal capitalism?

If much of the writing and research about global or international curricula highlights the difficulties involved in identifying and implementing it, there is another, relatively small yet still important body of opinion that questions whether school curricula should be 'globalised' or 'internationalised' at all – either in relation to global economic challenges or in relation to a humanitarian or moral imperative.[3]

One of the most cogent and sustained critiques of both the economic and the values-led approaches to (and rationales for) global education is provided by Alex Standish in his 2012 book *The False Promise of Global Learning: Why Education Needs Boundaries*. Taking us back to issues around knowledge discussed in Chapter 4, including issues concerning 'useful' and 'powerful' knowledge and the importance of its equitable availability, Standish argues that developments such as global education or global learning undermine the *knowledge content* of school curricula embedded within the traditional subject disciplines, which themselves serve to empower students as autonomous citizens and provide an important barrier to the infiltration of economic-global (and, Standish would add, values-global) elements that focus on the particular 'skills' and 'flexibility' required of post-Fordist capitalism. Within 'global education' (thus conceived) potentially empowering 'knowledge' gets confused with and effectively replaced by functional, non-empowering 'information', and the 'true purpose' of globalised or internationalised curricula (according to this understanding, to promote a compliant, neo-liberal citizenry) hides itself behind a critical, inclusive-sounding, evolutionary policy rhetoric. Aligning himself very clearly with educators who favour a knowledge-based approach to curriculum development and design, Standish's particular approach within this broad area of criticism accuses some educators interested in promoting global education as having 'an obsession with novelty' (2012, Foreword), and opposes such an obsession with the enduring usefulness of – but 'declining faith' in – 'academic knowledge' (2012: 4).

Standish's concerns (and those of others similarly minded) are understandable and worthy of attention. However, for those of us suspicious of curricula dominated by subject disciplines and subject knowledge, his alternative is hard to swallow for it is as if the choice we are being offered is between two equally unpalatable possibilities: a curriculum dominated by the instrumental logic of neo-liberalism, or a curriculum dominated by the foundationalism of conservatism. This leads me to suggest that there might be a fundamental difficulty with this particular argument against curriculum globalisation or internationalisation: not that globalising or internationalising the curriculum is not potentially dangerous or that it might be – perhaps in some cases already has – been hijacked or colonised by instrumental economic discourses rather than embedding itself within more strictly humanitarian, social liberal ones, but that, as argued in Chapter 3, we need to be wary about how we go about identifying curricular knowledge, how we understand the purposes and the interests that such knowledge serves or might serve in the future (might these not be 'neo-liberal purposes and interests'?), and what we believe, in any event, empirical knowledge alone (i.e. without the teaching of the practical knowledge to put it into practice) can achieve.

The knowledge that finds its way into any curriculum is, I have argued, essentially a matter of choice (even within Standish's own discipline of Geography, which finds its very existence as a separate discipline under threat in some national curricula) and consequently we need to be very careful and thoughtful about the extent to which we 'trust' such choices. It is also questionable whether knowledge alone – not just without the knowledge of how to use knowledge, but also without the critical acumen to question knowledge choices themselves – can really bring about or is essential to the formation of 'autonomous subjects' as Standish claims. A concern here is that arguments within the academic and teaching communities regarding the rightness or wrongness of internationalising school curricula can all too easily become a diversionary red herring: that the real battle, as has been suggested elsewhere in this book, may be between a curriculum that affirms and *reproduces* and a curriculum that *challenges*. A curriculum that challenges does not dispense with or underplay the importance of knowledge, but rather expands our definition of knowledge and of what might be included within it. For example, in addition to essentially empirical knowledge – much of whose 'empiricism' may, in any event, be of a somewhat dubious nature – it includes knowledge *about* (for example, about how social inequalities are produced). This is a political approach to education and knowledge, certainly, but no more so than in a curriculum which seeks to conceal such 'other knowledge', often through an over-emphasis on the acquisition and regurgitation of 'facts' or on the development of workplace related 'skills' and 'attitudes'. The curriculum that challenges, furthermore, does not confine itself to challenging existing orthodoxies related to the relative value of different knowledges; it also challenges orthodoxies concerning the hierarchisation of cultures, and orthodoxies concerning ways of understanding *ourselves* (individually and collectively) as learners and as human beings – and of the nature and purposes of the education we are (or might wish we were) experiencing. For all the scepticism about it, it seems to me that, as long as our imperative is more humanitarian than functional, globalising or internationalising curricula has the capacity to contribute very considerably to such an education.

Notes

1   Bates' argument resonates with McNiff's accounts of 'cosmopolitanism' and 'localism' (McNiff 2013; Inglis 2008). Cosmopolitans 'develop outgoing perspectives in relationships with others, usually through engaging with other people's cultures and forms of thinking, while locals are those who maintain a stay-at-home mentality, more comfortable in their own cultures and systems' (McNiff 2013: 502, summarising Hannerz 1990). Elsewhere, Hannerz (1990: 239) defines cosmopolitanism as 'a stance towards diversity itself, towards a co-existence of cultures in the individual experience'. The 'cosmopolitan mindset' (McNiff: ibid.) 'involves not simply learning to get on with the locals at a surface level (observing national days, particular forms of greeting and eating together)…but actually committing to a deep level of respect for the traditions and values of others and internalising the insights'.

2   Readers interested in looking at how a more 'internationalised' curriculum might be put into practice within the context of an alternative approach to curriculum design that starts with 'big questions' and impels the more traditional curriculum to adapt to rather than simply to accommodate *them* are recommended to consider the International Middle Years Curriculum (IMYC) for 11–14 year-olds, produced by the organisation Fieldwork Education and currently used by a number of private international schools. The IMYC begins not by asking each subject discipline to identify its own priorities and curriculum content, but adopts a cross-curricular approach constructed around what it calls 'big questions', 'big ideas' and 'guiding principles', constructing curriculum 'delivery' around 30 pre-specified cross-curricular 'units' (e.g. 'adaptability', 'balance', 'celebration', 'collaboration', 'consequences', 'creativity', 'discovery', 'resolution', 'risk', 'structures'). Undertaken in sequence, with specific, widely circulated suggestions as to how each unit might be approached within different subject areas, two additional elements – 'international mindedness' and 'dispositions' – run across each and every unit specification. Thus, in the cross-curricular unit called 'Challenge', students are required to 'look at how people around the world have overcome different kinds of challenges and how this improved and increased the opportunities in their lives and communities' – while in the same unit, under 'dispositions' (to hark back to issues discussed in the previous chapter), students are required to learn 'how to better cope with challenges and problems they have in their own lives, and better understand why overcoming challenges creates more opportunities for them'.

3   A not uncommon rationale (among others) for globalising or internationalising the school curriculum in so-called developed countries relates to a perceived need to educate young people about global problems such as poverty, hunger and sectarianism in order that they might better understand their nature and causes at the same time as developing an intolerance toward them and seeking in the future to be involved in action to tackle them.

Chapter 7

Curriculum decision-making

In a rapidly changing society, there is a need for an institution of some kind to be responsible for keeping the curriculum up to date. But such an institution will also need to develop principles and procedures for analyzing social developments and making careful judgments about necessary changes. [...] Both culture and curriculum should be concerned with "what might be" as well as "what is".

(Lawton 1996: 24–5)

Education, being a deliberate, purposeful activity directed to the development of individuals, necessarily involves considerations of value. Where are these values to be found? What is to be their content? How are they to be justified? They can be, and often are, values that reflect the interests of a minority group in society. They may be religious, political or utilitarian in character. They are always open to debate and detailed criticism, and are always in need of particular justification.

(Hirst 1998: 249)

Does it matter? Curriculum as self-justifying

A recurring theme in previous chapters concerned the questions 'Where does the curriculum "come from"? Who makes the important decisions about what should be in it? How should it be organised? And what should its relationship be to assessment and pedagogy?' These are important questions. As the Australian academic Malcolm Skilbeck observes:

Statements of educational aims are usually very general. Behind them are assumptions and values, perhaps principles of procedure and criteria which are largely unexamined, as part of the shared way of life of a society, or they may represent the interests and viewpoints of powerful minorities who command office or influence action without themselves being representative of society as a whole.

(Skilbeck 1984: 147)

Skilbeck's concern over who decides what a curriculum should include and look like, on what levels of understanding such decisions can be taken, and on what (other than self-appointed) authority curriculum policymakers act, leads him to question whether curriculum matters should (continue to) be left in the hands of the 'Establishment' – particularly in the 'rapidly changing world' whose existence, elsewhere in policy statements, that same Establishment appears to recognise the need to respond to – or whether it is time to empower other voices. Skilbeck (ibid.) continues:

> Is too much emphasis given to traditionalist views, held by government, officials and advisers, about what it is good for the nation to learn, know, and be able to do? Is it clear that the core curriculum will enable all individuals, as they grow and develop, to gain the knowledge, skills, values and freedom of mind to make wise choices on their own? How appropriate is the core to an open, democratic, multicultural, pluralist society?

(I imagine there is no need to spell out Skilbeck's implied answer.)

Naturally, the extent to which we regard these as important questions may depend on our view of knowledge, on whether or not we believe that any one individual or group of individuals can be entrusted with making appropriate nationally-applicable selections from that knowledge, and on whether we accept that, to a degree, all such decisions will be subjective – thereby, perhaps, focusing our attention on *which* subjectivity (or subjectivities) we most wish to give our trust and support.

Some curriculum theorists, for instance, Bobbitt (op.cit.), have suggested that curriculum inclusions are at least capable of being generally *self*-justifying, i.e. that there is some knowledge and there are some skills whose claim to curriculum importance is intrinsic and irrefutable, and which simply, therefore, demand some sort of forensic identification. The so-called 'scientific' method of carrying out this identification rather reduces the importance of the 'Who Decides?' question, since it is based on a belief that dispassionate, non-ideologically driven, evidence-based decisions can be made about what should and should not be included in the curriculum, and that as long as an equally dispassionate, non-ideologically driven, evidence-basing selection committee is entrusted with the task of identification, all will be well. Shedding any preconceptions it might have, such a committee (Bobbitt did not actually specify 'a committee', or make any definitive suggestions regarding who might be charged with this responsibility or how they might shed any potentially corruptive ideological or philosophical predispositions) would determine by 'analytic survey…the total range of human abilities, habits, systems of knowledge, etc., that one should possess' (Bobbitt 1971: 43). (An ambitious undertaking, we might argue, even without the 'et cetera'!)

This argument for an 'objective', ideology-free curriculum grounded in perceived 'needs' rather than guided by political intent is somewhat problematic. Despite his calls for curriculum change, for instance, there is something very reproductive about Bobbitt's approach, which is troubling for those of us who might wish for a more [r]evolutionary curriculum: that is to say, in Bobbitt's approach the job for curriculum is first to discover what the 'needs' of society – and therefore the needs of individuals within society – are, then to itemise these as accurately and comprehensively as possible, then to design or revise the curriculum as appropriate. Needs are thus seen as existing *in themselves* ('reified') rather than being constructed by those 'identifying' them, and curriculum itself is seen as *responding to* social conditions rather than encouraging and enabling students to wish or to seek to change them. There appears, too, to be a hidden hierarchical assumption in Bobbitt's proposition, that those whose 'needs' are to be met do not need to be consulted regarding such needs – presumably because they cannot be trusted to be impartial about the matter – whereas the constituency charged with the task of identifying them can.

Finally, there is the danger in such an approach of what we might call the 'imposter scientist': that is to say, the ideologically driven curriculum 'expert' who takes advantage of the intrinsically important, 'scientifically identifiable' construction of curriculum content, *posing* as the neutral, objective, ideology-free identifier capable of carrying out the necessary identifications while in reality imposing his or her own cultural and political preferences. (An oppositional view is articulated by Paolo Freire, in his assertion: 'Attempting to liberate the oppressed without their reflective participation in the act of liberation is to treat them as objects which must be saved from a burning building… Political action on the side of the oppressed must be pedagogical action in the authentic sense of the word, and, therefore, action with the oppressed' [Freire 1996: 47, 48]).

Many curriculum commentators have been less convinced than Bobbitt of the possibility of constructing 'objective', ideology-free curricula. As Young (1998: 1) puts it: 'The assertion by sociologists that all knowledge is socially produced for particular purposes in particular contexts is now relatively uncontentious'. Young does not dismiss the possibility of identifying 'important knowledge' for curriculum, so much as question the selection processes themselves, observing that 'whereas the curriculum is always partly designed to enable students to acquire concepts and forms of understanding and learn how to apply them in different contexts, it is also always organized to preserve vested interests and maintain the status quo' (Young 1998: 5; see also Riley 2011: xi). Young's rejection of any current claims to impartiality in this context extends to suggesting the need to question the apparent naturalness of how curricula are traditionally *structured*: for example, 'whether a particular form of curriculum organization, such as that based on school subjects, provides reliable frameworks for young people to make sense of the world they face, or the extent to which it is primarily a leftover of past traditions which have come to be seen as the only way to organize knowledge' (Young: ibid.).

While Young implies a difference between genuine objectivity and faux objectivity (i.e., to return to the 'imposter scientist', subjectivity self-presenting as objectivity) in making curriculum selections, we might additionally question whether curriculum content can *ever* be 'objective' and ideology-free, and whether, indeed, objectivity itself is a misleading concept adopted by politicians for rhetorical purposes. In the end, if we are not to take the 'objective', 'scientific' approach to curriculum selection seriously, a decision still has to be made between either regarding certain knowledge as having an intrinsic value that merits its inclusion for some or for all students, *or* understanding the importance attached to certain knowledge as essentially *invested* or *attributed* for ends which may or may not be related to inclusion and equity. This, I think, is rather different from, though clearly related to, questions around the potential usefulness and empowering attributes of particular knowledge discussed in Chapter 4. The reality, of course, is that in practice decisions *are* made about curriculum content, that they are made by specific groups of people on behalf of and for the alleged benefit of other groups of people, and that in understanding school curricula we need to give close and careful consideration as to:

- who does – and perhaps who *should* or who *might* – make such decisions;
- who, if the decisions are indeed self-justifying and scientifically achievable, should be considered sufficiently impartial to be entrusted with the task of making them;
- and on what *bases* curriculum decisions are (or we might wish to be) made.

Having expressed (I hope) my own scepticism concerning the scientific method, it is to this 'Who Decides?' question that I will now return.

'Centred' and 'decentred' possibilities

Next to the right to life itself, the most fundamental of all human rights is the right to control our own minds and thoughts. This means, the right to decide for ourselves how we will explore the world around us, think about our own and other persons' experience, and find and make the meaning of our own lives. Whoever takes that right away from us, by trying to "educate us", attacks the very centre of our being and does us a most profound and lasting injury.

(Holt 1976: 7–8)

In an interesting counterbalance to some of the standard (and for most of us, I imagine, perfectly acceptable) arguments in favour of free mass education – that it promotes equity (if not always equality), that it helps young learners make sense of the world, and that it should be perceived as a fundamental human right – Holt points to the potential that mass education has to *delimit* or *negate* a fundamental human right: not encouraging the individual's development at all, but, through its very universalising, 'entitling' tendency, constraining individuality and individual development, encouraging us all to think in much the same ways about much the same things and being tested and assessed in terms of our willingness and capacity to do so (with potentially very serious negative effects for us if we don't!). We might argue on this basis that mass education can never promote individuality in the way that we might wish it to (and in the way that some of its policy rhetoric might claim it does do), and indeed that given the need to provide a standard basic education for all it is simply impractical to do so. The question then becomes: Is individual development and self expression – to some degree – a necessary and worthwhile *cost* of the universal, national, entitlement curriculum? And if so, what sort of degree might we be talking about?

Holt's argument not only returns us to some of those questions we considered regarding the development of *national curricula*, but impels us to consider with perhaps greater urgency that other fundamental question: not just Who does decide on curriculum form and content? But also, What purposes (overt and covert, conscious and unconscious, articulated and concealed) might lie behind such decisions?

During my own time as a schoolteacher in England (that is, from the late 1960s until the late 1980s) the answer to the 'Who Decides?' question was, effectively, as follows:

- The organisation and broad content of the curriculum had been decided on by politicians many decades earlier, at the time of the introduction of universal education.
- It had subsequently and substantially been sustained in that form by tradition and custom.
- The regulation, broad development and detail of the curriculum, including some element of enforced consistency across educational providers, was undertaken essentially by a number of approved examination boards.
- Detail at the finest point (for example, what supporting textbooks to use, what particular examination syllabuses to follow, whether to teach this or that first) was left largely to the individual schools and teachers.

Over time, the working relationships between examination boards, schools and teachers in connection with this fine-tune decision-making had been through many different forms but had generally shifted, by the late 1970s and early 1980s, from one in which the examination boards had most of the say in selecting the specific curriculum elements that would be subjected to high-stakes assessment, toward one in which there was genuine dialogue between examining boards and teachers in some subject areas, not only over the content of the curriculum – which in some subject areas now allowed for considerable local variation within an agreed broad framework and set of criteria – but also in the manner in which students were assessed (see Moore 2005). This latter development, which appeared to be underscored by a trust in teachers' professionalism and sound judgement on the part of examination boards and (if to a lesser extent) central government, included a great deal more externally-moderated school-based assessment, adding significantly to a growing sense of curriculum 'ownership' on the part of teachers and (potentially) students too (Moore: ibid.).

For many of us teaching at that time, this still feels like a Golden Age of school-based curriculum development and practice in England: one which, it seemed, valued the collective expertise of external examiners and schoolteachers, and required no further modification or control on the part of central government. In the political terms used in earlier chapters, we might say it was a self-regulating system (public education had yet to be reconstituted as a quasi market), couched within a social liberal understanding and ideology of public education. State involvement in the curriculum itself was minimal, rendering its development, to use Bernstein's expression, more de-centred than it had ever appeared, with central government *policy* tending to focus its attention more on such economic matters as teachers' pay and the number of schools required to meet the demand of student numbers. Although there was no shortage of complaining voices, typically expressed through the nation's press or more directly from representatives from British business and industry, that schools and teachers were not (re)producing an appropriately knowledgeable and skilled *workforce*, central government appeared reluctant at this time to intervene in matters of curriculum, pedagogy or assessment.

Since the later 1980s, the relationship between schools and examination boards in England has shifted again – not out of any desire on the part of the boards or teachers themselves, but by virtue of the imposition of a state-centred and very prescriptive national curriculum which has effectively taken most important curriculum decision-making away from the boards and teachers, providing very detailed 'orders' concerning what should be taught and learned in every state school in the land. England now experiences a very centralised or (Bernstein 2000) 'centred' curriculum, zealously regulated via national student testing, school inspections and the publication of 'league tables' of schools' public examination results (which has had the added effect of designating and controlling pedagogy), and so explicit in the finer detail of required curriculum coverage as to leave very little room for local interpretation at all.[1]

There are many other things that might be said about this particular national curriculum in terms of its curricular emphases and its underpinning rationales, most of which cast a ghostly shadow over the debates introduced in previous chapters. The issue here, however, is a slightly different one. To return to our central question – Who Decides? – it prompts us to ask, more specifically:

- *Should* 'the State' (i.e. central government) decide?
- If so, for what reason, on what basis, and via what processes? (This includes questions concerning whether public education should, in any event, be predominantly state funded and controlled or predominantly privately funded and controlled.)
- How much, then (if anything), should be left to 'local decision-making', whether this means individual schools and teachers operating within the state sector, or individual schools and teachers working outside it?

Centralised guidance and control: The curriculum, the State and the Market

Some commentators (e.g. Skilbeck, op.cit.) have argued that *too much* involvement in curriculum content and design on the part of central or local governments can result in an overcrowded and partial curriculum that reduces opportunities for curricular pluralism, and that seriously undermines school-based curriculum development. Others, however – particularly in England, where the development of the national curriculum has proved something of an ideological and educational battleground – suggest an equal danger, that the *under*-involvement, or the wrong *kind* of involvement, on the part of central governments might critically undermine the school curriculum's defence-mechanisms against what they see as some of the less palatable values of the marketplace (see Hartley 2003; Young 2006). In other words, to return to the 'schizophrenia–paranoia' relationship introduced in Chapter 2, the curriculum supported and controlled *by* the State can serve as a buffer against or moderator of potentially unsocial, self-serving values, and protect more 'enduring' social values such as collaboration, tolerance, social justice and a respect for and love of learning itself. But it can also serve as a straitjacket constraining curriculum evolution.

One broad rationale for *increased* central government involvement in the school curriculum in the public sector of education is included within one of the central rationales for introducing *national curricula*. This concerns, essentially, the matter of curriculum entitlement, of promoting an education system that is more equitable and more inclusive – related to a suspicion that without strong central control the quality of a young person's education becomes something of a lottery, overly dependent on where they happen to live and which school they happen to go to.

Embedded within such a view (in the case of England) is a concern that what I have called a Golden Age of school-based curriculum development in the 1970s and early 1980s was not, from the student perspective, a Golden Age at all, having done nothing to regularise the curriculum experience across the nation, or to reduce perceived gulfs in quality within the teaching profession. Indeed, this period in England's educational history has often been demonised by politicians more recently, as a time in which large numbers of children were 'let down' by teachers pursuing their own ideologies rather than seeking to do what is best for their students, and during which a school- and examination-board led curriculum was not meeting the perceived needs of 'employers' (whoever they might be): consequently, that the system then in place had not been working.[2]

The very propensity that sometimes exists for the State to prioritise the perceived *economic* demands of the curriculum (and of the interests of those who most fervently pursue them) might be seen as a reason for *not* allowing the State alone to be responsible for the mandated curriculum – that indeed, and in any event, '[e]ducation is too important to be left to politicians…and those parents who believe them' (Pinar 2004: xiii).[2]

We should not be overly surprised, perhaps, by central governments' inclination to prioritise the concerns of the Economy's perceived representatives – often, those who provide them with the greatest support financially and at the ballot box. Governments, after all (see also Chapter 6), are centrally concerned with managing the national economy, and it is on their management of this, or at least the strength of the impression they can make that they are managing it effectively, that they are most likely to stand or fall. The extent to which we support or accept such prioritisation – as national citizens, as workers, as parents – depends on our particular view of what a school education should comprise and the extent to which we are prepared to compromise such views in the interests of pragmatism. We might, for example, argue that schooling should concern itself exclusively with preparing tomorrow's workforce, and that everything else can be taken care of outside of the school walls: that there is no real need for young people to be formally taught about literature, or to develop practical and appreciative skills in art or music or creative writing, or to study history or geography or any other subject which does not obviously connect on a significant scale to possible future employment. If we hold such a view, then we might well approve of a government's action in basing its curriculum policy on what it understands as the needs of the national Economy. I suspect, however, that few of us involved in education – and no one who has persisted thus far with this book – would wholeheartedly subscribe to such a view, and that we are therefore compelled to adopt a more critical stance toward the relationship – and the *possible* relationships – in curriculum policy within the economic domain between the State and the Market, asking if and how such a relationship works in the best interests of young students (or indeed of the nation as a whole) in terms of their personal, social and spiritual development.

One major criticism of the centralisation of curriculum policy to have emerged in some recent sociology and philosophy of education is that the State does not just 'listen to' alleged complaints, suggestions and demands from 'the Market' ('employers are telling us that young people are leaving formal education lacking this or that skill, knowledge or aptitude prior to entering the workforce'), but that it does so at the cost of other voices, and that in so doing it sacrifices what some educationalists see as a major reason *in favour of* a relatively high level of State control: that is to say, precisely its capacity to act in a regulatory, tempering manner in relation to what we might call 'Market values'. Such criticism calls for an education policy that ensures that vested interests and ideologies are not allowed to colonise education and thereby risk harming the interests of individual students, preferring an understanding of education as being both multi-functional and fundamentally ethical. John White, in recognising the potential importance of strong State involvement in compulsory education (albeit on the basis of full and appropriate consultation processes) argues, thus:

> government's role is not to enter into the curriculum world as just another interest-group alongside industry, universities and so on. …Its proper role is to stand aloof from interest groups as the guardian of liberal democratic values. Its job is to restrain the interest groups, to prevent their biases from warping the curriculum away from coherence and adherence to underlying values.
>
> (White 2004d: 189)

The difficulty, as some observers have pointed out, is that the State can only assume such a regulatory role as long as its own values run counter to those of other 'interest groups': that is to say, as long as it can make judgements and promote policies itself which are educational and ethical rather than simply supportive of the powerful interests of dominant groups in society. Such a position demands of central government that it puts aside concerns regarding the likelihood of its own re-election, and that it positions itself not only away from vested interests but outside of dominant discourses too: discourses which can, for example, have the effect of disguising curriculum *choice* as curriculum *inevitability*, thereby creating the illusion that the education systems and the school curricula that we already have are the 'only versions' realistically available to us. As Ruti (2009: 20–1) wisely observes, in what effectively amounts to a definition of hegemony:

> [I]t is those meanings, beliefs, and values that are most insistently and commonly utilized in a given social order that take on the status of truths; what becomes constituted as truth is never independent of power relations. Rather, those with sociosymbolic power – with *representational* power – have over the years been able to pass off *their* particular beliefs and values as universal truths. This means that to the extent that we lose track of the process by which fictions solidify into facts – that we are incapable of envisioning viable alternatives to the dominant fictions that govern our lives – we can become entangled in beliefs and values that are actually hurtful to us. (emphases added)

In England, there is a growing concern among some educational theorists – at least, among those on the political Left – that the possibility for central government to act in the way suggested by White, or to use its own 'representational power' critically to challenge the systems and beliefs which it may feel it has effectively been mandated to perpetuate and support – is becoming increasingly difficult and increasingly unlikely as the wider ideological stance of government moves ever closer to the values and practices espoused in and by the Market, both nationally and globally. As Kress (2006: 162) has argued with reference to education policy in the UK:

> [A] state which is becoming the servant of the market, and an economy based in consumption, have an entirely different relation to the "education system" than those of before. [...] In [an] environment where the market is increasingly the dominant social, cultural and economic force, a no doubt old question needs to be posed newly and urgently: What is the curriculum for, and what [in relation to currently configured academic disciplines] is *this* subject for?

Elsewhere, Coffield and Williamson (2011: 3) have described how even the *language* of public education and the language of the business world have come to be shared, further cementing a growing philosophical and ideological coming-together – not only in the eyes of politicians and policymakers themselves, but even in discussions among habitually sceptical practitioners and education theorists:

> [I]n the last 30 years the language of management and economics has virtually replaced the language of education. The process is insidious: at first hearing, such phrases as '*the bottom line*', '*the business model*' and '*more for less*' are clearly limited and

objectionable, but within a short time, so great is the power of money, that we catch ourselves using them without a qualm.

When the State fails to act in the way suggested by White (not a disinterested or 'neutral' way, since it will always be guided by certain ideologies and philosophies, but a way which does not simply represent or fall in line behind certain constituents' interests at the expense of others), the impact is plain to see – not just on the content of curriculum, but in relation to the discussions we are likely to have about curriculum and on how education is perceived, practised and understood more widely. Keck (2012), citing Besley and Peters' (2007: 133) 'neo-Foucauldian' analysis of the impact of neo-liberal politics in the wider social arena, argues that the promotion of 'autonomy' to schools in relation to such matters as managing budgets masks a project more concerned in reality with controlling and delimiting public education practice and experience through the risk of eliding autonomy and choice with responsibility, thus enabling institutions and their workers to be blamed if and when things either go wrong or are claimed (by central government) to have gone wrong. Keck argues, after Besley and Peters:

> [T]he neo-Foucauldian interpretation of the liberal project of modernity demonstrates how modern government has effectively attempted to divulge great responsibility to individuals whilst simultaneously circumscribing the accompanying power to self-determination. The truly modern subject has been invested with the responsibility to self-govern by the exercise of moral, economic, political and professional "freedom of choice", but these are only to be enjoyed within narrow parameters policed by government. It is, [Besley and Peters argue], the consummate sleight of hand of good government to divulge responsibility to the subject at the same time as circumscribing their freedom.
>
> (Keck 2012: 188, 190)

'Dynamism' versus 'repair'

It will be evident from the discussion so far that there are potential pros and cons to leaving curriculum decision-making largely in the hands of the State – and similarly, indeed, within the hands of schools and teachers. After all, as White (2004c: 21) argues, harking back to that period when, in England, schools and teachers had considerably more power and control over curriculum:

> There were practical problems about this, not least the often widely different provision between schools. But there was also a more fundamental issue. *Why* should teachers have this power? Do they have the expertise which equips them to make such decisions? [...] Where teachers *do* have an expertise is in deciding what specific aims and what pupil experiences best suit the particular children they teach in specific circumstances and at specific times. But this does not show why they should make macro-decisions – decisions about what aims to have in the first place.

White's issue of 'qualification' applies both to teachers and to politicians, though in different ways. Teachers might not be qualified to decide on the curriculum for an entire nation, for example (or even a substantial part of it), not least because, regardless of their obvious expertise, they have not been given a public mandate to do so and would not, either, necessarily feel the same need as politicians to make judgements related to the curriculum's relevance and impact nationally as opposed to locally or individually. On the other hand, it is very often the case that, apart from having been formally educated themselves, government ministers charged with responsibility for the education of the nation state may feel they have a *mandate* to make educational decisions on a national basis and yet typically come to the job extraordinarily unqualified to do so: having no obvious, broad-based experience or evidence of previous interest on which to base their judgements, not having had to apply for the specific position from which they are trusted to make such judgements in the first place, seldom (if ever) having had to be interviewed for the post or having been required to submit a curriculum vitae and supporting statement, and not necessarily being expected or instructed, once they are in post, to continue to extend what expertise they do have through wider reading or through making use of the expert advice that is available to them within the teaching profession and within the examination boards. To revisit a discussion developed in Chapters 2 and 6, another way in which the different perspectives and priorities of politicians and practitioners can render each susceptible to questions regarding their qualification for the task of curriculum construction and selection relates to the ability and preparedness of the main curriculum designer to remain flexible to changing circumstances in the wider society – or indeed the wider world – and to adjust the curriculum (whether national or 'local') accordingly. Schools and teachers, for example, operating largely alone *might* be less inclined to make such adjustments, since their chosen curricula are perhaps more likely to be based around enduring skills than on a body of knowledge perceived as being applicable to external circumstances, whatever they might be and however they might change.

Once again, much depends on our answer to the Big Question: What, principally, is the curriculum *for*? Is it mainly, for instance, for developing learning, thinking and a range of expressive and communication skills (including expression and communication through the visual and performing arts) which the learner can 'carry away' with them, so to speak, to put to their own use in their life beyond school? (In which case, the skills might vary in nature and emphasis, though the skills *base* would remain the same.) Or do we believe that the curriculum is less about developing and honing what already exists (Bernstein's 'competence' approach), and more about addressing a perceived problem or a deficiency in society and in its young citizens: for example, that literacy and numeracy levels are unacceptably low, or that young people are politically disengaged, or that previously accepted and expected standards of behaviour have slipped, or that we are not adequately preparing students for the future world – that is to say, a 'deficit' approach to curriculum development akin to Bernstein's 'performance' orientation?

An inspection of centrally devised school curricula around the globe suggests that school curricula are likely to be partly 'competence' oriented and partly reactive – although at different times, in different countries, and under different governments the emphasis might change so that sometimes the curriculum sways in the direction of identifying desirable content and outcomes, while at other times it sways more toward correcting some perceived deficiency or deficiencies.

The 'deficiency' or 'repair' approach to education and curriculum reform is very evident in the more recent history of curriculum reform in the UK, most notably perhaps in a famous speech given at Ruskin College Oxford in October 1976 by the then Prime Minister James Callaghan – heralding the commencement of what in England came to be known as 'The Great [Education] Debate'. Callaghan's argument had been based on an attack on prevailing educational practice at the time, proclaiming (if on the basis of somewhat spurious evidence) that there had grown an intolerable mismatch between what children learned in school and what was required 'beyond' school in a rapidly changing workplace: in particular, by the nation's 'industry'. Callaghan's analysis was one that started out with a claim to deficiency, inviting 'repair' as the only way forward: it was not so much that public education had got worse over the years, as that it had simply failed to 'keep up' or to get better: 'It is not enough to say that standards in this field have or have not declined. With the increasing complexity of modern life we cannot be satisfied with maintaining existing standards, let alone observe any decline. We must aim for something better' (Callaghan 1976).[3] There is much in Callaghan's speech to appeal to a wide spectrum of educationalists, including those on the Left, for example, in its endorsement of creativity, its attack on institutionalised sexism (which had seen so few young women take up science as a school option), in its reference to the importance of personal development and individual 'flowering', in its recognition of the underhand rhetorics of 'those who claim to defend standards but who in reality are simply seeking to defend old privileges and inequalities', and in its attempt to raise the status of vocational routes and subjects in public education. However, it also (arguably) launched the troublesome discourse of 'standards' into public education debate, first in the UK, then 'going global', as well as heralding a new age of government influence on the detail of what teachers and students do in school which, though it sounded sensible enough at the time, many feel has grown out of hand in the years that have followed and which set an unfortunately pathologising tone in which teachers appeared to be constructed as setting themselves above the wishes and needs of society and of refusing to accept either discussion or change:

> It is almost as though some people would wish that the subject matter and purpose of education should not have public attention focused on it: nor that profane hands should be allowed to touch it. ...I cannot believe that this is a considered reaction. The Labour movement has always cherished education: free education, comprehensive education, adult education. Education for life. There is nothing wrong with non-educationalists, even a prime minister, talking about it again.
>
> (Callaghan: ibid.)

It could be argued that observations such as this, though it might not have been their intention, have helped to support in England a growing lack of trust not simply in teachers' openness to criticism, discussion and change, but in their broader professionalism: one which has provided an excuse for drastically reducing their input into matters of curriculum content and design and for dramatically increasing that of central government. Certainly, by the late 1990s, by which time Callaghan's Labour government had been superseded first by a Conservative government and then by a 'New Labour' government, central government in England was very much in control of curriculum design, and was placing its emphasis very much on economic issues rather than on personal 'flowering'.

In 1976, Callaghan's centre-left stance was able to float a criticism of teachers and schools that they had failed to produce 'balance' in the curriculum, leaning far too heavily in the direction of the social, therapeutic aspects and purposes of public education at the expense of some of the more pragmatic, instrumental ones to the detriment of the life chances of the less privileged members of society in whose interests public education had (so we are asked to believe) been established in the first place. Perhaps overlooking the shortage of jobs available for young people even then, and indeed the steps that might have been taken by central government to alleviate the difficulty, Callaghan (ibid.) continued: 'There is no virtue in producing socially well-adjusted members of society who are unemployed because they do not have the skills. Nor, at the other extreme, must they be technically efficient robots.'

Alas, it becomes all too easy to forget the latter part of this equation, and to concentrate almost exclusively on the first part – or, rather, the second part of the first part – so that 'socially well-adjusted' and 'no virtue' become elided within a 'discourse of derision' (Ball 1990). By the late 1990s, the emphasis had certainly shifted – but so too, arguably, had the balance: this time, too far toward 'skills' and 'technicism' as successive governments had become increasingly anxious about the nation's economic competitiveness in a rapidly expanding global marketplace and about social cohesion in the equally rapidly changing character of multi-cultural, multi-racial, multi-faith Britain. In its 1997 publication *Excellence in Schools*, the new UK Department for Education *and Employment* (during Callaghan's term of office, still the Department for Education *and Science*) was thus able to assert, with a passing reference to the therapeutic aspects of public education: 'In the 21st century, knowledge and skills will be the key to success. Our goal is a society in which everyone is well-educated and able to learn throughout life. *Britain's economic prosperity and social cohesion both depend on achieving that goal*' (emphasis added, DfEE 1997, para. 1:1).

While the role of central government in curriculum development is not to be dismissed or its potential for good underestimated, there is, I think, an abiding problem when it appears to be based, as in England, not on fundamental questions such as 'What – and who – should public education be for? What are the various things we want it to achieve?' but on this more reactive approach that adopts an essentially 'corrective' stance in which perceived economic demands act as the defining curriculum compass. When this occurs, rather than being responsive to changes in the wider socio-economic and physical world, curriculum can become *enthralled* by such changes (in both senses of the word), resulting in an endless cycle of 'catch-up' change and ultimately futile pursuit. Policy then can provide a stark contrast with the idea of the *dynamic curriculum* explored in Chapter 2. While the dynamic curriculum is concerned to keep curriculum in a continuous state of *evolution*, remaining endlessly open to responding to and taking advantage of changes in the social and natural worlds and in new and developing knowledge, the *repair curriculum* is engaged in a never-ending cycle of 'fixing things'. As with the dynamic curriculum, its work is never (and can never be) 'done'; but unlike the dynamic curriculum, it is burdened with a belief in and commitment to eventual completion, and a seductive image of perfection – never happy until every imagined problem is fixed, and therefore never happy at all and never ceasing from its constant corrections. Not only does the repair curriculum seek to restore curriculum to the path from which, it believes, it has been allowed to deviate (perhaps by being 'too dynamic'), but it contains within it a corresponding view of learning and the learner: that is, not of Bernstein's 'competent', ever-evolving learner engaging freely and creatively with knowledge of and about the world, but of a body of learning that can be identified as essential and of a learner whose own work is done (again and again) each time such learning is acquired and its acquisition 'demonstrated'.

Linking such practices to politics and political ideologies and to their impact on how education constructs its population of learners, Wendy Brown (2006), in her essay 'American Nightmare: Neoconservatism, Neoliberalism and De-democratization', talks, after Apple (2006), of how, in the USA, neo-liberalism and neo-conservatism have worked together 'to undermine the public sphere and democracy, producing governed citizens who looks to find solutions in products, not political processes', while the French sociologist, Alain Touraine, elaborates a not dissimilar concern:

> The world of markets does not constitute a social system, but rather a field of strategic action in which actors strive to use an uncontrolled or even unknown environment. That is why it is more and more difficult to locate individuals on a scale of qualifications or even authority: they are defined, rather, by their position in a market, or, in other words, by their ability to master change or, conversely, their tendency to fall victim to it. Change replaces order as the framework for analysis and social action, because the field of strategic action is a constantly changing set of possibilities, opportunities and risks.
>
> (Touraine 2000: 27, cited in Bates 2005: 102)

'Shock Doctrine': The impact of 'politicking' on policy judgement

This notion of the 'repair curriculum', based on a deficit view both of curriculum and of the students following it (we might add, too, the teachers teaching it!), raises another concern regarding the discharging of curriculum decision-making too completely to the hands of politicians in central government. In pursuing this further, I make no apologies for dwelling a little longer on the matter of State control: it is, after all, the case that, globally, it is currently the State, more so than ever with the advent and proliferation of centrally mandated national curricula, that assumes major responsibility for the school curriculum, the only variation, and admittedly it is a very significant variation, being the extent of its consultations and its devolution of curriculum selection to schools and local authorities.

A particular difficulty that can arise as a development of the reactive, remedial approach to curriculum policy occurs when, caught up in that compulsion to fix things, problems which may in reality not exist, or might be relatively minor, are 'identified' as major concerns by politicians anxious both to justify their professional existence and to justify it to others. In this latter case, the imperative is not so much about doing something in itself, as about *being seen to be doing something about something*. After all, if there is nothing wrong, nothing for something to be done about, why would we ever need politicians in the first place?

One suggested response to such a concern – elaborated in Naomi Klein's book *The Shock Doctrine: the Rise of Disaster Capitalism* (2007) – is that politicians (more specifically, those particularly wedded to the virtues and values of free-market capitalism) do not only seek to justify their existence by taking advantage of national and global crises in order to implement new policies that demonstrate that they are doing something about them; in the absence of a sufficient number of crises, particularly 'at home', they might be inclined to create or construct a problem that can – even if only to a limited degree – prove solvable within existing arrangements, rather than to face actual problems which might require bringing about a radical *change* to those existing arrangements. The real problem of poverty within a generally prosperous nation state, for example, might require a radical change in the ways in which the nation's wealth is distributed, threatening the social and economic status quo, whereas the constructed problem of failing schools or a failing curriculum can be more easily addressed by 'get tough' policies in relation to schools and teachers, by transferring blame to schools and teachers (and perhaps parents), or by instigating yet another curriculum review).[4]

Commenting on 'good government', Foucault observes: 'The end of good government is the correct disposition of things – *even when these things have to be invented to be well-governed*' (emphasis added, Foucault and Rabinow 1991: 21). It might be argued that recent examples of such 'good government' strategies in England concern the current (2013) government's portrayal of mass illiteracy among young people, which provides the excuse for what many teachers and education researchers see as an ill-informed policy of phonics-based reading development, old-fashioned grammar teaching, and an over-concentration on correct spelling among infants, and of public examinations having become 'too easy' on the (questionable) basis that results in them continue to improve year on year, as an excuse for a policy aimed at re-vamping the examination system. In either case, if we adopt the Foucauldian line of argument, it is not the nature and supposed intent of the policy that makes for 'good government'; it is, rather, the making of policy itself – we might almost say, of any policy – and the impact that this *faux* attempt to improve society is expected to have.

If not...then who? Other experts: teachers, parents, students

> Professional autonomy is a principle of action wherein the knowledge, understanding and values of the teacher are given full play, not a sphere or arena shielded from other influences and forces wherein the teacher can exercise unchecked control. [...] Claims to power and influence over the curriculum are not the exclusive prerogative of any one group or office holder. We have to identify those who have some measure of legitimate authority, whether legal, moral, institutional or traditional. If we are to avoid authoritarianism or anarchy, there must be a meshing of their interests, a reconciliation of roles, a quest for consensus over what is legitimate authority and how control is to be shared and distributed.
>
> (Skilbeck 1984: 144)

The point has already been made that one of the major difficulties to arise when a single body such as the State has complete or dominant control over the school curriculum concerns the important matter of regulation and control. Often, it is the State that adopts the controlling, regulatory function of curricula, ensuring, for example, that it remains 'relevant' (in all its interpretations) and fairly and consistently implemented across a nation or a designated region. If the State also has central responsibility for devising the curriculum, however, who is left to take on this regulatory function? The answer, very often, is that the State continues to take on regulatory responsibility, thus regulating its own practice. While this may not necessarily be a problem, depending on how the regulatory mechanism is established, how it operates and whether it is itself subject to some kind of regulation, some curriculum theorists have suggested that such a situation is far from ideal. White, for example, answering his own question 'Do democratically elected ministers have the right to introduce *whatever* aims and curricula gain parliamentary approval [on the basis *that* they have been democratically elected]?' (2004c: 21), observes:

> It is clear that there must be some kind of check on *ministerial and parliamentary arbitrariness.* [But] What kind of check? To answer this, we have to go back to the rationale for a politically-imposed curriculum in the first place. It assumes a democratic society in which everybody is politically equal. Nationally determined aims and curricula are only justifiable if they are fashioned within and support such a framework. ...Aims for the school curriculum must at the very least be aims which foster democratic society. (emphasis added)

White's concerns, which relate also to matters of authority (whose authority in the matter of decision-making is recognised, and on what grounds) and to the *assumption of wisdom* on which authority (sometimes somewhat precariously) depends, are shared by Dewey, who echoes Skilbeck's argument with which this section opened, that there is an important distinction to be made between the central *implementation* of public policy and the central *imposition* of public policy – the former committed, as far as the system allows, to take full and democratic account of the wishes and concerns of its electorate, the latter tending rather to pursue its own ideological agenda regardless. The folly of the latter approach is neatly summed up by Dewey in the suggestion that: 'All reforms which rest simply upon the enactment of law, or the threatening of certain penalties, or upon changes in mechanical or outward arguments, are transitory and futile' (Dewey 2009: 40).

But if curriculum decision-making is not to be the sole preserve of central government, who should be given the responsibility and authority to do so, and by what mechanisms might effective decision-making be ensured? The answer is unlikely to be as simple – or as desirable – as 'schools and teachers': not because schools and teachers are irresponsible or unqualified or (as a previous UK Prime Minister suggested) 'extremist' in their approach, but because, as White has more sensibly argued, there are 'practical problems about this, not least the often widely different provision between schools', and because teachers may not necessarily possess the specific expertise to devise curricula that are of *national* relevance and suitability. White asks: '*Why* should teachers have this power? Do they have the expertise which equips them to make such decisions?', continuing:

> Where teachers *do* have an expertise is in deciding what specific aims and what pupil experiences best suit the particular children they teach in specific circumstances and at specific times. But this does not show why they should make macro-decisions – decisions about what aims to have in the first place.
>
> (White 2004c: 20)

Martha Nussbaum (2010) and Coffield and Williamson (2011) respond to the 'Who then?' question in a way that echoes Callaghan's call for 'balance'. This is not, however, Callaghan's balance between the practical and therapeutic aspects of curriculum (though these are clearly seen as important too). Rather, it is what might be called a 'selection balance', in which different interested and capable parties are brought to the curriculum table to be listened to respectfully as their particular expertise demands, without any one party having excessive influence over the outcomes, even though it may fall, finally, to central government to determine the extent to – and manner in which – the various contributing voices are accommodated and to fashion the official policy to have emerged from the discussion (implementation rather than imposition).

The suggestion that different interested parties ('stakeholders' as they are often called these days: another example of the infiltration of business-speak into public education policy and reform) should be permitted to contribute to curriculum development *nationally* as well as locally is not a new or far-fetched one; nor does it need to fall foul of the objection that such processes are apt to result in endless rounds of committee meetings resulting in fudged compromises or, worse, never getting anything done at all. It is worth reminding ourselves that Callaghan, in his call for curriculum reform, couched it in terms of a 'debate', and that he acknowledged the importance of including all major 'stakeholders' in the process:

> I take it that no one claims exclusive rights in this field [public education]. Public interest is strong and legitimate and will be satisfied. We spend £6bn a year on education, so there will be discussion. But let it be rational. If everything is reduced to such phrases as "educational freedom" versus state control, we shall get nowhere. I repeat that parents, teachers, learned and professional bodies, representatives of higher education and both sides of industry, together with the government, all have an important part to play in formulating and expressing the purpose of education and the standards that we need.
>
> (Callaghan: ibid.)

We might consider two broad approaches to the kind of curriculum decision-making implicit in these suggestions. The first approach is to adopt what might be termed a 'consultative approach', i.e. an attempt (a genuine attempt) to seek out and respond positively but critically to a range of knowledge and wisdom. Such consultation can be fashioned, broadly, in one of three ways, the decision often having much to do with the practicalities of the exercise:

- Form consultative committees, drawing on the representatives of interested parties, either selected by their own constituents or by the committee convenors – perhaps the kind of committee suggested in Denis Lawton's observation that '[i]n a rapidly changing society, there is a need for an institution of some kind to be responsible for keeping the curriculum up to date. ...[S]uch an institution will also need to develop principles and procedures for analyzing social developments and making careful judgments about necessary changes. [...]' (Lawton 1996: 24, 25).
- Seek out a wider range of opinion via an 'open response' mechanism or 'call for views' – often these days making use of websites and email.
- Adopt some form of combination of both.

Teachers and other educationalists in most countries will, I suspect, be familiar with these consultative approaches, and know that they can be done well or badly and can be useful and constructive or an apparent waste of everyone's time and effort. In the UK, central government has, over the years, conducted a number of such consultations, often forming expert groups to report on issues and charging them with the wider, open response consultation process – one recent example being the Cambridge Primary Review whose final report (sometimes known as 'The Alexander Report') was published in 2009 under the title *Children, Their World, Their Education* (Alexander 2009). If such careful and important work ends up, as it sometimes does, in nothing being done, we might argue that this has less to do with the process itself, more to do with a reluctance on the part of central government to treat it with the seriousness we might think it deserves.

The second approach, which does not exclude the consultative approach, is for an agreement to be reached whereby different actors in the educational field are entrusted with different roles and responsibilities according to what might reasonably be asked of them in light of their likely expertise. Such an approach might involve (for example) central government being charged with organising the 'broad framework' of a national school curriculum, and schools and teachers of 'the details' (White 2004d: 189). Such an approach accepts that individual teachers might not be best placed to decide on a curriculum's overarching aims – especially when there is a national curriculum in place – but that they are likely to be better placed than most politicians to decide upon appropriate teaching methods and perhaps specific curriculum content in the context of their particular schools and classrooms. This approach is prepared to back teachers' professionalism, ingenuity and imagination, recognising the importance of having a workforce that is not only qualified and talented but also happy and secure in its work; feeling it has the support and respect of central government and the public.

Not to belabour a point, the difficulty for some countries – England included – in adopting such a division of responsibility and labour as suggested by White occurs when a national curriculum is designed and imposed that is so detailed and prescriptive in its content that the flexibility demanded by shared decision-making makes it virtually impossible – at least in anything but a very rudimentary and lopsided form. The English National Curriculum, for example, even in a currently slimmed-down form, remains very specific in its requirements, offering little scope for local variation, and indeed refusing, in its 'universalising', one size fits all approach, to accept that (apart from in the private sector, where it is actively encouraged within discourses of 'difference' and 'choice') local variation is acceptable. Where there is no room for variation or negotiation there is correspondingly little room for choice. Other nations, on the other hand, *have* believed in and created the space and conditions for local decision-making, and therefore for the kind of shared decision-making we have considered, partly through the adoption of less detailed and specific 'core' or 'minimum' curricula which set out broad principles, aims and requirements but very specifically encourage negotiated variations to account for local and regional differences. The 'Who Decides?' question then becomes a very different – and somewhat easier – one, which may even be set out in a nation's national curriculum documentation. Consider, for example, the following instruction, taken from the National Core Curriculum for Basic Education [Primary Education] for Finland:

> The National Core Curriculum is the *national framework* on the basis of which the *local curriculum* is formulated. The education provider takes responsibility for the preparation and development of the local curriculum. …The curriculum may be formulated so as to include a segment specific to the municipality, or segments specific to the region or school, as decided by the education provider. …The coherence of the curriculum for basic education requires cooperation among different teacher groups in drafting the curriculum. In particular, the pupils' parents and guardians must be able to influence the definition of the curriculum's educational objectives. The pupils may also be involved in the curriculum work. …[T]he

> curriculum must [also] be drafted in collaboration with authorities charged with tasks that are part of the implementation of the local authority's social and health services.
>
> (The National Core Curriculum for Basic Education 2004: 8. www.oph.fi/ english/publications/2009/national_core_curricula_for_basic_education, emphases added)

While the Finnish government provides very clear instructions regarding the skills and knowledge that all children are to have access to and to develop, they are yet at a level of generality sufficient to enable such local decisions to be undertaken democratically: these are not decisions that run the risk of 'disabling' students by producing curricula so idiosyncratic as to damage their future life chances, but decisions which seem likely to ensure a sense of 'ownership' and 'togetherness' among various interested parties. This (importantly) extends Ruti's 'representational power' to constituents who within other systems might be excluded from the decision-making process (Ruti 1999, op.cit.): creating a sense, on the part of teachers and, equally importantly, on the part of students and their parents, that this is 'our curriculum' and we are all pulling in the same direction. It is an approach to curriculum development, design and management that is by no means confined to the political preferences of one nation. The national curriculum for New Zealand, for example, offers the following concise account of a similar commitment to curriculum responsibility-sharing:

> Curriculum is designed and interpreted in a three-stage process: as *the national curriculum, the school curriculum, and the classroom curriculum.* The national curriculum provides the framework and common direction for schools, regardless of type, size, or location. It gives schools the scope, flexibility, and authority they need to design and shape their curriculum so that teaching and learning is meaningful and beneficial to their particular communities of students. In turn, the design of each school's curriculum should allow teachers the scope to make interpretations in response to the particular needs, interests, and talents of individuals and groups of students in their classes.
>
> (The New Zealand Curriculum Online 2007 http://nzcurriculum.tki.org.nz/ Curriculum-documents/The-New-Zealand-Curriculum/ The-school-curriculum-Design-and-review.)

Here, interestingly, local variation is not simply perceived as a possibility or a need-that-might-arise, but rather as a key aspect of the curriculum as practised and experienced in schools and classrooms, resulting in central policy insisting upon it and taking on its own responsibility for ensuring that it can happen. The central rationale for this appears to lie in a recognition of the inevitable existence – and significance – of the idiosyncratic and contingent in both teaching and learning, and their need and capacity to be incorporated within a universal or 'common' entitlement: that is to say, a particular understanding of 'entitlement' that stops short of being overly specific and prescriptive, but does so not at the cost of facilitating an unofficial turn within schools and classrooms to supplying different curricula to different students on the basis of judgemental estimations of individual worth or anticipated life chances.

This inclusion of the student's life and perspective into curriculum development and curriculum choices is particularly strong in the Finnish curriculum documentation, including the suggestion that students as well as their parents should, if and where possible, be included in the processes of local curriculum decision-making. As such, it raises important issues regarding student voice, the democratisation of schools and classrooms, and what is sometimes called 'chronological imperialism' (whereby adult teachers and politicians bearing adult values and perspectives impose their own world views on young learners rather than taking the trouble to find out more about the lived experiences of their students and responding accordingly). Few would suggest, I imagine, that committees of school students should be set up to determine the shape and content of their curriculum, or that it would be anything other than irresponsible to deny young students the wisdom of those who have lived longer and perhaps (though this is not always the case) seen 'more of the world'. But the involvement – again, the *genuine* involvement – of student voices in curriculum decision-making and curriculum evaluation is another matter altogether, suggestive of Coffield and Williamson's account of a 'democratic education' which 'would encourage learners to form an image in *their* heads of the kind of society in which *they* want to live and how *they* can bring it into being' (emphasis added, 2011: 11–12). This is not just a matter of 'democratisation' either: it also concerns democracy's development more broadly, and returns us to issues concerning the potential stagnation both of curriculum and of democracy itself when oppositional and critical voices are silenced, and when alternative approaches are easily dismissed as faddish or extreme.[5] As Mark Fisher asks – somewhat disturbingly: '[H]ow long can a culture persist without the new? What happens if the young are no longer capable of producing surprises?' (Fisher 2009: 3)

Notes

1   Interestingly, there are many politicians, most often on the political Right, who believe that central government should not arbitrate on important educational matters – although their objection is more likely to be predicated on a view that education should not be a 'public sector' matter at all. Chitty, for example, reports on how a former Conservative Secretary of State for Education in the UK – somewhat bizarrely, given his title – complained, in a radio interview after leaving office:

> We have a…state system I wish we hadn't got. I wish we'd taken a different route in 1870. We got the ruddy state involved. I don't want it. I don't think we know how to do it. I certainly don't think Secretaries of State know anything about it. But we are landed with it. …We've got compulsory education, which is a responsibility of hideous importance, and we tyrannise children to do that which they don't want, and we don't produce results.
> (Quoted in Chitty 1997: 80 and 2002: 29)

   Such views do nothing to contradict a suspicion that teachers in England have often voiced to me, that the increasing curriculum demands on schools and teachers enforced by central government are designed to make life so difficult that the government's offer of full or partial opt-out of the public, State-managed sector of education becomes the only manageable choice.

2   This view that large numbers of children were being 'let down' by school and teachers is not a view to which I can easily subscribe. The picture often drawn by politicians – of teachers allowing their young students to do what they wanted within the context of an extremist alliance to student-centred and 'discovery' learning – is not one that I recognise as a teacher who practised in the 1970s and 1980s. While it may be true that some schools and teachers – and thereby some students – might have benefited from higher levels of curriculum regulation and school inspection during this period, it is equally the case that a great deal of highly effective, creative, and, I would argue, empowering developments in curriculum, pedagogy

and assessment were also taking place, and very widely so. This was certainly the case in the schools I had the privilege to work in during this period, and in the neighbouring schools with whom we shared curriculum developments. We also need to be very careful and clear about what we mean when we talk of curriculum 'not working', bearing in mind that the judgement is bound to reflect what we had intended or wanted our curriculum to achieve in the first place. Typically, within central policy and its rhetoric, 'not working' is appended to concerns that, so we are advised, emanate from the world of business and industry, sometimes expressed as 'employers' (the term apparently excluding potential employers in the public sector). We might argue, however, that 'not working' might equally refer to any number of curriculum aspects: for example, we might argue that our curriculum is not producing happy, confident, lifelong learners; or that it is not adequately promoting creativity, invention, and idiosyncratic expression; that it is making young people too competitive and insufficiently collaborative and cooperative; that it is not doing enough to help break down existing class barriers, or to help students from less privileged backgrounds to become sufficiently academically accomplished as to obtain places in Higher Education. These are all possible reasons that might be given for saying that a curriculum is not working. If most of them also appear in the *rhetoric* of central education policy in England, I would suggest that it is only occasionally, and at best half-heartedly.

3   The full text of Callaghan's speech can be accessed online at: http://education.theguardian. com/thegreatdebate/story/0,,574645,00.html. Accessed 19 March 2014.

4   The invention of social problems that required fixing and the subsequent blaming for them of (in this case) schools and teachers was a strategy widely used by Margaret Thatcher during her periods as Education Secretary and Prime Minister in the UK in the 1970s and 1980s. In justifying the introduction of the first official National Curriculum for England and Wales, for example, Thatcher (by now Prime Minister) famously and very publicly demonised many teachers, schools and education authorities, misrepresenting their concern about and resistance to the influence of neo-liberal and conservative values in public education as evidence of an anti-democratic, Marxist plot aimed at undermining the nation. Carefully presenting her argument as a crusade in support of her society's less privileged communities, Thatcher opined:

> We want education to be part of the answer to Britain's problems, not part of the cause. …
> Too often, our children don't get the education they need – the education they deserve. And in the inner cities – where youngsters must have a decent education if they are to have a better future – that opportunity is all too often snatched from them by hard-left education authorities and extremist teachers.
>   And children who need to be able to count and multiply are learning anti-racist mathematics – whatever that may be.
>   And children who need to be able to express themselves in clear English are being taught political slogans.
>   Children who need to be taught to respect traditional moral values are being taught that they have an unalienable right to be gay.
>   And children who need encouragement – and children do so much need encouragement – they are being taught that our society offers them no future.
>   […]
>   I believe that government must take the primary responsibility for setting standards for the education of our children. And that's why we are establishing a national curriculum for basic subjects.
>   It is vital that all children master essential skills: reading, writing, spelling, grammar, arithmetic; and that they understand basic science and technology.
>
> (Thatcher 1987)

Thatcher's invention of 'anti-racist mathematics', the falsehood that children were 'being taught political slogans', and the implication that teachers were not only encouraging homosexuality but that homosexuality itself is in contravention to and threatens 'traditional moral values' provide another example of the discourse or politics of derision, whereby an alternative political view is itself (mis)represented in an extreme (and untruthful) way so that it can be mocked and dismissed.

5   See also Rose and others (e.g. Rose 2006) on the development within wider neo-liberal politics of 'biopolitics'. Akin to Foucault's 'governmentality' and embracing notions and practices of 'marketization', 'autonomization' and 'responsibilization', biopolitics works on people's desires to promote internalised yet externally instituted ideas and beliefs about the kinds of people we (think) we want ourselves and our children to be in current and future life. As education theorists and practitioners, we might then ask where our wishes and priorities for the future 'come from' – and the extent to which they might merely represent the internalised wishes and priorities of those who seek to sustain and maintain their own privilege through the consent of those to whom such privilege is denied.

Chapter 8

Hidden, absent, lost

From misrepresentation to myth-recognition

[T]he world is not a school. Schools, for one thing, are buildings in which schooling is practised by teachers and students who encounter each other in their role as teachers and students. The world, on the other hand, is everywhere and allows for a multitude of roles, identities and encounters. In this respect, schools are not only confined spaces, they also entail confined practices with limits and boundaries. Perhaps one of the most prominent limits that is set and enacted by schools is a limit on interpretation. ...To the extent to which schools are set up as institutions for the transmission of knowledge, skills and values, they are not simply there to transmit but also to sanction certain knowledge, skills and values as valuable, as correct, or even as true.

(Bingham and Biesta, with Rancière, 2010: 148)

Which knowledges are authorized and conferred a particular status, which are silenced, and who has access to or is excluded from these knowledges, are all bound up with relations of power and are key mediators of students' participation in and experience of schooling.

(Youdell 2011: 8)

The 'null curriculum' I: Legitimised and subjugated knowledge

In the preceding pages, a number of critiques have been offered in relation to current knowledge- and subject-based school curricula, along with some indications – little more than that – as to what shape alternative curricula might take (or indeed, in some locations, are already endeavouring to take). The translation from intention to practice is, it must be acknowledged, not always an easy one, and there is an additional problem in relation to radical curriculum change in that the traditional curriculum itself – very widespread globally in its form (see Meyer et al. 1992) – is a highly stable construct that actively and stubbornly *resists* such developments. As other commentators have pointed out, this inherent stability (equally capable of being experienced as stasis or stagnation), which is also, by and large, reflected in wider education *systems*, is 'locked into place' (Ridgway and McCusker 2003) by equally rigid elements such as assessment systems or inflexible programmes for professional development (see also McFarlane 2006: 140).[1]

In this chapter, I want to move on from the 'Who Decides?' questioning of the previous chapter, to begin to consider the relationships between decision-making perspectives, philosophies and ideologies and the actual curricula they produce. Having paid some considerable attention (e.g. in Chapter 4) to what tends to be *in*-cluded in school curricula,

I am inviting readers to make such a consideration somewhat obliquely, by taking into account what is popularly *ex*-cluded – and why this might be. We might then begin to envision what curricula might look like should those *ex*-clusions become *in*-clusions and vice-versa: a process which, I shall suggest, involves identifying and distancing ourselves first from some popular educational and curricular 'myths' which, through custom and the passage of time, may have come to be 'misrecognised' not as mythic at all but rather as simply the way things (inevitably) are. In the process, we will inevitably return to the concept of the 'entitlement curriculum', and in particular the problem that entitlement itself is both a slippery and a prescribed term. As White (2004d: 179) pointedly asks: '[W]hat is the entitlement *to*?' (We might point out, by way of example, that prisoners have certain 'entitlements' in common with one another: the entitlement to certain provided meals, to certain periods of exercise and recreation, to certain visits from family and so forth. However, prisoners are not entitled to come and go as they please, and certainly not to leave the prison grounds except under exceptional circumstances or at the end of their sentence. This is, of course, another metaphor – and, as with all metaphors, does not provide a perfect match. The point is, however, that for every entitlement there is a dis-entitlement, and we might not unreasonably ask, what is the 'disentitlement curriculum'?)

In December 2012, The Fifth Psychosocial Studies Network Conference (PSNC), held at the Institute of Education University of London (IoE),[2] announced its intentions in the following terms and with the following set of questions:

> The social world is saturated with powerful formations of knowledge that colonise individual and institutional identities. Some knowledge emerges as legitimised and authoritative; other knowledge is resisted or repressed.
>
> Psychosocial approaches highlight the unstable basis of knowledge, learning and research; of knowing and not knowing. How do we come to formulate knowledge in the ways that we do? Are there other possible ways of knowing that are too difficult or unsettling for us to begin to explore? Do we need the authority of legitimised institutions and regularised methods to build secure knowledge? What might it mean to build insecure edifices of knowledge? How can/should we trouble notions of knowledge in processes of teaching, learning and research? How does knowledge circulate and how is it implicated in exclusionary social processes?
>
> The conference will generate discussions to help us to explore and develop psychosocial conceptualisations of knowing and not knowing, learning and resistance: the flows and blockages positioned within individuals and institutions, and within the discursive and material processes that constitute these social identities.

Such an agenda – such an orientation to 'knowledge' – is evidently a far cry from the discussions and debates we often find in official curriculum policy, in which knowledge itself is treated unproblematically, the only issue then being which knowledge from a tacitly accepted 'knowledge pool' is deemed worthy of inclusion. In Chapter 4, consideration was given to what is sometimes called 'useful' knowledge and 'powerful' knowledge. The Psychosocial Studies Network Conference also appears to be interested in such knowledge; however, it is at the same time a somewhat different knowledge. Indeed, there is a clear suggestion that much of the potentially empowering knowledge that it advocates – including, centrally, 'knowledge *about* knowledge' – is routinely and politically excluded from the curriculum: not least, perhaps, because of its potentially disruptive nature, both (potentially) for the individual, and in relation to the curricular and wider socio-economic status quo. (For a notable exception, see the post-16 International Baccalaureate curriculum, which specifically – and highly unusually – includes a course on the theory of knowledge.)

The alternative take on knowledge embedded in the PSNC call for papers takes us back from the question posed in the previous chapter – 'Who Decides?' – to revisit an earlier one: 'What Is Decided?' and, in particular, 'On what basis are curriculum elements either included or excluded from the official curriculum? What do such inclusions and exclusions tell us about how public education – and indeed society more broadly – is understood and managed, including, and perhaps most importantly, by politicians?'

In responding to these questions, it is useful to turn to the notion from sociology of the 'null curriculum' (Eisner 1979; Flinders et al. 1986), referring to all of the knowledge, the skills and the culture that the curriculum chooses not to 'legitimise' or to encourage (even to 'allow' us to talk about): to use Foucault's term, that is 'subjugated'. The null curriculum (effectively, the 'disentitlement curriculum' referred to above) will be different in different countries and even within different schools *within* different countries; however, it will always be characterised in terms of its political, ideological or philosophical biases and marginalisations.

Reiss and White (2013) have observed that in the case of the national curriculum in England, there is nothing of note to be found in relation to the workings of national economies or, other than in a somewhat watered-down version in citizenship education, to understanding society, or to sex and relationships, including issues around gender and sexuality. We might add to this that there is little or no *Philosophy* – a subject discipline with a very long and impressive history, whose absence from most formal school curricula may, if we think about it, seem somewhat surprising. (Why is it, we might ask, that in the UK so very few people have even heard of some of the major European philosophers of our time – let alone the non-European ones – or have at best a passing familiarity with the ideas of the great philosophers in history? And why do our curricula tend to marginalise or discourage explorations and understandings concerning the nature of existence, of knowledge, and of the universe – other than those embedded within various forms of religious education?)

The same questions arise when we look at what is excluded within the subject disciplines that *are* considered worthy of curricular inclusion (histories of class and racial oppression in England, for example, in History; or the celebration of local dialects in English language and literature classes).[3] More fundamentally, however, the null curriculum excludes large swathes of *experience*: typically, the lived experience – and its potential for promoting learning in the formal educational setting – of students from backgrounds which might be described as non-dominant or deprivileged – and thus, symbolically, though it will be felt very tangibly, the exclusion of such students themselves.[4]

Others have suggested that the null curriculum might include more specific *learning experiences*, such as those to do with pleasure, and of what Walsh has described as the 'ecstatic' dimension of the school curriculum (Walsh 1993; see, too, Steers 2004, White 2004d: 181): in other words, a therapeutic love of knowledge and learning 'for its own sake' in which (for example) science is approached and experienced more as a 'spiritual' than a purely cognitive affair, so that a dry, factual study of the universe is replaced by questions, understandings, and explorations that enable students to respond to it as 'awesome, wonderful, marvellous, beautiful!' (Walsh 1993: 103). (Such an approach is not unreminiscent of Bennett's notion of 'enchantment' and the ways in which it might be encouraged and experienced through educative practice. Bennett's suggestion that '[t]o be enchanted is to be struck and shaken by the extraordinary that lives amid the familiar and the everyday' [Bennett 2011: 4] may for many readers suggest a stark contrast with the practice that very often dominates the formal educational landscape, in which, to return to Walsh's point, the potentially 'enchanting' is habitually constrained by and confined within the parameters of the 'familiar and the everyday'.)

Variations within the 'null curriculum', both in terms of its content and in terms of how it is conceived, and the sheer extent of what it *might* include, manifest themselves in some commentators' configuring of the null curriculum in terms of 'uncomfortable knowledge': that is to say, knowledge which (unlike the knowledge we shall consider shortly in relation to the individual psyche) might prove as uncomfortable to politicians as it does to students and teachers, not least because of its potential to reveal the hidden stories, motives, relations of power and inequalities that legitimised knowledge buries beneath its own reassuring façade (Foucault's 'subjugated knowledge' again). Coffield and Williamson's (2011) list of ignored or marginalised curriculum content thus includes an inventory of major 'threats' in the social, economic and natural worlds that may comprise very real issues and concerns in relation to students' lived experience outside the school classroom, but that are typically marginalised within school curricula in favour of decontextualised lessons in grammar, mathematics, science, geography, history and so forth. These marginalised issues and concerns include 'global warming, growing inequalities, competition for resources [and] managing complexity'. In a not dissimilar vein, Noddings links the null curriculum to political efforts to marginalise *criticality* in the curriculum and therefore (we might add) to promote a curriculum that is reproductive and compliant rather than [r]evolutionary and questioning. Referencing the banning of teachers' discussing the 2003 invasion of Iraq with their students in the USA, Noddings thus observes in her book *Critical Lessons: What Our Schools Should Teach*:

> although free debate is rarely so directly forbidden, the suppression of discussion and critical thinking in our educational system is widespread. Usually, it is accomplished by defining the curriculum so narrowly and specifically that genuinely controversial issues simply do not arise. [...] *Without controversial issues, critical thinking is nonexistent or, at best, weak.*
>
> (emphasis added, Noddings 2006: 1)

Noddings' chapter headings in *Critical Lessons* read almost like an alternative curriculum in their own right. Replacing Maths, English, History, Science, Art and so forth, we have: 'Self Understanding'; 'the Psychology of War'; 'House and Home' (not to be confused with Home Economics); 'Other People'; 'Parenting'; 'Animals and Nature'; 'Advertising and Propaganda'; 'Making a Living'; 'Gender'; 'Religion'. It is doubtful whether a curriculum with quite such a base exists in practice (*extremely* doubtful that it might do so in the central mandates of any *national curriculum*), although elements of it may be traced in and across the curricula that we do have – a situation which prompts Noddings to ask: 'How can teachers be prepared to conduct critical lessons and, in particular, to conduct such lessons on issues that do not appear in the standard curriculum?' (ibid.: 282) Noddings' answer, which may provide little comfort for many teachers, is that the curriculum itself must change – away from a tidy, universal, step-by-step approach to development, with its own internal, fundamentalist justifications, to one that is more immediately relevant to students' lives and experience and in which, even where pre-planned sequential elements are considered appropriate, these are brought to the service of that alternative rationale rather than *vice versa*.

Noddings' critique draws our attention to another important aspect of the null curriculum, i.e. that it is not just a matter of *what* is left out, but of *why* it is left out; not just a matter of overlooking something as of lesser importance, so much as a deliberate expunging. Keck (2013: 107) reminds us in this regard that an essential part of the null curriculum, in line with Noddings' 'Critical Lessons', is that it effectively bans classroom discussion *of itself*. Summarising Bernfeld's (1973) argument on this matter, Keck asks:

> Does the school hide the knowledge of an order more difficult and unpalatable than the priorities of curriculum? Could this knowledge refer to the relations between knowledge, power and subjectivity as expounded or "unveiled" so forcefully by Foucault in *Discipline and Punish*? (1977) The suspicion that something is being done to us at school which is other than its express purpose is, according to Bernfeld, ubiquitous, and rightly so given education's attachment to the economy and to power (1973: 68). Bernfeld's view was that this something being done is ultimately prescriptive: education is not giving us the tools to construct our freedom; "more than preservation or reproduction of what has been attained, it becomes conservation for the purpose of preventing anything new".
>
> (Bernfeld 1973: 83)

(Interestingly in relation to our earlier considerations regarding uncertainty and change, prospective and retrospective identities, and reproductive and [r]evolutionary curricula, Keck adds: 'Were Bernfeld's suspicions to be true, we might conclude that teachers exist not to ensure the new social order of the future, but rather to prevent the future occurring other than as a repetition of the present' [ibid.: 107].)

Keck's and Bernfeld's suggestion of *deliberation* and *manipulation* in curricular rejections and suppressions is reflected in Bourdieu's theories of symbolic violence and misrecognition (e.g. Bourdieu and Passeron 1977), returned to below, and Giddens' (1979: 193) suggestion (taking us back to issues of curriculum selection and what 'counts as knowledge') that one of the primary 'modes in which domination is concealed as domination' is the 'representation of sectional interests as universal ones'.

The null curriculum 2: Marginalising affect

> Wherever one finds systematicity, one can, from a psychoanalytic point of view, ask the question of what unbearable piece of reality is being defended against by means of the system.
>
> (Blass 1998: 426)

> How is it possible for education as a discourse and as a practice, as an institution and as an experience, to listen to its own exclusions, repressions, and silences? What could education be like if its interest began with Winnicott's notion of "making elbow room for the experience of concern"?
>
> (Britzman 1998: 59)

The suggestion that the official curriculum hides or masks or attempts to stand in place of something else is no longer unusual. Britzman (1991), for example, drawing on Freudian dream theory, invites us to think not just of the 'manifest' (immediately visible, 'masking') and 'latent' (underlying, forceful, yet in hiding) meanings in student writing and teachers' practice, but those too that may be uncovered within school curricula – suggesting, perhaps, that the curriculum's very function (its key function at least) is not so much to induct young people into a world of important knowledge as to present before them – and to persuade them to internalise – a safe, untroubling way of understanding and experiencing themselves and the world: a different kind of preparation for present and future life than is usually understood by 'preparation', and one that must remain hidden from learners themselves, since for it to become visible would result in that very de-stabilisation that it strives to resist.

Other commentators (e.g. Dreeben 1967; Lynch 1989) have talked of a 'hidden curriculum' which lurks behind the overt, official one – distributed not so much via official taught curriculum content as through such things as school rules, codes of conduct, and pedagogic cultures reinforcing particular learner–teacher, child–adult hierarchical relationships. (The 'hidden curriculum' might also refer to matters of selection and choice, i.e. the possible ideological and political *rationales* lying behind curriculum selections, presented themselves as 'neutral' or contingent choices, may themselves be understood as 'curriculum'.) To return to Rancière's analysis, while students might, for example, be encouraged to perceive themselves as independent thinkers and learners within official curriculum rhetoric, and even via some official curriculum materials, their daily experience of themselves and of the way they are actually understood and treated by adults as thinkers and learners may be one of absorption and regurgitation; while they may be encouraged to think of themselves as future 'active citizens' taking a full part in democracy, their experience of such encouragement might be that it is taking place within decidedly undemocratic classrooms and non-negotiable curriculum content; and while curriculum rhetoric might speak of promoting community, collaboration, tolerance and mutual respect, the curriculum as offered, as negotiated and as assessed might speak, rather more loudly, of competition, of being better or worse than others, of the importance and desirability of individual entrepreneurship.

The notion of the 'hidden curriculum' (in which certain dominant values and preferred practices are omitted from the specified curriculum only to be resurrected within institutional organisation and conduct, teacher pedagogy, and test and examination criteria) will be returned to in the next section. First, it might be helpful to briefly consider the possibility of that other 'hidden purpose' identified by Britzman and others that might lie behind some school curricula. This is the suggestion that the official curriculum serves not simply to mask certain political intentions, thus presenting itself as neutral and beyond serious disagreement, but that it might serve to offer a particular 'comfortable' body of skills, knowledge and understandings that, so to speak, stands in place of a raft of other skills, knowledge and understandings that are far more difficult for us to engage with or confront. Whether we think this is a good idea or not will depend partly on the extent to which we are happy to accept the potential therapeutic qualities of such a 'safe' curriculum, or whether, in line with Holt's view (op.cit.), we believe it is a fundamental right to be encouraged to explore all aspects of human experience and the universe in which we live, and, even if we accept that some decision-making might have to be made at a national level regarding what is and is not included in the school curriculum, not to have such decisions made for us patronisingly and not to be always told what is acceptable knowledge and what is not.

The particular curriculum omissions referenced by Britzman concern not just matters related to power relations or the nature of 'knowledge', but those to do with specific, often 'not-talked-about' human characteristics: namely, those to do with feelings, emotions, or 'affect', related to the development of *self*-knowledge or self-understanding. Within school curricula characterised – at least superficially – by 'rationality', the 'irrational' is not only not discussed, but rather, where its presence does make itself felt willy-nilly, becomes domesticated within rationalist discourses such as 'emotional *intelligence*', or in terms of 'good and bad', 'acceptable and unacceptable' behaviour.

Many years ago, Sigmund Freud memorably observed of education that it was 'behaving as though one were to equip people starting on a Polar expedition with summer clothing and maps of the Italian lakes' (Freud 1930: 134). Freud was referring specifically to the complex, often difficult and painful emotional experiences of young people, including those related to sexuality and gender as they grow into and beyond adolescence, which are seldom allowed into schools and classrooms as subjects worthy of serious teaching and learning (Reiss and White, op.cit.), ousted instead by knowledge of the physical rather than the psychic/affective world. Embedded within discourses of modernism and reason, within which that which is readily explicable is welcomed and that which is harder to explain and perhaps more painful and difficult in the process is not, the dominant curriculum project thus focuses on that which is 'external' to the individual and to relationships, rather than on understandings of the self, of others, and of inter-relations between the two.

We might argue, of course, that there are spaces – nooks and crannies – in which the psyche is allowed some curricular recognition and debate (within some language and literature lessons, for example, or within the humanities and creative subjects from time to time); however, Keck (2012: 184) has a point when he identifies and critiques 'modernity's regime of truth – that truth is the fruit of reason and therefore incompatible with and threatened by emotion…and corporality', concluding: 'There are always, then, two or more worlds in the classroom: the world of teaching and learning, and the world of what Foucault termed the *bios philosophicos*, the animality of being human.' (Keck: ibid.) The consequences for curricula which acknowledge and celebrate the rational at the expense of the affective are plain to see, and connect very powerfully with previous arguments concerning 'curriculum dynamikos'. They are neatly encapsulated in Ruti's account of the relationship in public institutional(ised) life between the symbolic order (principally, language) of the rational world – which acts precisely *to* rationalise, contain, make some kind of provisional, workable sense of Foucault's not-to-be-talked-about 'animality of being human' – and that 'animality' itself, that 'Real' (as Lacan puts it) of the seldom discussed but ever present force of desire that drives and motivates us beneath the surface of our neatly ordered, rational lives (and of our neatly ordered, rational curricula): 'Whenever the symbolic gains *too much power* at the expense of the Real, our existence loses its passion and forward-moving cadence' (emphasis added, Ruti 2012: 160). Ruti is not (any more than others advocating the de-marginalisation of affect in school curricula), advocating the elimination of traditional social structures and organisations (like school curricula) with new ones which occupy another extreme in which the 'rational' symbolic world's role is negated in favour of a surrender to our instincts and desires. On the contrary, along similar lines to earlier arguments concerning the necessary controlling, mediating, regulating (yet not *over*-controlling/mediating/regulating) function of the State, of government, of 'paranoia', she recognises and argues: 'When the symbolic fails to adequately mediate the disorderly energies of the real …we fail to gain a steady foothold in cultural narrative and other collective landmarks that would be able to anchor us in the symbolic world.' (Ruti 2012: 160–1). Translated into curriculum philosophy, Ruti's argument as a whole might suggest the desirability of curricula that:

- allow for openness and exploration, for the inclusion of emotionality and experience as legitimate curriculum content, but that at the same time accept the need for common structures on and within which to support such learning (as indeed with all other learning);
- embrace rather than run away from the notion of 'unresolved meaning' (Kennedy 2004);
- accept the impossibility of a 'single history' rather than inventing and endlessly pursuing one as if it exists;
- understand the world as process not as fact;
- appreciate and turn to their own advantage Foucault's 'rich uncertainty of disorder' (Foucault 1969: 76) and the acceptance of our ontological condition as 'beings of uncertainty' (Ruti 2009: 42)[5] – mining, perhaps, the rich seam of the 'mass of largely silent development' that lies 'beneath the thin surface of discourse' (Foucault: ibid.);
- recognise (Ruti 2009: 9) that '[o]ur attempts to know ourselves more fully… tend to expand the realm of the unknowable', while '[o]ur social embeddedness… narrows down the possibilities that the future holds by connecting us to collective conceptions of what is and is not possible' (2009: 37);
- open up the way to – and equally recognise the value of – new directions of questioning toward which to aim our human curiosity;
- and in practical, pedagogical terms, without eschewing thorough, professional planning, feedback, reflection and organisation, acknowledge 'the messy complexity of the classroom' and its only 'partially apprehendable practice' (Goodson and Walker 1991: xii) – giving full recognition to 'the central role that people play in the educational process and educational systems' (ibid.: 1), legitimising a *range* of approaches and behaviours, and understanding that 'much of the most expert practice in schools is based on intuitive judgement'.

(McIntyre et al. 1994: 57)

In sum, such a philosophy might suggest school curricula that are constructed around Ruti's powerful assertion that 'the world imposes itself on us, but we also impose ourselves upon the world' (Ruti: 2009: 38; see also Moore 2012 and below, on the 'responsible–responsive curriculum'), and on the broad principles outlined by Coffield and Williamson, in which education represents a 'dynamic combination' of elements, including:

[T]he means of creating the kind of society we want by opening minds, transforming lives and civilising society;

A critical understanding of society by encouraging independent thinking and collective action;

[…]

A simultaneous matching of society to the needs of learners and of learners to the anticipated and debated future needs of society;
The preparation of all citizens as full, active members of a democratic society.
(Coffield and Williamson 2011: 5)
(Coffield and Williamson importantly elaborate this last principle as follows: '[O]pportunities for learning at all stages of life are a necessary feature of an open, democratic society to which citizens have an entitlement, and therefore should be free. The costs of providing such opportunities will be paid back in abundance by socially responsible citizens engaged in a lifetime of creative work and civic engagement' [ibid.: 60].)

Coffield and Williamson's emphasis on the development and flourishing of the individual within a revised curriculum content and structure underlines the relationship between what curriculum looks like, how it is experienced, and the understanding(s) of – and plans for – the human psyche that underpin and are reflected in it: in short, the relationship in curriculum policy and design between epistemology and ontology. For Britzman, as for Keck (op.cit.), the 'rational' or 'rationalised' curriculum constructs itself on a view of the rational or rationalised *human being*, and seeks to reproduce and validate such beings – in the process, destroying what it fears: i.e. that which is inventive and creative in the young learner, that which, given freer rein, imagines and 'dreams'; that which challenges the contrived rationality of the curriculum itself. Contrasting the 'child who dreams' with the knowledgeable scholar-child constructed within much formal education, Britzman argues:

It is not only the child who dreams but the dream of the child, indeed, the child as dream that interferes with the question of knowledge in education. Can educators face the same sort of choice, between the empirical child made from the science of observation, behaviourism and experimental and cognitive psychology and the libidinal child who dreams and yet still desires knowledge? The field's dominant tendency is to choose the empirical child over the dream, the child the adult can know and control. But in so doing, education has reduced the child to a trope of developmental stages, cognitive needs, multiple intelligence, and behavioural objectives. And these wishes defend against a primary anxiety of adults: what if the dream of learning is other to the structures of education?

(Britzman 2003: 54)

'Hidden' or 'in hiding'? The curriculum's secret self

I have suggested that our decision to embrace or reject (entirely or in part) a curriculum philosophy such as that outlined above is likely to depend both on our acceptance of the analysis and on whether, even if we do accept it, we think that it might be appropriate and practicable: in short, what we think the overall purpose and responsibility of a curriculum is, embedded within broader questions regarding how we understand such concepts as entitlement, inclusion and human rights. Giving greater emphasis to getting young people to learn about and discuss some of those things that we 'don't normally talk about' (essentially, our fears, our desires, our frustrations, our hates, our loves, our prejudices; how they impact on us and on society; how things might be different if we bring into the open that which is normally 'hidden') might have its virtues, and might contribute to a radical change (it would be hoped, an improvement) in the ways in which we experience our own lives and behave towards one another. On the other hand, the argument has already been acknowledged that there might be much to be said for the 'safe' curriculum with its 'safe' knowledge; that if the curriculum itself not only offers students knowledge and skills that will be of use to them in a variety of ways in their current and future lives but also an opportunity for denial in relation to things which we might not normally talk about 'with good reason', we should not be too quick to condemn it on those grounds. As Frosh has argued, denial might have a restrictive quality, concealing from us certain truths which might serve to empower us, but it also conceals less palatable truths that we might be better off *not* acknowledging, for

> not only are denial and other types of defence very common, but there are occasions on which they are advisable too. This is not only when there is a threat to selfhood from overwhelming emotion [...] but also as a more mundane issue: sometimes we just have to get on with life and postpone our feelings to allow us to do so.
>
> (Frosh 2011: 25)

An issue to be addressed here (not a new one for us) is: To what extent do we include 'difficult', 'challenging' knowledge in the curriculum – if at all? And (as always) which difficult, challenging knowledge *might* we include? The broad answer, too, is likely to be framed as a question – the same question which always faces curriculum theory and design: What do we want our curriculum inclusions to achieve? In this case, if our intention is to shield students, to 'protect' them from troubling (and perhaps trouble-some) knowledge, we might reject uncomfortable, 'difficult' knowledge altogether – especially if we are also guided by an aim to maintain a social status quo rather than to question it. If, on the other hand, we wish to produce a critically educated citizenry that might challenge the status quo, difficult knowledge might force itself more into the forefront of our reckoning. (Even then, we will have decisions to make regarding what kind[s] of difficult knowledge to include. Where do we draw, so to speak, the curriculum line?)

Marx's famous reference to Perseus' magic cap might be useful here: 'Perseus wore a magic cap so that the monsters he hunted down might not see him. We draw the magic cap down over our eyes and ears so as to deny that there *are* any monsters' (emphasis added, Marx 1976: 91). Without wishing to prejudice the issue further, we might, I think, ask of the curriculum: Does it/in what ways might it encourage learners to draw a 'magic cap' down over their ears and eyes in order to avoid engaging with or confronting social and psychic 'monsters'? Which 'monsters' might we wish our learners to recognise and engage with – and which might we wish to shield them from? And if there are indeed 'monsters' with which our curriculum refuses engagement, do we not seriously undermine our intention to *educate* by severely restricting *what* we educate in and for, imposing parental-like judgements not just about usefulness but also regarding appropriateness and 'suitability'?

This last possibility has been explored further in Britzman's idea of curriculum as 'fantasy' (see also Chapter 4).[6] First, there is the (Enlightenment) fantasy of orderliness and control that we have already considered: the supposition or implication that everything is knowable and under control – or will be if we can only get our act together; so that the curriculum simultaneously ratifies as it promotes the illusion of an ordered, orderly world and universe. Then, in parallel with the 'repair curriculum', there is the fantasy of the faulty child, the imperfect human needing correction or 'cure' in order for orderliness – social and economic – to be maintained or restored: a deficit curriculum model, constructed, as in Bernstein's 'performance' orientation (op.cit.), on a notion of that which is 'missing' or that which has become weakened, rather than on that which is present, that which might serve to carry us forward.

The notions of 'hidden' and 'hiding' in Marx's metaphor, and how they might be relevant to our understandings of school curricula, bear a little additional development, beginning with a concept already referred to – that of the 'hidden curriculum' – but going further to explore some of the ways in which the curriculum, now itself Perseus-like, might be seen to be engaged in selective 'hiding'.

One of the ironies of the marginalisation of affect and the exclusion of uncomfortable knowledge in school curricula is that the official curriculum itself may be said to sustain itself, for all the 'rationality' of its rhetoric and its curriculum selections, precisely by a hidden reliance on the actual existence of that whose existence it denies. What I mean by this is that the curriculum may be seen to depend on the emotionality – the emotional responses and experiences – of both students and teachers in order to sustain both its rational appearance *and* its rational justification. There are two ways in which this can happen. One is by encouraging and rewarding emotional investment in success *within* the stated curriculum: the joy and guilt of teachers in relation to their students' examination results, for example, or the drive for parents to do their utmost to ensure their children's success regardless of the system within which it is located, or the desire of young children to win their teachers' love and respect through the repetition of 'correct answers' (Moore 2013), or the internal doubt affecting teachers and parents when experiencing philosophical and political opposition to dominant, hegemonised policy[7] – perfectly normal emotions, we might say, that are allowed, encouraged and enabled to play so strong a part in curriculum reproduction and implementation precisely because of their marginalised (we might say pathologised) status within the curriculum as officially presented.

The second way is via what Thornton (2009) calls 'Silence'. This concerns the way in which something – particularly something which has become invested over time with a great deal of affective content – that is marginalised or excluded from the official curriculum has its marginalisation endorsed and perpetuated precisely because it is not talked about, and because its not being talked about, its silen*cing*, reinforces and confirms the justification of its pathologisation. Thornton uses the example of homosexuality, coining the phrase 'The Hidden Curriculum Everybody Sees' (2009: 364), referencing the general absence of recognition not just of homosexuality but of gay and lesbian *people* in school curricula in the USA. The tacitly accepted reason for homosexuality's curriculum absence might not be that it is uncomfortable or not sufficiently relevant or 'useful' enough to merit discussion, but that there is something wrong with homosexuality itself and therefore something wrong – perhaps something to be ashamed of – either in being homosexual or in wanting to talk about it.[8] Homosexuality is 'seen' by students (i.e. they physically see and interact with homosexuals both in and outside school), but what is simultaneously seen (perhaps because it is so visible in the non-official experience of school life) is its exclusion from the official discourse.

Although different from Britzman's 'missing curriculum' (if we can call it that), Thornton's 'hidden curriculum that everybody sees' has at least one very important thing in common with it. Both suggest that what is typically referred to as the hidden curriculum[9] (though it clearly exists, and very powerfully too) might have the effect of obscuring or 'eclipsing' *another* hidden curriculum: one that is, so to speak, doubly hidden. We might call this the 'hidden hidden curriculum'. The recognition or discovery of the hidden curriculum as normally understood might simply, then, act to obscure this other hidden hidden curriculum; a curriculum whose discovery or outing cannot be so easily contemplated by society, let alone by politicians, policymakers, teachers and – dare we say it? – many curriculum commentators, since to do so might undermine both public education as we know it (its structure, yes, but also its very rationale, its most profound functions and purposes) and our own carefully arrived at convictions as to what is wrong and what is right.[10]

Concealing-strategies: Some educational myths

The concept of hiddenness, like so many other key curriculum issues, has a substantial history in the field of critical social and educational theory. Both Basil Bernstein (2000) and Pierre Bourdieu (Bourdieu and Passeron 1977) have, in their different ways, made some attempt to illustrate the *mechanisms and processes* by which such concealment is carried off: how that which is hidden remains 'invisible' in the experience of those from whom it is hidden. Both commentators suggest that, apart from the possibility I have suggested of the hidden being eclipsed by the visible, the hidden may also (or instead) preserve its hiddenness through the practice of *disguise*: relying on what Bourdieu refers to as 'misrecognition' and what Bernstein links to the development of certain educational myths. Here, misrecognition (Bourdieu and Passeron 1977; Moore 2012) refers to the way in which arbitrary cultural selections (within, for example school curricula) are experienced and understood not as arbitrary at all, or as representative of the particular tastes, preferences and priorities of a specific (powerful) social group, but as 'natural', 'god-given', intrinsically worthwhile. Failure to perform well within the misrecognised curriculum when others are clearly performing very well then leads to another, related misrecognition on the part of the learner, that he or she must be deficient or inadequate – just as the *successful* performer might misrecognise success as indicative of some inherent *superiority* over those seen to be failing. (For a fuller account of this process, see Moore 2012, Chapter 4.)

Bernstein, in an analysis not unlike Bourdieu's, locates such processes not simply within the 'official recontextualising field' of public policy, but within schools and schooling too, suggesting ways in which the school disconnects its internal hierarchy of success and failure from ineffective teaching or from the 'external hierarchy of power relations between social groups outside the school' through attributing success and (in particular) failure to 'inborn facilities...or to the cultural deficits relayed by the family which come to have the force of inborn facilities' (Bernstein 2000: xxiv). Education taken as a whole thus 'preserves structural relations between social groups but changes structural relations between individuals' (ibid.). One result is that 'orientation is displaced towards national consciousness and struggle rather than class consciousness and its conflicts' (ibid.). That is to say, to return again to national curriculum matters, the mandated curriculum, in particular perhaps when it has strong national-*ist* leanings, may seek to unite its students within some conceptualised national identity and some shared national problems and aspirations at the same time as preserving economic, social and status differentials *between* students within the (conceptualised) organic society; indeed, such a curriculum might be said not simply to preserve but to promote and effect the continuation of such differentials through its very nationalist character.

If we accept Bourdieu's and Bernstein's analyses, we might contend that in order not just to envision but to put into practice curricula that are radically alternative to those most commonly in existence (rather, that is, than simply replicating in a slightly different form their existing aims, objectives and content) – and in particular if we feel that our existing curriculum might be overly and inappropriately culturally biased or unacceptably socially unjust – we might first need to identify and reject some of these myths, replacing Bourdieu's misrecognition with what we might call a process of myth-recognition, exposing them in the process as acts of deliberate *misrepresentation* concealing unequal and inequitable relations of power. This, essentially, is the process and the project identified by Popkewitz (2009: 303–4) of: 'Making visible the authority of existing systems of reason [as] a strategy to open to the future the possibilities of alternatives other than those already present'.[11]

What, then, are the myths of public education and school curricula that present themselves most obviously for interrogation? We will all have our ideas, and our lists may inevitably be incomplete, both to ourselves and to others. Those which have particularly exercised me personally over 44 years in education (I am excluding from this my time as a school- and undergraduate-student) are broadly as follows:

- the myth of curriculum neutrality, which denies its cultural biases and the partiality of its selections;
- the myth of intelligence, which narrowly defines the concept and then argues that some are 'naturally more intelligent' than others;
- the myth of orderliness, that refuses to embrace and take advantage of disorder and uncertainty, seeking to confine us as learners within the 'safe', reproductive world of 'The Answer';
- the myth that competition improves quality and efficiency, whether in the national and global marketplace or within the school classroom;
- and the myths of meritocracy and equal opportunity, which make it easy to blame students and/or their teachers or families or local communities for failure to 'achieve' in the prescribed manner, rather than acknowledging the profound potential impact on learning of differential social conditions supported and maintained by the wider socio-economic system.

As Jaramillo observes in relation to this last myth (preferring the term 'Imaginary'):

The problem with the Imaginary of equal opportunity in capitalism is that it consequently obscures the structural limitations and boundaries that condition human activity in social institutions, such as schools. Rather than drawing attention to the social organisation and social relations between and among different actors in education, the Imaginary of capitalist democracy reproduces the belief that academic failure is largely the result of individual characteristics. Whether the blame is placed on educators and administrators as ineffective, lazy, unqualified, and so forth or on the families themselves as poor, uninformed, culturally dissonant, or otherwise, the predominant belief systems in education attribute blame to either or both groups for paltry academic outcomes. This forms part of what Wilden calls the projection identification, and objectification of the "other" for legitimizing the pervasive Imaginary social view.

(Jaramillo 2010: 48)

Adopting a more specific – potentially, perhaps, a more practical – approach, Denis Lawton has critiqued the English school curriculum as being based on 'a series of false assumptions'. Lawton lists seven of these, which might also prove a useful starting point for interrogating the curricula of nations other than England:

1   That it is possible to plan a curriculum for today and tomorrow by looking backwards to what schools have always done.
2   More specifically, it is assumed that a curriculum should be planned by listing ten or eleven subjects and then specifying detailed content.
3   That planning by objectives is the best way.
4   That in all subjects the most important aspect is memorisation of content.
5   That cognitive development is more important than the social, moral and aesthetic development of pupils.
6   That assessing pupils' achievement on the curriculum can be used to grade teachers and their schools (assessment as social control).
7   That assessment by external tests is better than teacher assessment (more control).

(Lawton 2000: 30–31)

Lawton's list is one that will be broadly approved of by education ministers in some nations, broadly dismissed by those in some others. In the case of England at the current time, the latter would appear to apply, and it has often been pointed out that even if we as teachers and academics approve of such a curriculum there are likely to be very powerful forces of conservatism opposing and resisting it. The following metaphor, likening the English school curriculum to an 'old fashioned juggernaut', taken from Coffield and Williamson (2011: 2), sums up rather neatly and dramatically the concerns that many of us here have, not only at the content of our national curriculum but at its lack of fitness even for the purposes it publicly espouses:

There is…thick fog ahead on the motorway along which this juggernaut is trundling, but it is now being forced to increase speed without a clear view of the dangers in front of it. The many drivers on board are all pulling different levers to improve its performance, with only a vague notion of where it is headed: a society of aspiration and opportunity. This is a laudable ambition until the fog lifts and suddenly there is a pile-up ahead, and no one knows what has caused it or how to remove it or how to stop the juggernaut in time. We need to act before the old juggernaut crashes into the back of the queue of cars ahead.

Coffield and Williamson embed their account within references to resistance in central government policy which refuses to change the system, only elements within it, talking of policies 'the summit of [whose] ambition is to reform, yet again and in different ways, the present "system"' – a system, however, 'that is deeply undemocratic, inequitable, inefficient and inadequate to address our present problems and future threats' – a system 'that does not need to be reformed [but] needs to be replaced' (ibid.: 1).

Theoretical alternatives

> [T]he more we cling to the notion of predictability, the less dexterously we are able to deal with life as the erratic and capricious stream of unanticipated events, encounters, and developments that it often is. No matter how carefully we strive to organize our lives around certain centers of security – ideals, ambitions, or relationships, for instance – it is our lot as human beings to learn to survive less than secure circumstances.
>
> (Ruti 2009: 45)

To say that something is faulty is one thing. To come up with something that we might think is better – something that might also work in practice – is another. Not only is there the issue of designing our alternative; there is also the very big task of persuading others – including, essentially, those with 'representational power' (Ruti 1999, op.cit.) – that our alternative is preferable. The strength of the gravitational pull of tradition and conservatism is not to be underestimated in this endeavour – not just in England, either. At the front end of his damning indictment of schooling in *America* in the 1970s and 1980s – though it might confidently be argued to apply equally today – Jonathan Kozol quotes at length from the Introduction to Doris Lessing's *The Golden Notebook* (Lessing 1973: xvii):

> It may be that there is no other way of educating people. Possibly, but I don't believe it. In the meantime it would be a help at least to describe things properly, to call things by their right names. Ideally, what should be said to every child, repeatedly, throughout his or her school life is something like this:
>
> > "You are in the process of being indoctrinated. We have not yet evolved a system of education that is not a system of indoctrination. We are sorry, but it is the best we can do. What you are being taught here is an amalgam of current prejudice and the choices of this particular culture. The slightest look at history will show how impermanent these must be. You are being taught by people who have been able to accommodate themselves to a regime of thought laid down by their predecessors. It is a self-perpetuating system. Those of you who are more robust and individual than others will be encouraged to leave and find ways of educating yourself – educating your own judgment. Those that stay must remember, and all the time, that they are being moulded and patterned to fit into the narrow and particular needs of this particular society."
>
> (quoted in Kozol 1993)

Transforming education might indeed prove every bit as difficult as many of us would argue it is necessary – especially in some countries, such as England, where the democratic power of Teachers' Trades Unions, along with their own 'representational voice', has been severely reduced by central governments and where what power they have left is too often and too completely siphoned off in the defence of basic rights, salaries and conditions of service rather than in arguing and debating matters of social and educational principle. However, this should not stop us first from theorising some alternatives and then seeing if we can find some examples of curriculum development around the globe that might, reassuringly perhaps, suggest the viability of such alternatives in practice – all the while recognising that radical, global curriculum change is likely to require a 'long revolution' (Williams 1961) rather than an overnight *coup*, and that, to quote Coffield and Williamson again (looking back on past reforms by way of understanding the nature and possibilities of future ones): 'At each stage in the process, the pioneers of reform had to overcome the resistances of tradition, of élite power determined to keep education exclusive, or of economic arguments that it could not be afforded, or the psychological arguments that few had the ability to benefit' (Coffield and Williamson 2011: 55).

Lawton's own contribution to the 'long revolution' is not insubstantial, and it is a pity that there is no room to do his work anything like full justice here. In response to the 'What would you do instead?' question, he identifies five proposals in recommending 'a massive reorganisation of the curriculum' (2000: 32–35). Offering a stark contrast with the 'core knowledge' approach favoured within some national curriculum initiatives, these are:

1   From content and objectives to skills and processes;
2   From subjects and cognitive attainment to cross-curricular themes and the affective domain;
3   From didactic teaching to self-directed learning;
4   From academic or vocational to integration of both aspects of experience;
5   From a national curriculum 5–16 to life-long learning.

Lawton concludes (ibid.) in similar vein to Coffield and Williamson:

> We face the twenty-first century with two major unresolved problems in our schools: first, the culture and organisation of schools; second, the curriculum. Both problems are still dominated by nineteenth-century thinking about education. Politicians and others still tend to think of a school where young people have to be made to work: control of students by teachers now themselves controlled by late twentieth-century centralism is the order of the day. Then there is a curriculum which is out of date and simply does not meet the needs of young people growing up in a rapidly changing democratic open society. They are both aspects of the same problem.

Taking my cue from Lawton, I want to suggest that we might consider the development of curricula that are characterised by the following distillations of what has gone before in *Understanding the School Curriculum*: that is, curricula that are characterised as:

- forward-looking and proactive (in addition to paying full and appropriate attention to the present and to the value of the past);
- both respons-*ive* and respons-*ible* in their orientation (responsive to wider social and physical change, responsible in encouraging students to envision and to wish and know how to contribute to the creation of a safer, more equitable future);
- prioritising individual and collaborative problem-solving skills, 'useful knowledge' and the promotion of a love and capacity for learning, for self-expression and for

investigation over 'knowledge for knowledge's sake' within active, student-centred classrooms;

- taking a more deliberate and thought-out ethical stance in relation to concerns and issues that are global rather than local or national;
- ensuring that education – learning – is both relevant (to society and to the learner) and enjoyable;
- providing the stability that schools and teachers need while at the same time continuing to evolve and to self-evaluate;
- seeking as far as possible to base their judgements on curriculum inclusions and exclusions on educational and social principles rather than on political ideology or on educational myths or illusions of objectivity;
- promoting both *collective*, communitarian values *and* the development of the *individual* citizen as a happy, creative, well rounded and culturally enriched human being.

These are very broad curricular aims, but I hope they will not be dismissed for that. (An even broader and at the same time more fundamental aim is offered by Reiss and White [2013] in their eloquently argued work *An Aims-based Curriculum: the Significance of Human Flourishing for Schools*, in which their curricular 'bottom line' [with apologies to Coffield and Williamson] is that education should seek to equip young learners *to be able to lead a personally fulfilling life and to help others to do likewise*.) These aims are underscored by a particular view of human beings as learners and creators who are driven by a desire for the reassurance of knowing but also by a restless desire to explore. They are fashioned in response to some of the 'what if' questions that have been raised earlier in this book, i.e.:

- What might a school curriculum look like if we decided to reject sameness as the dominant discourse in favour of difference, and if we rejected orderliness in favour of dealing with a certain amount of disorderliness – of recognising uncertainty, perhaps, and learning how to live with it rather than hoping or pretending it wasn't there?
- What if we listened more attentively and respectfully to the voices of young learners and to their own articulations of their needs?
- What if we envisioned, in line with Bates' suggestion (Bates 2005: 98), a curriculum that set out to serve the interests of 'the working class, women, ethnic minorities, etc.?' and in doing so perhaps considered how 'the insurrection of subjugated knowledges [might] be made part of the curriculum of schools?'
- What if we predefined our curriculum in some alternative way, calling it, for example – and fashioning it accordingly – the Critical Curriculum, or the Democratic Curriculum, or (to hark back to a previous chapter) the Global Curriculum, or the Activity Based Curriculum, or (in a reminder of the tyranny of The Answer) the Inquisitive or Questioning Curriculum?
- What if, after Atkinson (2013: 19), we structured our curriculum on Deleuze's 'notion of immanence, where learning emerges from within the contingencies, differences and diversity of each individual life', in which we focused our attention 'not with a pre-ordained subjectivity but with a subject-yet to-come' transforming our and our students' conception of the world 'from something given, that is to say already grounded in established knowledge, to something to be explored and continuously created not in terms of what exists but more in terms of "what this world is capable of"' (ibid.: 12)?

It is conceivable that any such approaches could be materialised without the abandonment of traditional subject disciplines. However, the specific emphasis – one which, in each case, is on an overall purpose or set of purposes rather than on the *a priori* identification of subject knowledge – might suggest some reorientation regarding their inter-relationship and the ways in which they are pressed to the service of our overriding curriculum principles, in particular, it might be suggested, promoting 'cross curricular' work much more forcefully and centrally than is often the case. Nussbaum's 'critical', 'reflective', 'democratic' curriculum, for example, might be easily mapped on to subject disciplines across the curriculum, suggesting not so much a major adjustment to 'knowledge content' (though this might also prove desirable) as a more radical change in relation to pedagogy and assessment, including a more questioning stance in relation to the knowledge that *is* included and perhaps the welcoming (again) of 'subjugated knowledge' into the previously exclusive curriculum club. The adoption of an 'Aims based Curriculum' or an 'Activity based Curriculum', too, might not require us to dispense with traditional subject disciplines, but might impel us rather to reconsider what those disciplines might include, and, in particular, what specific purpose there is in their inclusion and how it might be of genuine benefit to the learner.

Lawrence Stenhouse, whose theory of the 'Process based Curriculum' we have already considered, offers us a potentially helpful way into such considerations in his account, after Raths (1971), of 'worthwhile activities' that a young student might be engaged in and which therefore present a strong case for themselves for curriculum inclusion – the list focusing, importantly, and in ways that also allow for local and chronological curriculum flexibility and choice, on the *activity's purpose* rather than on identifying the specific activity itself. That is to say – to adopt Tyler's blueprint [Tyler op.cit.], albeit in a less than orthodox way – we must first decide what kinds of experience we wish our students to have and what we intend them to achieve as a result, and then decide on the activities that will, and those that will not, best provide these experiences. 'All other things being equal', Stenhouse says, 'one activity is more worthwhile than another' if:

1 It permits children to make informed choices in carrying out the activity to reflect on the consequences of their choices.
2 It assigns to students active roles in the learning situation rather than passive ones.
3 It asks students to engage in inquiry into ideas, applications of intellectual processes, or current problems, either personal or social.
4 It involves children with realia (i.e.real objects, materials and artefacts).
5 Completion of the activity may be accomplished successfully by children at several different levels of ability.
6 It asks students to examine *in a new setting* an idea, an application of an intellectual process, or a current problem which has been *previously studied*.
7 It requires students to examine topics or issues that citizens in our society do not normally examine, and that are typically ignored by the major communication media in the nation.
8 It involves students and faculty members in "risk" taking – not a risk of life or limb, but a risk of success or failure.
9 It requires students to rewrite, rehearse, and polish their initial efforts.

10 It involves students in the application and mastery [sic] of meaningful rules, standards, or disciplines.
11 It gives students a chance to share the planning, the carrying out of a plan, or the results of an activity with others.
12 It is relevant to the expressed purposes of the students.

(Stenhouse 1975: 86–7)

We might not agree wholeheartedly with everything on this inventory: I must own up to having issues with some of them myself, and would want to add to the list something concerning the encouragement of wonder, excitement and pleasure through an activity. The point is, however, that, as with Nussbaum's critical curriculum, Stenhouse's Process based Curriculum, linked to the concept of worthwhile activity, can suggest a radical revision of the most common curriculum structure, based around subject disciplines, but can also invite a 'mapping and readjustment' exercise in which the curriculum content of each subject area, the relationships between subject areas, and the modes of pedagogy and assessment are themselves subjected to revision and critique. (An interesting activity, which I have sometimes used with Beginning Teachers in a variety of subject areas, is to try to map each of Stenhouse's 'worthwhile activities' on to an existing subject curriculum, identifying any problems that arise, whether and how we might reconcile such problems, and how our curriculum priorities, our teaching and our assessment might change as a result. This might consider the feasibility and desirability of modes of assessment that do not overly focus on the demonstration of 'acquired knowledge' in formal pencil and paper tests, but prioritise forms of 'formative assessment' or 'assessment for learning' whereby teachers and students together make sophisticated, informed judgements regarding students' capacity to operate in a range of settings and in response to a range of challenges.)

Notes

1 I was recently asked how some of the more democratic, 'flatter', open-ended curricula proposed by Somekh in Chapter 5 might possibly be assessed and examined, and regulated for quality. The obvious answer is that such curricula would demand not only different modes of assessment and evaluation than those we have become very familiar with, but also a change of attitude toward the whole concept of assessment itself: not a rejection of assessment, but a radical reappraisal of what it means, who undertakes it, and what, essentially, it is *for*. Issues of assessment have always been an important aspect of curriculum theory and curriculum design, and some have argued that assessment practices effectively establish their own curriculum alongside – and perhaps in dominance over – the curriculum as officially designated in national curricula. Some years ago, for example, with reference to circumstances in the USA, George Madaus argued that:

> In recent years, it seems that the aims of education, the business of our schools, and the goals of education reform are addressed not so much in terms of curriculum – the courses of study that are followed – as they are in terms of standardized tests. It is testing, not the "official" stated curriculum, that is increasingly determining what is taught, how it is taught, what is learned, and how it is learned.

(Madaus 1988: 83)

2 'Knowing and not knowing: thinking psychosocially about learning and resistance to learning', The Institute of Education, University of London, Monday 17th and Tuesday 18th December 2012.

3 Sometimes things do slip – temporarily – through the net. For example, in the 1970s and into the 1980s in England and especially in inner-city schools, Language Awareness Programmes encouraged students to appreciate English in its many dialectal forms, to explore the power relations behind (and perpetuated through) language, to recognise Standard English as a powerful and important dialect rather than simply as 'correct' English, and to expand young people's linguistic repertoires rather than 'correct' their linguistic 'errors'. It enjoyed an extensive if somewhat short-lived popularity. In the early 1990s, this approach to English language teaching (and some Modern Foreign Language teaching) even found its way into the 'Official Recontextualising Field' of central education policy, in the form of national curriculum support materials and exemplary video-recorded materials for classroom teachers. One such recording, presented as exemplary of good practice (and in contradiction to the views expressed previously by Margaret Thatcher and subsequently by Michael Gove), showed young secondary school students re-writing and re-telling well-known fairy stories in local dialects and in heritage languages, and a class of older students discovering, via a 'What's My Line?' activity, that accent and dialect can be very unreliable indicators of intelligence.

4 For an expansion of this point, see Moore 1999: 101–11: also Dalphinis 1988 (cited in Moore 1999: 101).

5 When Ruti speaks of 'beings of uncertainty' she is not referring to the uncertainty discussed in Chapters 5 and 6 involving 'external' threats to the psyche (poverty, global warming, breakdowns with loved ones and so on) but rather to a deeper, less 'accessible' uncertainty that characterises us as individual human beings: an uncertainty of what or who we are in the world, of how we are or will be received by others; of doubt, and guilt, and shame.

6 The curriculum itself is not a fantasy, of course, but a reality that is experienced as such by students and teachers. The argument here is that it is constructed on or out of a fantasy – or more accurately, perhaps, a set of fantasies. It could be argued that any proposed curriculum of the future will also be constructed on a fantasy or set of fantasies: however, we might identify a difference between fantasy which seeks to mask and conserve (which is, centrally, about denial and control), and fantasy which is more about possibility and hope, about change and resolution.

7 Hegemony itself, of course, is very dependent on affect for its sustenance – an aspect of theory developed and supported in the schizoanalysis of Deleuze and Guattari introduced in Chapter 2.

8 It would appear that not all countries exclude discussion and education about homosexuality in this way. The Maltese National Curriculum, for example, includes as one of its '14 educational objectives' 'Education on Human Sexuality'.

9 The hidden curriculum as usually understood might best be understood as a set of assumptions, or 'takens': assumptions about 'good behaviour', about the reasons for including or not including a topic or subject area in the prescribed curriculum, about differences and different roles between adults and children or adolescents, about the kind of society 'we' all want and the kind of citizen 'we' wish to see in it, and of how learning takes place and what effective teaching looks like. It is that which may not be specifically 'written down' in the official curriculum but nevertheless requires and demands, very explicitly, certain things on the part of learners and teachers.

10 In talking of hidden and 'hidden hidden' curricula in this way, we are pushing the boundaries of what curriculum means – and what might or might not be appropriate theory and research within Curriculum Studies. Not all of my Curriculum Studies colleagues would agree that there is much value in pursuing some of the ideas explored in this chapter around the 'null curriculum' and different conceptualisations of the 'hidden curriculum'.

11 In referencing 'myth' and 'misrepresentation' as I am, I am aware that I may be taking something of a linguistic liberty. I am suggesting a distinction between 'myth', which is embedded in the public consciousness where it is experienced as 'truth', and 'misrepresentation', which is the active process of myth-creation undertaken by powerful people, whether consciously or not,

for social, economic and political ends. It is only when the mythic understanding is, so to speak, de-internalised and de-naturalised, and its 'truth' relocated in the domains of politics and power, that its resistance and rejection can occur – a notion not dissimilar to Marx's of the development of 'class consciousness'.

Chapter 9

Alternatives in practice

I am aware that some readers, in some countries, might be thinking in relation to the previous chapter 'Well, this is all very well in theory but how can it be put into practice? Is it possible here, in my own country? How do I know if the alternatives are going to be any better or any worse than what we already have?'

In certain other countries, however, and in some fortunate educational establishments within some other countries, many of the alternative proposals I have mooted will not appear as alternatives at all but as common sense and (at least in part) existing practice. In this final short chapter, I want to reference some of the ways in which some of these 'alternative' proposals are already being developed and invested in, along with some of the rationales behind them (policymakers' rationales, that is, rather than simply those of educational theorists). These models and rationales act as important reminders not only that such curriculum alternatives can and do operate around the globe but also that radical departures in relation to traditional views of knowledge and skills, of curriculum 'content', of pedagogy and assessment should not be dismissed lightly as eccentric, as 'pie in the sky' or (as we are often encouraged to think in England) as 'extremist', as 'ideologically driven' or as being contrary to children's best interests. I have elected to present these examples relatively blandly, with little more than a brief contextualising introduction by way of encouraging readers to make of them what they will, deciding for themselves if and how that might impact on or work within or be used as change agents to their own school curricula, whether 'national' or not.

The examples I will be drawing on are of recent curriculum developments[1] in five countries: two (Malta and Sri Lanka) that, in terms of population, might be regarded as 'small' (with no intention of disparagement) and which share a history of relatively recent independence following longer periods of (UK) colonisation;[2] two (China and Japan) that are, in terms of population but also in relation to global trade and influence, 'large' and do not have that same history of colonisation and independence; and one (the one with which I will begin) – Singapore – which is often cited by education policymakers in other countries (nowhere more so than in England) as a model of success in the field of public education.

Details of recent curriculum developments in a sixth nation, England, have also been explored in some detail in the preceding pages, with particular reference to its political conservatism and cultural traditionalism. While it is not a topic for discussion here, there might be some merit in considering the ways in which what might be regarded as an ex-colonising nation such as England responds within public education to changes in the world and in its own relationships with the rest of world, and the responses of previously colon*ised* nations. In either case, the connections between the development of a *national* curriculum and a national 'identity' are clearly of interest. In the case of some former colonies, for example, national identification, like curriculum development, might be more inclined to adopt a 'start again' approach: Who are we [now that we are no longer part of the British Empire, adopting British educational, legal and administrative practices]? Who/what do we want to be? How do we envision our new future role in a world we are entering [at least to a greater extent] on our own terms? In England, on the other hand, there might be a greater inclination to hang on to a past identity – to ease the loss of Empire, as it were, by acting as though it was still there; to find the prospect of having to change how we see ourselves and *how we see ourselves being seen by the rest of the world* as considerably more difficult to contemplate.

Singapore's 'holistic' approach

One of the most significant and (to many of us) 'alternative' curriculum histories is to be found in the case of Singapore – a case that presses itself on our collective attention partly because of the apparent success its past reforms have achieved in the eyes of the watching world, and partly because (on the back of such perceived success) of the reforms it continues to plan even as this chapter is being written. (For a detailed account of Singapore's most recent education reforms, which connect particularly closely with the major curriculum issues explored in *Understanding the School Curriculum*, readers are strongly recommended to access 'Towards a Holistic Education: Enhancing Our Curriculum', at http://www.moe.gov.sg/corporate/contactprint/pdf/contact_jul06.pdf: Singapore Ministry of Education 2009.)

I have written elsewhere (Moore 2012) of the Singapore National Curriculum's rhetorical positioning of teachers and schools as reflexive, theory-driven facilitators of student learning, and of its aim to develop independent and engaged lifelong learners. More recently, Stewart (2013) has reported on subsequent developments in the same curriculum, as announced by the Director of Singapore's National Institute of Education Lee Sing Kong at an education conference in London. Noting that Singapore's performance in international school league tables 'has placed it among the world's élite and won it praise in the West for its rigorous approach to education', Stewart adds:

> [A]s reformers in the UK and the US emphasise the importance of core knowledge and traditional teaching methods, Singapore is sending its schools on a different trajectory. Holistic child development, student-centric lessons [and] a less prescriptive curriculum…are among the radical reforms being introduced by the country.

A new emphasis on equipping children to contribute to a more equal and caring society, and on changing from traditional, autocratic pedagogies, has involved, among other things, redesigning classrooms in ways which 'encourage collaboration, with rows of desks replaced with circular or hexagonal tables' (Stewart: ibid.) – interestingly, the kind of arrangement which was particularly popular in England in the 1980s and 1990s! Suggesting both a more student-centred approach to teaching and learning, and one in which student voice is encouraged and responded to, Lee Sing Kong is reported as advising conference attendees: 'We are dealing with 21st-century digital learners who have a very different expectation of what learning is about' – who prefer to learn from their experience and who 'like to study as a group' (Stewart: ibid.).

As with the other national curriculum initiatives, even the most innovative ones, there are, not unexpectedly, self-imposed limitations to such reform: the pervading influence of conservative 'paranoia', perhaps. As Stewart continues (ibid.: 9), for all the drive to develop '21st-century skills': 'Didactic teaching and an emphasis on basic numeracy and literacy will survive the latest developments' – while a reference elsewhere in the Director's own speech to the demands of 'employers' ('telling us that they cannot predict what kind of jobs will be available in five years' time') might lead us to suspect that the Singapore reforms are driven as much by neo-liberal concerns with national and international economies as with students' personal development and 'enrichment'. However, we might yet argue, with some reason, that whatever its *motives* (the policy *effects* arguably being of greater importance here than their causes) the Singaporean National Curriculum has ventured considerably further in terms of policy and design than many others, not least in its return to those fundamental questions (cited also in the Singapore Ministry's own website) that were identified in Chapters 2 and 3: What is the curriculum – what is education – *for*? Do we think it might be for some of the same things as in the past, or might it be for some different things too? And if we do think it is no longer as 'fit for purpose' as it might have been in the past, what changes are required in terms of content, of pedagogy, of assessment, *and of our overarching aims, values and principles?*[3]

Malta's 'principles' and 'objectives'

The first 'small nation' I want to reference by way of example is Malta (see also Moore 2012). At the point of achieving independence from the UK in 1964, Malta still had a very conservative, 'traditional' education system based on an extreme model of the dominant British version: one which was very teacher-led and textbook focused, which mimicked the British subject-based curriculum structure, and which made use of British test and examinations systems, including an examination taken at age 11 to determine what kind of education a young learner would receive on entering high school. At the turn of the century, however, a new 'national minimum curriculum' was devised, partly in response to a wider re-identification process brought about by independence, partly as a requirement of the country's efforts to be included in the European Economic Community as a separate nation (which eventually happened in 2004). Returning to the same fundamental curriculum questions we have considered in the preceding pages, this new national minimum curriculum ('minimum' in the sense that it set out its requirements in ways that allowed for and encouraged a considerable amount of school-based curriculum development) comprised, centrally, a set of 15 'educational principles' and 14 'educational objectives', each elaborated at some length in terms of the kinds of classroom experience they would demand, but doing so in a way that drew short of recommending specific texts and support materials or (except in the case of the requirement for group learning) specific teaching strategies.

The selection of principles and objectives – not least, the educational and curricular *priorities* they reveal – is an interesting one, particularly, I imagine, for teachers in countries like England whose curricula continue to be structured around subject areas and knowledge content and who might be surprised to see highlighted in the Maltese curriculum some elements of what might, in other countries, be consigned to the 'null curriculum'. The 15 'principles', for instance, are as follows:

- Quality Education For All
- Respect For Diversity
- Stimulation of Analytical, Critical and Creative Thinking Skills
- Education Relevant for Life
- Stable Learning Environment
- Nurturing Commitment
- Holistic Education
- An Inclusive Education
- A More Formative Assessment
- The Strengthening of Bilingualism in Schools [Malta has two official languages: Maltese and English]
- Gender Equality
- Vocation and Competence
- The Importance of Learning Environments
- Increasing Participation in Curriculum Development
- Decentralisation and Identity

The educational 'objectives' are listed as:

- Self-awareness and the Development of a System of Ethical and Moral Values
- The Development of Citizens and a Democratic Environment
- Developing a Sense of Identity Through Creative Expression
- Religious Education
- Strengthening of Gender Equality
- Education on Human Sexuality
- Preparing Educated Consumers
- Media Education
- Effective and Productive Participation in the World of Work
- Education for Leisure
- Wise Choices in the Field of Health
- Greater Awareness of the Role of Science and Technology in Everyday Life
- Competence in Communication
- Preparation for Change

As mentioned above and earlier on in this book, group work is included as a key element running across the curriculum, being repeatedly highlighted in the detail of the curriculum and thus becoming a curriculum element/requirement in its own right, linked to a single overarching pedagogic requirement described as 'a pedagogy of co-operation':

> [A] pedagogy of co-operation, based on group work, should transform…classrooms into a hive of synergetic collective endeavour. …The vehicles for the development of critical and independent thinking are: questions, systematic investigation and the exchange of ideas with others. …Genuine group work implies that the control over the production of knowledge does not remain in the hands of teachers but is shared

among students. An educational context based on holistic principles is essentially a democratic context in which a balance between individual and participatory learning is achieved.

(Maltese Ministry of Education 2000: 25ff)

As has already been suggested, the effective inclusion of group work and, we might add, the co-construction of knowledge as 'curriculum' rather than 'pedagogy' presents an interesting challenge to traditional conceptualisations of curriculum 'content' as referring exclusively to items of knowledge and 'practical' skills.

Sri Lanka's 'educational goals'

The next example of what for many readers might look like an 'alternative' curriculum approach is from another former member of the British Empire, Sri Lanka. Like Malta, Sri Lanka is a small country in terms of size and population and has also, for many years, followed a very traditional English model of education using traditional public examinations (some of which are not even used in England any more), emphasising student discipline (including strictly observed and somewhat dated school uniforms, and a 'do not speak unless spoken to' philosophy) – focusing very stringently on academic work and academic achievement, arguably at the expense of the creative and the expressive. As any visitor to Sri Lanka will be aware, school students are still under a great deal of pressure from parents as well as from the wider system to compete with one another for top grades that may lead to better paid, more prestigious jobs, and large numbers of children attend weekend schools and after-school evening classes by way of additional exam preparation.

Sri Lanka, however, like Malta 15 years previously, is in the process of developing its own national curriculum, albeit after an arguably longer period of independence, and, as will be immediately evident, the two attempts have much in common. The Sri Lankan curriculum, for example, is underscored and guided by some key educational 'goals', which are summarised as follows:

- To develop and understand the cultural and religious heritage and the democratic traditions of the country, as well as an appreciation of the contributions made by the different ethnic groups to the national culture.
- To develop a basic understanding of the environment and skills relevant to the needs of life and society.
- To cultivate an appreciation of the arts, literature and science.
- To develop attitudes conducive to harmonious relations among the different ethnic groups.
- To promote moral, spiritual and physical development.
- To inculcate a sense of commitment to national development.
- To develop and promote a system for the acquisition of technical knowledge and vocational skills to meet the manpower needs of the country.
- To promote lifelong education and knowledge renewal through programmes of formal and non-formal education.
- To promote the democratization of education.

(Karunasinghe and Ganasundara 2013: 120)

In relation to the primary school curriculum:

> The reforms will see the countrywide introduction of a highly integrated curriculum at the lower primary stage, with the subject-area environment-related activities, which encompasses several disciplines. ...Additionally, there is a provision for co-curricular work in all the key stages. ...The number of subject areas in the curriculum is now being limited to four: (1) languages; (2) mathematics; (3) religion; and (4) environment-related activities. ...In the past, even at primary level, the content of subjects received the greatest emphasis. However, nowadays the focus will be placed on competencies that children are expected to have acquired at the end of their general education. ...The new teaching/learning methodology will incorporate an appropriate mix of play, activity and deskwork, the proportion of each component varying gradually with successive grades. The new curriculum also incorporates cross-age play and activity opportunities, where KS-1 children interact with children from grade 6. ...There will be continuous classroom-based assessment, with increased emphasis on the use of informal methods. This represents an attempt to deviate from past assessment techniques (which encourage comparative student achievement) and move towards criterion-referenced assessment techniques.
>
> (ibid.: 121–22)

As with many 'alternative' curricula, there is nothing to stop this approach – even with its references to the role of play in learning and to the development of 'informal assessment' practices – from continuing to adopt much of the traditional, front-of-class teaching that has characterised Sri Lankan classrooms from the time of British rule, or to enforce a complete move away from traditional subject boundaries, and, in any event, curriculum change of this degree is unlikely to be accomplished overnight. However, it is clear that the revised Sri Lankan curriculum is making a conscious effort to distance itself from past practice, to challenge previous hegemonic understandings of and approaches to education and curriculum, and to re-imagine curriculum in a way that is free from outside interference. Interestingly, rather than detailing what is to be taught within each of a number of pre-identified subject disciplines, this new national curriculum also organises itself around 'aims', encourages cross-curricular work, and, in the case of primary education, actually reduces the number of pre-identified subject areas to four, including a new one called 'environment-related activities'. The curriculum is interesting in other ways, too: for example, in its emphasis on 'competences' as opposed to 'knowledge', and in its shift away from end-of-course, one-fit-for-all assessments in which students compete with one another for finite symbolic resources (in the form of test and examination grades) to an assessment approach which consciously 'deviates' from such techniques, moving towards 'criterion-referenced assessment' (ibid.).

China and Japan: From 'Master' to student

It is not just 'smaller' countries that provide us with examples of curriculum alternatives (in particular, curricula which may not necessarily dispense with traditional subject disciplines, but do not, so to speak, *start out with them* or use them as the principal guide for curriculum content, purpose and design). Colleagues and students in England are often surprised to learn of the development of inclusive, student-centred, process-based national curricula in China and Japan – two countries which, in the West, (rightly or wrongly) have traditionally been viewed (and largely represented via the mass media) as wedded to formal whole-class teaching and to knowledge acquisition and regurgitation.

In the past (including the relatively recent past), the public education systems in each of these two countries, according to their own national curriculum documentation, were to a considerable extent characterised by validating and emphasising the 'explicator Master'/receptive student pedagogy discussed in Chapter 2, and (over-)valuing repetition and imitation over critical engagement. Japan's recent curriculum reforms, however, have shown both a desire to move away from such a pedagogic model towards a far more 'progressive' one, and a challenge to traditional curriculum content and structure that bears strong echoes of many of the issues we have discussed in earlier chapters. Recently, for example, the Japanese government has sought to introduce a new 'integrated curriculum' based on '5 criteria':

- ability for problem identification
- problem-solving capability
- learning and thinking skills
- active and creative study attitudes
- reflecting on people's lifestyles.

Alongside more traditional subjects, a new 'integrated study period' specifically designed to enforce cross-curricular thinking and teacher creativity, includes such themes as:

- international understanding
- digital-age literacy
- global learning
- social welfare and health
- environmental issues.

(Aranil and Fukaya 2010: 65)

Addressing its own question regarding 'How education should be in the 21st century', the new curriculum highlights the following five key curriculum strategies:

- enriching the experiential and problem-solving learning of each course subject to cultivate the ability to learn and think voluntarily;
- cultivating ways of learning and thinking and an attitude of trying to solve or pursue problems independently and creatively;
- encouraging students to learn 'more freely and in a more leisurely way';
- 'internationalising', and recognising the need to educate students in and for 'an information-oriented society';
- giving schools more freedom to engage in school-based curriculum development.
  (Education in Japan Community Blog. http://educationinjapan.wordpress.com/
    education-system-in-japan-general/what-is-the-national-curriculum/)

Earlier reforms in Japan also bore the hallmark of a change of culture of education and curriculum policy towards more student-centred, contingent and flexible approaches to teaching and learning as well as to what is taught and learned – highlighting priorities to:

(1) encourage the emotional development of the youth, to make them well equipped to contribute to society and to have an increased self-awareness as a member of the international community;

(2) enhance children's ability to learn and to think independently;

(3) develop a comfortable educational environment, which successfully equips children with essential basic contents as well as develops children's individual personalities;

(4) encourage each school to discover its own special characteristics and redefine itself as a unique site of distinctive education.

(Shigeo Yoshikawa, n.d.)

In the People's Republic of China, recent reforms have seen curriculum policy move in a similar direction. Jin (2010), for example, describing the evolution of China's New Curriculum of Basic Education (NCBE) from its inception in 2005, talks of its call for reforms in both subject content and pedagogy, and its embracing of flexibility, school choice and innovation. As Zhu puts it: 'The NCBE advocates teacher–student interaction, teachers' guidance in sharing, student autonomy and inquiry study' (Zhu 2010: 374).

Parallel developments in the implementation of the new curriculum in senior middle schools have promoted a number of changes to existing curricular and pedagogical approaches, for example:

• giving students greater opportunity to choose courses;
• focusing on promoting students' generic skills related to independent inquiry, cooperation, communication, and problem-solving;
• assessing students' academic performance via a 'growth portfolio' as part of the development of a more formative evaluation system;
• the encouragement of school-based curriculum development.

In their 2012 survey 'Curriculum Transformation in China: Trends in student perceptions of classroom practice and engagement', Adams and Sargent (2012: 2) describe a policy move in China starting in the 1990s, away from 'exam-oriented education to student-centred learning':

Traditional education practices have expected students to passively accept and memorize material presented by teachers, and to reproduce the knowledge in often high-stakes examinations. The new curriculum is designed to reduce teacher-centred instruction in favour of student-centred learning characterised by active learners creatively solving problems, *challenging existing knowledge*, and participating in lively discussion.

(emphasis added, Adams and Sargent: ibid.)

Adams and Sargent acknowledge that to many Westerners such developments may come as a surprise, offering the following additional elaboration of curriculum developments in both Japan and China:

Perhaps most surprisingly, the more collectively-oriented and examination dominated educational systems in East Asian nations such as China, Korea and Japan have embraced the belief that schools need to provide students with more than exam skills to prepare them for the future. Each of these nations have implemented new curriculum policies emphasizing student autonomy, creativity and problem-solving with the hopes of reducing rote memorization and exam pressure while developing creativity, initiative, and innovation.

(ibid.: 19–20)

Interestingly, the authors relate such developments not to fundamentally social or humanitarian reasons, nor to theories of learning, but rather to those same perceived economic needs that have led some other countries to re-focus on the development of competitive skills and practices via *increased* testing and examination, and the absorption of the superficial or 'surface' knowledge demanded for success in such assessments: 'Educational policies promoting inquiry-based, research-based, and problem-based learning have been promoted as a way to develop *citizens who are ready to compete internationally in the knowledge economy.*' (emphasis added: ibid.)

Adopting a purely Economic perspective for a moment, we might be tempted to detect between these initiatives and those in countries like England and America a key difference between: (a) seeking to encourage individuals to compete with one another and to demonstrate their superiority or inferiority in one-off, transient contests of memory regurgitation (a residual legacy, perhaps, of 'old capitalism'); and (b) seeking to develop in individuals and groups the lifetime skills to compete nationally and internationally within arenas whose precise conditions cannot be accurately predicted in advance: a feature, perhaps, of 'new capitalism'. From a non-Economic perspective, these curriculum developments offer another interesting example of how differing ideologies, priorities and politics can lead, nevertheless, to identical or very similar conclusions regarding curriculum content and design and related pedagogic and assessment practices. Group work, problem-solving and continuous assessment, for example, can be equally appealing to national politicians, regardless of whether one adopts a 'humanitarian', learning-theory based approach to curriculum development or a more 'hard nosed', nationalist, economic-related one. In England, it is unclear whether the country's current curriculum priorities serve either humanitarian needs or the economic needs that they often claim to. Perhaps politicians in Japan, in China and in many other nations in the world know something that their counterparts in England do not – something that John Dewey recognised so many years ago that it might seem stubborn to ignore it:

With the advent of democracy and modern industrial conditions, it is impossible to foretell definitely just what civilization will be twenty years from now. Hence it is impossible to prepare the child for any precise set of conditions. To prepare him for the future life means to give him command of himself; it means to train him that he will have the full and ready use of all his capacities that his eye and ear and hand may be tools ready to command, that his judgment may be capable of grasping the conditions under which it has to work, and the executive forces be trained to act economically and efficiently.

(Dewey 2009: 35)

In conclusion

These final two chapters of this book have sought to return to some of the key issues introduced in previous chapters – issues of 'Who Decides?', of curriculum 'balance' of various kinds, of 'content' versus 'process', of the various needs and demands (and the *possible* needs and demands) of a school curriculum, of the possible tension between commonality and individuality, between compulsion and flexibility, of what is considered important in relation to knowledge and skills, of the desire to preserve and maintain certain aspects of the past while preparing students for a future that is in part manufacturable and in part uncertain, of deciding what knowledge needs to be 'given' and what needs to be 'constructed' – suggesting not only how curricula different from those traditional versions that are still in place in many parts of the world may be theorised, but also how they might be beginning to take shape in countries that have chosen to return to the basic curriculum questions, seeking to inscribe their new curricula on the nearest approximation to a clean slate that current socio-economic circumstances allow:

- What is public education – what is a school curriculum – *for?*
- In whose interests is it designed and implemented?
- What imagined future do we wish it to promote?

I have suggested that some curricula, those that are perhaps more resistant to change for a variety of reasons, might do well to free themselves from a 'paranoid', conservatising curriculum mindset, and that this might need to entail, in order for change first to be countenanced by politicians and then to be accepted in the wider public domain, a change of culture and attitude toward a more critical, politicised reading of how schools and schooling operate and how conservatism in curriculum policy reproduces and sustains itself. It is a move that inevitably involves recognising and exposing a number of educational and curricular myths by way of understanding their function as misrepresentations: misrepresentations which we have been encouraged to misrecognise, and perhaps have become accustomed to misrecognise, as 'truths'.

I suggested in the first chapter of this book that 'understanding', located within the realm of 'reason', is itself something of a political choice ('political' in the sense that it will be guided in some degree by a particular ideology, and by some level of allegiance to political acts emerging from and supporting that ideology). It is one, too, that only with difficulty – often the greatest difficulty – disengages itself from deeply embedded discourse, from hegemonic versions of 'reality' and 'truth', and from often long-held conceptualisations of the world and ourselves within it. It is, I think, best 'understood' itself in terms of an ongoing process of 'becoming': to return to the tyranny of The Answer, a determination to continue questioning, to continue challenging the 'truths' that are laid before us, rather than treating them in terms of 'completion', of 'being', of complete-ness. It is my hope that the preceding pages may, in some way, have offered readers something to support that ongoing process of understanding – in addition to suggesting what might be some useful references for follow-up investigation. Above all, I hope that readers who are also teachers may find some encouragement in relation to their endeavours, as they seek to continue to do their best to help their students become thoughtful, creative, critical and kindly learners – sometimes within cultures and policies that may appear at times to conceptualise young people purely in terms of their potential 'usefulness'. To repeat Reiss and White's 'educational bottom line', this is no less than a continuing curriculum project of equipping young learners with the wherewithal and the desire to be able to lead personally fulfilling lives themselves, and with the ability and the determination to help others to do likewise.

Notes

1 A note of warning needs to be sounded here. Curriculum policy developments do not always equate entirely with (actual changes in) curriculum practice, and there is often a gap or a mismatch between policy rhetoric and policy intention. It would be naïve of us to believe otherwise. This is not to question or to undermine the policy initiatives outlined in this chapter; rather, it is to take some account of the fact that radical policy initiatives may or may not be prompted by and effect truly radical curriculum development. What is undeniable, and is of particular interest, is the change in the *language* of curriculum aims and objectives revealed in these examples – and the possible significance that such a change might bring with it (always keeping in mind that language can also be 'colonised' not only to encourage thinking and doing 'outside' dominant discourses but also to perpetuating such discourses – adopting, and in the process domesticating, discourse that is oppositional).

2 The colonial relationship between the UK and three of the countries I have referred to in this book – Malta, Sri Lanka and Hong Kong – are not identical, of course. However, the powerful and, up to a point, persistent influence of the traditional English school curriculum in each country is unmistakably similar.

3 As with many of the findings and suggestions of his own expert curriculum review panel, the Secretary of State for Education in England appears to have undertaken what might be perceived as a selective reading of the panel's accounts of Singapore's education system, rather overlooking its more progressive, student-centred approaches in favour of highlighting that 'in Singapore, pupils are expected to know all their times tables and related division facts by the end of Year 4, [while in England] our national expectation is at Year 6', and 'pupils in Singapore are also expected to learn about plant and animal cells in Year 6, including how cell division forms the basis of growth, while we leave this until secondary'. (The National Curriculum Review, Department for Education, 7 February 2014. www.education.gov.uk/schools/teachingandlearning/curriculum/nationalcurriculum2014/nationalcurriculum/a00201093/review-of-the-national-curriculum-in-england.)

References

Adams, J.H. and Sargent, T.C. (2012) 'Curriculum Transformation in China: Trends in student perceptions of classroom practice and engagement', *Scholarly Commons*. Available at: http://repository.upenn.edu/gansu_papers/34. (Accessed 21 March 2014.)

Ahmad, S. (2010) 'Rethinking Britain's role in the world: a global responsibility'. In B. Little (ed.) *Radical Futures: politics for the next generation*. London: MacMillan, Soundings/Compass Youth and Education, pp. 103–108.

Aitkenhead, Decca (2012) 'Slavoj Žižek: Humanity is OK, but 99% of people are boring idiots'. *The Guardian*, 11 June, p. 9. Available at: www.theguardian.com/culture/2012/jun/10/slavoj-zizek-humanity-ok-people-boring. (Accessed 7 April 2014.)

Alexander, R. (2004) 'Still no pedagogy? Principle, pragmatism and compliance in primary education', *Cambridge Journal of Education, 34*(2): 7–33.

——(ed.) (2009) *Children, Their World, Their Education: Final report and recommendations of the Cambridge primary review*. London: Routledge.

Althusser, L. (1964) 'Problèmes étudiants', *La Nouvelle Critique* (152) January (cited in Ross 1991, xvi).

Anderson, L. and Krathwoll, D.A. (2001) *Taxonomy for Learning: Teaching and Assessing. A revision of Bloom's taxonomy of educational objectives*. New York: Longman.

Apple, M. (1995) *Education and Power*. 2nd edition. New York and London: Routledge.

——(2004) *Ideology and Curriculum*. 3rd edition. New York and London: Routledge/Falmer.

——(2006) *Educating the Right Way: Markets, standards, God and inequality*. 2nd edition. New York and Abingdon: Routledge.

Aranil, M.R.S and Fukaya, K. (2010) 'Japanese National Curriculum Standards Reform: Integrated study and its challenges'. In J. Zajda (ed.) *Globalisation, Ideology and Education Policy Reforms*. Dordrecht: Springer, pp. 63–78.

Atkinson, D. (2013) 'The blindness of education to the 'untimeliness' of real learning' paper presented at the School of Social Science and Public Policy, King's College London, February. Available at: www.kcl.ac.uk/sspp/departments/education/web-files2/JBurke-Symposium-/Dennis-Atkinson.pdf. (Accessed 21 March 2014.)

Ball, S. J. (1990) *Politics and Policy Making in Education: Explorations in policy sociology*. London: Routledge.

——(2008) *The Education Debate*. Bristol: Policy Press.

——(2013) 'Education, justice and democracy: The struggle over ignorance and opportunity', Policy paper, London: Centre for Labour and Social Studies. Available at: http://classonline.org.uk/pubs/item/education-justice-and-democracy. (Accessed 4 April 2014).

Barnes, D. (1986) 'Language in the secondary classroom.' In Barnes, D., Britton, J. and Torbe, M. *Language, the Learner and the School*. 3rd edition. Harmondsworth: Penguin, pp. 9–88.

Barthes, R. (1990) *S/Z*. Translated by R. Miller. Oxford: Blackwell.

——(2000) *Mythologies*. Translated by A. Lavers. London: Vintage Books.

Bates, R. (2005) 'Can We Live Together? Towards a global curriculum', *Arts and Humanities in Higher Education, 4*(1): 95–109.

Ben-Peretz, M., Brown, S. and Moon, B. (eds) (2000) *The Routledge International Companion to Education*. London: Routledge.

Bennett, J. (2011) *The Enchantment of Modern Life: Attachments, crossings, and ethics*. Princeton, NJ: Princeton University Press.

Bennett, S., Maton, K. and Kervin, L. (2008) 'The "digital natives" debate: A critical review of the evidence', *British Journal of Educational Technology, 39*(5): 775–786.

Bentley, T. (1998) *Learning Beyond the Classroom*. London and New York: Routledge.

Bernfeld, S. (1973) *Sisyphus, or The Limits of Education*. Oakland, CA: Quantum Books/University of California Press.

Bernstein, B. (1971a) *Class, Codes and Control, volume 1*. London: Routledge and Kegan Paul.

——(1971b) 'On the classification and framing of educational knowledge'. In M.F.D. Young (ed.) *Knowledge and Control*. London: Collier-Macmillan.

——(2000) *Pedagogy, Symbolic Control and Identity: Theory, research, critique*. Oxford: Rowman and Littlefield.

Besley, T. and Peters, M. (2007) *Subjectivity and Truth: Foucault, education, and the culture of self*. New York: Peter Lang.

Bingham, C. and Biesta, G.J.J. with Rancière, J. (2010) *Jacques Rancière: Education, truth, emancipation*. London and New York: Continuum.

Blake, N., Smeyers, P., Smith, R. and Standish, P. (2003) *The Blackwell Guide to the Philosophy of Education*. Oxford: Blackwell.

Blass, A. (1998) 'Sigmund Freud: the Questions of a Weltanschauung and of Defense'. In Marcus, P. and Rosenberg, A. (eds) *Psychoanalytic Versions of the Human Condition: Philosophies of life and their impact on practice*. New York/London: New York University Press, pp. 412–447.

Blenkin, G. and Kelly, A.V. (1981) *The Primary Curriculum*. London: Paul Chapman Publishing.

Bloom, B.S., Engeklhart, M.D., Furst, E.J., Hill, W. and Krathwoll, D.R. (1956) *Taxonomy of Educational Objectives: The classification of educational goals Handbook 1: Cognitive Domain*. New York: Longman.

Bobbitt, F. (1971) *The Curriculum*. New York: Arno Press and the New York Times.

Bogue, R. (1989) *Deleuze and Guattari*. London and New York: Routledge.

Bourdieu, P. and Passeron, J-C. (1977) *Reproduction in Education, Society and Culture*. London/ Beverley Hills, CA: Sage.

Bourn, D. and Hunt, F. (2011) 'Research paper No.1: Global Dimension in Secondary Schools'. London: Development Education Research Centre (DERC), Institute of Education, University of London.

Bowles, S. and Gintis, H. (1972) 'IQ and the Social Class System', *Social Policy, 3*(4).

——(1976) *Schooling in Capitalist America: Educational reform and the contradictions of economic life*. London: Routledge and Kegan Paul.

Britzman, D. (1991) *Practice Makes Practice: A critical study of learning to teach*. Albany, NY: State University of New York Press.

——(1998) *Lost Subjects, Contested Objects: Toward a psychoanalytic inquiry of learning*. Albany, NY: State University of New York Press.

——(2003) *After-education: Anna Freud, Melanie Klein, and psychoanalytic histories of learning*. Albany, NY: State University of New York Press.

Brown, G. (2010) 'Opening remarks', Progressive Governance Conference, 19 February, London: Policy Network.

Brown, J.S., Collins, A. and Duguid, P. (1989) 'Situated Cognition and the Culture of Learning' *Educational Researcher 32*: 32–42.

Brown, W. (2006) 'American nightmare: Neoconservatism, neoliberalism and de-democratization', *Political Theory 34*: 690–714.

Bruner, J. (1996a) *The Culture of Education*. Cambridge, MA: Harvard University Press.

——(1996b) 'The complexity of educational aims'. In *The Culture of Education*. Cambridge, MA: Harvard University Press, pp. 66–85.

Burbules, N. (2004) 'Ways of thinking about educational quality', *Educational Researcher, 33*(6): 4–10.

Burchell, G., Gordeon, C. and Miller, P. (eds) (1991) *The Foucault Effect: Studies in governmentality*. Chicago, IL: University of Chicago Press.

Callaghan, J. (1976) 'Towards a national debate'. Speech to Ruskin College, Oxford University, 8 October. Available at: http://education.theguardian.com/thegreatdebate/story/0,,574645,00. html. (Accessed 19 March 2014.)

Carr, W. (1995) *For Education: Towards critical educational inquiry*. Buckingham: Open University Press.

Carrington, V. (2008) '"I'm Dylan and I'm not going to say my last name": Some thoughts on childhood, text and new technologies', *British Educational Research Journal, 34*(2): 151–66.

Carse, J. (1986) *Finite and Infinite Games: A vision of life as play and possibility*. New York: The Free Press.

Chitty, C. (1997) 'Interview with Keith Joseph'. In Ribbins P. and Sherrat B. (eds) *Radical Educational Policies and Conservative Secretaries of State*. London: Cassell, pp. 78–86.

——(2002) *Understanding Schools and Schooling*. London/New York: Routledge/Falmer.

Clarke, M. (2012) 'The sublime objects of education policy: Quality, equity and ideology', paper presented at the annual conference of the Australian Association for Research in Education (AARE), Sydney: University of Sydney.

Clarke, M. and Moore, A. (2013) 'Professional standards, teacher identities and an ethics of singularity', *Cambridge Review of Education, 43*(4): 487–500.

Coffield, F. and Williamson, B. (2011) *From Exam Factories to Communities of Discovery: The democratic route*. London: Institute of Education Press.

Commonwealth of Australia (2012) 'Global Education: Teacher resources to encourage a global perspective across the curriculum'. What is Global Education? Available at: www.globaleducation. edu.au/global-education/what-is-global-ed.html. (Accessed 16 October 2013.)

Connell, R.W., Ashenden, D.J., Kessler, S. and Dowsett, G.W. (1982) *Making the Difference: Schools, families and social division*. Sydney: George Allen and Unwin.

Cummins, J. (1996) *Negotiating Identities: Education for empowerment in a diverse society*. Covina, CA: CABE.

Dalphinis, M. (1988) Keynote Address, Anti-Racist Movement in Education Annual Conference, April. Manchester.

Deleuze, G. and Guattari, F. (1977) *Anti-Oedipus: Capitalism and schizophrenia*. Translated by R. Hurkley, M. Seem and H.R. Lane. New York: Viking Press.

——(1991) *What Is Philosophy?* Translated by H. Tomlinson and G. Burchell. New York: Columbia University Press.

——(2004) *A Thousand Plateaus: Capitalism and schizophrenia*. Translated by B. Massimi. London: Continuum.

Department for Education and Employment/Qualifications and Curriculum Authority (DEE/ QCA) (1999) *The National Curriculum Handbook for Secondary Teachers in England*. London: DEE/QCA.

Derrida, J. (1993) 'Structure, sign and play in the discourse of the human sciences'. In Natoli, J. and Hutcheon, L. (eds) *A Postmodern Reader*. Albany, NY: SUNY, pp. 223–242.

DES (Department of Education and Science) (1977) *The Curriculum 11–16*. London: HMSO.

——(1984) *Curriculum 11–16: Towards a Statement of Entitlement*. London: HMSO.

——(1991) *The European Dimension in Education*. London: DES.

——(1992) *Policy Models: A guide to developing and implementing European dimension policies in LEAs, schools and colleges*. London: DES.

Dewey, J. (1922) *Human Nature and Conduct: An introduction to social psychology*. London: George Allen and Unwin.

——(1933) 'Dewey outlines Utopian schools', *New York Times*, 23 April, p. 23.

——(1960) *The Quest for certainty: A study of the relation of knowledge and action*. 12th impression. New York: Capricorn Books G.P. Putnam's Sons.

——(2009) 'My Pedagogic Creed', in D.J. Flinders and S.J. Thornton (eds) *The Curriculum Studies Reader*. 3rd edition. New York and London: Routledge, pp. 34–41. (Originally published in *School Journal* vol. 54, January 1897: 77–80.)

DfE (Department for Education) (2011) *The Framework for the National Curriculum. A report by the expert Panel for the National Curriculum Review*. London: DfE.

——(2014) The National Curriculum Review, 7 February 2014. Available at: www.education.gov.uk/schools/teachingandlearning/curriculum/nationalcurriculum2014/nationalcurriculum/a00201093/review-of-the-national-curriculum-in-england. (Accessed 21 March 2014.)

DfEE (Department for Education and Employment) (1997) *Excellence in Schools*. London: DfEE.

DfES (Department for Education and Skills) (2005) *Developing the Global Dimension in the School Curriculum*. London: DfES.

Dolby, N. and Rahman, A. (2008) 'Research in international education', *Review of Educational Research*, 78(3): 676–726.

Dreeben, R. (1967) *On What is Learned in School*. London: Addison-Wesley.

Education in Japan Community Blog (nd) 'What is the National Curriculum?'. Available at: http://educationinjapan.wordpress.com/education-system-in-japan-general/what-is-the-national-curriculum/. (Accessed 21 March 2014.)

Edwards, D. and Mercer, N. (1987) *Common Knowledge: The development of understanding in the classroom*. London: Routledge.

Edwards, G. and Kelly, A.V. (eds) (1998) *Experience and Education*. London: Paul Chapman.

Eisner, E. (1979) *The Educational Imagination: On the design and evaluation of school programs*. New York: MacMillan Publishing.

Elliott, J. (2000) 'Revising the national curriculum: a comment on the Secretary of State's proposals', *Education Policy*, 15 (2): 247–255.

Ernest, P. (1998) 'Questioning school mathematics'. In Edwards, G. and Kelly, A.V. (eds) *Experience and Education*. London: Paul Chapman Publishing, pp. 20–45.

Fieldwork Education (2013) *International Middle Years Curriculum: Making meaning, connecting learning, developing minds*. London: Fieldwork Education.

Fien, J. (ed.) (1989) *Living in a Global Environment: Classroom activities in development education*. Brisbane: Australian Geography Teachers Association.

Finkelstein, B. (1984) 'Education and the retreat from democracy in the United States', *Teachers' College Record*, 86(2): 273–282.

Finnish National Board of Education (2004) *The National Core Curriculum for Basic Education*, Helsinki: Finnish National Board of Education.

Fisher, M. (2009) *Capitalist Realism: Is there no alternative?* Winchester and Washington: Zero Books.

Flinders, D., Noddings, N. and Thornton, S. (1986) 'The null curriculum: Its theoretical basis and practical implications', *Curriculum Inquiry*, 16(1): 33–42.

Flinders, D.J. and Thornton, S.J. (eds) (2009) *The Curriculum Studies Reader*. 3rd edition. New York and London: Routledge.

Foucault, M. (1969) *Archaeology of Knowledge*. London: Routledge.

——(1977) *Discipline and Punish*. London: Allen Lane.

Foucault, M. and Rabinow, P. (1991) *The Foucault Reader*. Harmondsworth: Penguin.

Freire, P. (1996) *Pedagogy of the Oppressed*. Translated by M. Bergman Ramos. 2nd edition. London: Penguin Books.

Freud, S. (1930) 'Civilisation and its discontents'. In J. Strachey (ed.) *The Standard Edition of the Complete Psychological Works of Sigmund Freud (vol.XVIII 1920–22)*. London: Vintage, pp. 65–143.

Frosh, S. (2011) *Feelings*. London: Routledge.

Fukuyama, F. (1992) *The End of History and the Last Man*. New York/London: Free Press.

Gardner, H. (1983) *Frames of Mind: The theory of multiple intelligences*. New York: Basic Books.

——(1993) *Multiple Intelligences: The theory in practice*. New York: Basic Books.

Gardner, J. and Walsh, P. (2000) 'ICT and world mindedness'. In Bailey, R. (ed.) *Teaching Values and Citizenship Across the Curriculum: Educating children for the world*. London: Kogan Page, pp. 80–91.

Gee, J.P. and Lankshear, C. (1995) 'The New Work Order: Critical language awareness and "Fast Capitalism" Texts', *Discourse, 16*(1): 5–19.

Gibbs, P. (2011) 'Adopting consumer time and the marketing of higher education'. In Molesworth M., Scullion R., and Nixon E. (eds), pp. 52–63.

Giddens, A. (1979) *Central Problems in Social Theory: Action, structure and contradiction in social theory*. London: Macmillan.

Giroux, H. (1988) 'Critical theory and the politics of culture and voice: Rethinking the discourse of educational research'. In Sherman, R. and Webb, R. (eds) *Qualitative Research in Education: Focus and Methods*. London: Falmer Press, pp. 190–210.

Giroux, H. (1992) *Border Crossings: Cultural Workers and the Politics of Education*. New York and London: Routledge.

Goodlad, J.I., Solder, R. and McDaniel, B. (eds) (2008) *Education and the Making of a Democratic People*. Boulder, CO: Paradigm Publishers.

Goodson, I. and Walker, R. (1991) *Biography, Identity and Schooling*. London: Falmer Press.

Gough, N. (2003) 'Globalization and school curriculum change'. In Scott, D. (ed.) *Curriculum Studies: Major themes in education vol. IV 'Boundaries: Subjects, assessment and evaluation'*. London and New York: Routledge/Falmer, pp. 148–162.

Green, A. (1997) *Education, Globalisation and the Nation State*. Basingstoke and New York: Palgrave MacMillan.

Hacking, I. (1990) *The Taming of Chance*, Cambridge: Cambridge University Press.

——(2006) *The Emergence of Probability: A philosophical study of early ideas about probability, induction and statistical inference*. 2nd edition. Cambridge: Cambridge University Press.

Halpin, D. and Walsh, P. (eds) (2003) *Educational Commonplaces*. London: Institute of Education.

Hamilton, D. (1989) *Towards a Theory of Schooling*. London: Falmer.

Hannerz, U. (1990) 'Cosmopolitans and locals in world culture', *Theory, Culture and Society 7*: 237–251.

Harris, H. (2013) 'Abolish "Victorian" GCSEs says headmaster of Eton: Tony Little argues teenagers should not take any exams until they are 18 to "loosen" what schools teach', *Mail Online* 30 September. Available at: www.dailymail.co.uk/news/article-2398556/Eton-headmaster-Tony-Little-calls-Victorian-GCSEs-abolished.html. (Accessed 30 Sept 2013.)

Harris, K. (1979) *Education and Knowledge: The structured misrepresentation of reality*. London: Routledge.

Hartley, D. (2003) 'The instrumentalisation of the expressive in education', *British Journal of Educational Studies, 51*(1): 6–19.

Harvard Committee (1946) *General Education in a Free Society: Report of the Harvard Committee*. Oxford: Oxford University Press.

Harvey, D. (2007) 'Neoliberalism as creative destruction', *The ANNALS of the American Academy of Political and Social Science: 610*: 21.

Hellström, T. and Sujatha, R. (2001) 'The commodification of knowledge about knowledge: knowledge management and the reification of epistemology', *Social Epistemology, 15*(3): 139–154.

Hicks, D. and Steiner, M. (eds) (1989) *Making Global Connections: A world studies workbook*. Edinburgh: Oliver and Boyd.

Hirsch, E. (1987) *Cultural Literacy: What every American needs to know*. Boston, MA: Houghton Mifflin.

Hirst, P.H. (1965) 'Liberal education and the nature of knowledge'. In Hirst, P.H. and White, P. (eds) (1998) vol 1. London and New York: Routledge, pp. 246–266.

——(1974) *Knowledge and the Curriculum: A Collection of Philosophical Papers*. London: Routledge.

——(1979) 'Professional studies in initial teacher education: Some conceptual issues'. In R.J. Alexander and E. Wormald (eds) *Professional Studies for Teaching*. Guildford: Teacher Education Study Group, Society for Research into Higher Education, pp. 15–29.

——(1998) 'Liberal education and the nature of knowledge'. In Hirst, P.H. and White, P. (eds) *Philosophy of Education: Major themes in the analytic tradition Vol. 1 Philosophy and Education*. London and New York: Routledge, pp. 246–266.

Hirst, P.H. and Peters, R.S. (1970) *The Logic of Education*. London: Routledge and Kegan Paul.

Hirst, P.H. and White, P. (1998) (eds) *Philosophy of Education: Major themes in the analytic tradition volume 1, Philosophy and Education*. London and New York: Routledge.

Hofkins, D. (2008) *Enhancing the Experience of Schooling: A commentary by the Teaching and Learning Research Programme*. London: TLRP, IoE.

Hoggett, P. (2004) 'Strange attractors: Politics and psychoanalysis', *Psychoanalysis, Culture and Society, 9*: 74–86.

Holland, E.W. (1999) *Deleuze and Guattari's Anti-Oedipus: An introduction to schizoanalysis*. London: Routledge.

Holt, J.C. (1976) *Instead of Education: Ways to help people do things better*. Harmondsworth: Penguin.

Huckle, J. (1988) *What We Consume: The teachers' handbook*. Surrey: Richmond Publishing Company.

Hunt, F. (2012) 'Global learning in primary schools in England: Practices and impacts', Research Paper no. 9, DERC, Institute of Education, University of London.

Ikeda, D. (2005) 'Foreword'. In Noddings, N. (ed.) (2005) *Educating Citizens for Global Awareness*. New York and London: Teachers College Press.

Illich, I. D. (1973) *Deschooling Society*. Harmondsworth: Penguin.

Inglis, T. (2008) *Global Ireland: Same difference,* New York: Routledge.

James, M., Pollard, A., Wiliam, D. and Oates, T. (2011) *Framework for the National Curriculum: A report by the expert panel for the National Curriculum Review*. London: Department for Education.

Jaramillo, N.E. (2010) 'Liberal Progressivism at the Crossroads: Towards a Cultural Philosophy of Teacher Education' in Hill-Jackson V. and Lewis C.W. (eds) *Transforming Teacher Education: What went wrong with teacher education and how we can fix it*. Sterling, VA: Stylus.

Jin, T. (2010) 'A case study of the challenges for middle-school teachers' continuing professional development in China', unpublished MA Dissertation. University of Leicester.

Karunasinghe, A. and Ganasundara, K.W. (2013) *Sri Lanka Curriculum Design and Implementation for Upper Primary and General Secondary Education*, UNESC. Available at: www.ibe.unesco.org/curriculum/Asia%20Networkpdf/ndreplk.pdf. (Accessed 3 January 2014.)

Keck, C. (2012) 'Radical reflexivity: Assessing the value of psycho-spiritual practices of self as a medium for the professional development of teachers'. Unpublished PhD thesis. Institute of Education, University of London.

Kelly, A.V. (1999) *The Curriculum: Theory and practice*. 4th edition. London: Paul Chapman Publishing.

——(2009) *The Curriculum: Theory and practice*. 6th edition. London: Sage.

Kennedy, D. (2004) *Legal Education and the Reproduction of Hierarchy: A Polemic against the system*. New York and London: New York University Press.

Kimball, B.A. (1986) *Orators and Philosophers: A history of the idea of liberal education*. New York: Teachers College Press.

Klein, N. (2007) *The Shock Doctrine: The rise of disaster capitalism*. New York: Metropolitan Books/ Henry Holt.

Kliebard, H.M. (2004) *The Struggle for the American Curriculum, 1893–1958*. 3rd edition. New York and London: Routledge/Falmer.

Kozol, J. (1993) *On Being A Teacher*. Oxford: One World Publications.

Kress, G. (2006) 'Learning and curriculum: Agency, ethics and aesthetics in an era of instability'. In Moore, A. (ed.), pp. 158–178.

Kysilka, M.L. (ed.) (2011a) *Critical Times in Curriculum Thought: People, politics and perspectives.* Charlotte, NC: Information Age Publishing.

——(2011b) 'The rise and demise of the comprehensive school'. In Kysilka, M.L. (ed.) *Critical Times in Curriculum Thought: People, politics and perspectives.* Charlotte, NC: Information Age Publishing, pp. 269–293.

Lacan, J. (1977) *Écrits.* London: Tavistock.

Lauder, H., Brown, P., Dillabough, J-A. and Halsey, A.H. (eds) (2006) *Education, Globalization and Social Change.* Oxford: Oxford University Press.

Lave, J. and Wenger, E. (1991) *Situated Learning: Legitimate peripheral participation.* Cambridge: Cambridge University Press.

Lawton, D. (1975) *Class, Culture and the Curriculum.* London: Routledge.

——(1989) *Education, Culture and the National Curriculum.* London: Hodder and Stoughton.

——(1996) *Beyond the National Curriculum: Teacher empowerment and professionalism.* London: Hodder and Stoughton.

——(2000) 'Values and education: A curriculum for the twenty-first century'. In Cairns, J., Gardner, R. and Lawton, D. (eds) *Values and the Curriculum.* London: Woburn Press, pp. 25–36.

Lessing, D. (1973) *The Golden Notebook.* New York: Bantam.

Little, B. (ed.) (2010) *Radical Futures: politics for the next generation.* London: MacMillan, Soundings/ Compass Youth and Education. Available at: www.lwbooks.co.uk/ebooks/radicalfuture.html. (Accessed 21 March 2014.)

Lopez Schubert, H.A. and Schubert, W.H. (2011) 'Overcoming misconceptions in actualizing Dewey's philosophy of education'. In M.L. Kysilka (ed.), pp. 89–111.

Lynch, K. (1989) *The Hidden Curriculum: Reproduction in education, a reappraisal.* London: Falmer Press.

Lyotard, J-F. (1984) *The Postmodern Condition: A report on knowledge.* Translated by G. Bennington and B. Massumi. Minneapolis, MN: University of Minneapolis Press.

Madaus, G.F. (1988) 'The influence of testing on the curriculum'. In Tanner L.N. (ed.) *Critical Issues in Curriculum.* Chicago, IL: NSSE and University of Chicago Press, pp. 83–117.

Mahoney, P. and Hextall, I. (2001) '"Modernizing" the teacher', *International Journal of Inclusive Education,* 5(2/3): 133–149.

Maltese Ministry of Education (2000) *Maltese Minimum Curriculum: All Our Futures. Shaping the Future Together.* Floriana: Maltese Ministry of Education.

Marcus, P. and Rosenberg, A. (eds) (1998) *Psychoanalytic Versions of the Human Condition: Philosophies of life and their impact on practice.* New York/London: New York University Press.

Marx, K. (1976) *Capital, vol. 1.* Translated by B. Fowkes. Harmondsworth: Penguin.

McCormick, R. and Murphy, P. (2000) 'Curriculum – The case for a focus on learning', in Ben-Peretz, M., Brown, S. and Moon, B. (eds), pp. 204–234.

McFarlane, A. (2006) 'ICT and the curriculum canon: Responding to and exploring alternative knowledge'. In Moore, A. (ed.), pp. 130–141.

McIntyre, D., Hagger, H. and Burn, K. (1994) *The Management of Student Teachers' Learning.* London and Philadelphia, PA: Kogan Page.

McNiff, J. (2013) 'Becoming cosmopolitan and other dilemmas of internationalisation: Reflections from the Gulf States', *Cambridge Journal of Education,* 43(4): 501–515.

Meyer, J., Kamens, D. and Benavot, A. (1992) *School Knowledge for the Masses: World models and national primary curricular categories in the twentieth century.* London: Falmer.

Miller G., Bowes, E., Bourn, D. and Castro, J.M. (2012) 'Learning about development at A Level', Research Paper No.7, DERC, Institute of Education, University of London.

Miller, J. (1994) *The Passion of Michel Foucault.* New York: Doubleday.

Molesworth, M., Scullion, R. and Nixon, E. (eds) (2011) *The Marketisation of Higher Education and the Student as Consumer.* Abingdon: Routledge.

Moore, A. (1999) *Teaching Multicultured Students.* London: Falmer Press.

——(2000) *Teaching and Learning: Pedagogy, curriculum and culture.* London: Routledge.

——(2004) *The Good Teacher: Dominant Discourses in Teaching and Teacher Education.* Abingdon and New York: Routledge.

——(2005) 'Culture, knowledge and inclusion. What place for pluralism in the common curriculum?' In Halpin, D. and Walsh, P. (eds) *Educational Commonplaces.* London: Institute of Education, pp. 85–101.

——(ed.) (2006) *Schooling, Society and Curriculum.* Abingdon and New York: Routledge.

——(2012) *Teaching and Learning: Pedagogy, curriculum and culture.* 2nd edition. London: Routledge.

——(2013) 'Love and fear in the classroom: How validating affect might help us understand young students and improve their experiences of school life and learning'. In O'Loughlin, M. (ed.) *The Uses of Psychoanalysis in Working with Children's Emotional Lives.* Lanham, MD: Jason Aronson, pp. 285–304.

Moore, A., Klenowski, V., Carnell, E., Askew, S. and Jones, C. (2003) *Revising the National Curriculum: Teachers' and pupils' perspectives at KS2 and KS3.* Report of a DfES-funded research study *An Evaluation of Recent Changes to the National Curriculum,* London: Institute of Education, University of London.

NCEE (National Commission on Excellence in Education) (1983) *A Nation at Risk,* Washington DC: US Government Printing Office.

New Zealand Ministry of Education (2007) *The School Curriculum.* Wellington: Learning Media Ltd for the New Zealand Ministry of Education.

Noddings, N. (ed.) (2005) *Educating Citizens for Global Awareness.* New York and London: Teachers College Press.

——(2006) *Critical Lessons: What our schools should teach.* Cambridge and New York: Cambridge University Press.

Nussbaum, M.C. (2010) *Not For Profit: Why democracy needs the humanities.* Princeton, NJ: Princeton University Press.

Oakeshott, M. (1962) *Rationalism in Politics and Other Essays.* London: Methuen.

Olafsdottir, O. (2010) 'Editorial' Education for Sustainable Democratic Societies: the Role of Teachers: Special issue for the 23rd Session of the Council of Europe Standing Conference of Ministers of Education, Ljubljana, Slovenia.

Ollman, B. 'Why So Many Exams? A Marxist Response'. Available at: www.nyu.edu/projects/ollman/docs/why_exams.php. (Accessed 2 September 2013.)

Ozga, J. (2000) *Policy Research in Educational Settings: Contested terrain.* Buckingham: Open University Press.

Parr, A. (ed.) (2005) *The Deleuze Dictionary.* Edinburgh: Edinburgh University Press.

Peters, R.S. (1966) *Ethics and Education.* London: George Allen and Unwin.

Pike, G. and Selby, D. (1987) *Global Teacher, Global Learner.* London: Hodder and Stoughton.

Pinar, W. (2004) *What is Curriculum Theory?* Mahwah, NJ: Lawrence Erlbaum Associates.

Pollard, A. (2012) 'Proposed primary curriculum. What about the pupils?' Institute of Education University of London (IoE) blog, 12 June. Available at: http://ioelondonblog.wordpress.com/2012/06/12/proposed-primary-curriculum-what-about-the-pupils/. (Accessed 8 April 2014.)

Popham, W.J. (1972) *An Evaluation Guidebook: A set of practical guidelines for the educational evaluator.* Los Angeles, CA: The Instructional Objectives Exchange.

Popkewitz, T.S. (2009) 'Curriculum study, curriculum history, and curriculum theory: The reason of reason', *Journal of Curriculum Studies, 41(3):* 301–319.

Posch, P. (1994) 'Changes in the culture of teaching and learning', *Educational Action Research, 2(2):* 153–61.

Power, M. (2007) *Organized Uncertainty: Designing a world of risk management.* Oxford: Oxford University Press.

Rancière, J. (1991) *The Ignorant Schoolmaster: Five Lessons in intellectual emancipation.* Translated by K. Ross. Stanford, CA: Stanford University Press.

Raths, J.D. (1971) 'Teaching without specific objectives', *Educational Leadership April*, 714–720.

RE (2013) 'Homo Collaboratus'. Available at: www.doomsteaddiner.net/blog/2013/03/05/ homo-collaboratus/. (Accessed 5 March 2013.)

Reardon, B.A. (ed.) (1988) *Educating for Global Responsibility: Teacher-designed curricula for peace education, K-12*. New York and London: Teachers College Press.

Reiss, M.J. and White, J. (2013) *An Aims-based Curriculum: The significance of human flourishing for schools*. London: IOE Press.

Ridgway, J. and McCusker, S. (2003) 'Using computers to assess new educational goals', *Assessment in Education, 10*(3): 309–328.

Riley, K.L. (2011) 'Preface'. In M.L. Kysilka (ed.) pp. xi–xii.

Rischard, J-S. (2010) 'It is high time for Global Issue Networks', Progressive Governance Conference, 19 February. London: Policy Network.

Rizvi, F. and Lingard, B. (2010) *Globalizing Education Policy*. New York: Routledge.

Roberts, P. (1998) 'Reading Lyotard: Knowledge. Commodification and higher education', *Electronic Journal of Sociology 1998*. Avaliable at: sys.glotta.ntua.gr/Dialogos/Politics/1998_ roberts.html. (Accessed 24 March 2014.)

Rose, N. (2006) *The Politics of Life Itself: Biomedicine, power and subjectivity in the twenty-first century*. Princeton, NJ and Oxford: Princeton University Press.

Ross, A. (2000) *Curriculum: Construction and Critique*. London: Falmer Press.

Ross, K. (1991) 'Translator's Introduction'. In Rancière J., pp. vii–xxiii.

Rowling, J.K. (2013) *Harry Potter and the Order of the Phoenix*. London: Bloomsbury.

Ruskin, M. (2008) 'Taming the forces of globalisation'. *The Guardian*, 29 October. Available at: http://www.theguardian.com/commentisfree/2008/oct/29/climatechange-labour. (Accessed 8 April 2014.)

Ruti, M. (2009) *A World of Fragile Things: Psychoanalysis and the art of living*. Albany, NY: SUNY Press.

——(2011) *The Summons of Love*. New York: Columbia University Press.

——(2012) *The Singularity of Being: Lacan and the immortal within*. New York: Fordham University Press.

Schiro, M.S. (2013) *Curriculum Theory: Conflicting visions and enduring concerns*. Los Angeles, CA: Sage.

Scott, D. (2006) 'Curriculum discourses: Contestation and edification'. In Moore, A. (ed.), pp. 31–42.

——(2008) *Critical Essays on Major Curriculum Theorists*. London: Routledge.

Sfard, A. (1998) 'On two metaphors for learning and the dangers of choosing just one', *Educational Researcher, 27*(2): 4–13.

Singapore Ministry of Education (2009). 'Towards a holistic education: Enhancing our curriculum', *Contact* (2): July. Available at: http://www.moe.gov.sg/corporate/contactprint/pdf/contact_ jul06.pdf. (Accessed 4 April 2014.)

Skilbeck, M. (1984) *School-Based Curriculum Development*. London: Harper Row/Paul Chapman.

Smith, H. (2003) Tim Berners-Lee says "surveillance threatens web". Available at: www.bbc. co.uk/news/technology-25033577. (Accessed 12 April 2014.)

Smith, M. (2004) 'Contradiction and Change? NGOs, schools and public faces of development', *Journal of International Development 16(5)*: 741–749.

Somekh, B. (2006) 'New ways of teaching and learning in the digital age'. In Moore, A. (ed.), pp. 119–129.

Spring, J.H. (2009) *Globalization of Education: An introduction*. New York and London: Routledge.

Stagoll, C. (2005) 'Plane'. In Parr, A. (ed.) *The Deleuze Dictionary*. Edinburgh: Edinburgh University Press, pp. 204–206.

Standish, A. (2012) *The False Promise of Global Learning: Why education needs boundaries*. London and New York: Continuum.

Steers, J. (2004) 'Art and Design'. In White, J. (ed.) *Rethinking the School Curriculum: Values, aims and purposes*. London and New York: Routledge/Falmer, pp. 30–44.

Stenhouse, L. (1975) *An Introduction to Curriculum Research and Development*. London: Heinemann.

——(1983) 'Curriculum research and the art of the teacher'. In Stenhouse, L. *Authority, Education and Emancaption: A collection of papers by Lawrence Stenhouse*. London: Heinemann, pp. 155–162.

Stewart, W. (2013) 'Singapore heads in a bold new direction', *TES News*, 20 September, pp. 8–9.

Tanner, L.N. (ed.) (1988) *Critical Issues in Curriculum*. Chicago, IL: NSSE and University of Chicago Press.

Thatcher, M. (1987) Speech to Conservative Party Conference, 9 October. Available at: www.margaretthatcher.org/document/106941. (Accessed 7 April 2014.)

Thornton, S.J. (2005) 'Incorporating internationalism into the social studies curriculum'. In Noddings, N. (ed.), pp. 81–92.

——(2009) 'Silence on gays and lesbians in social studies curriculum'. In Flinders, D.J. and Thornton, S.J. (eds), pp. 362–367.

Touraine, A. (2000) *Can We Live Together? Equality and difference*. Translated by D. Macey. Oxford: Polity Press.

Tseng, Chun-Ying (2013) 'A discourse analysis of teacher professionalism in England since the 1980s', PhD thesis, Institute of Education University of London.

Tye, K.A. (2003) 'Global education as a worldwide movement', *Phi Delta Kappan, 85*(2): 165–168.

Tyler, R. (1949) *Basic Principles of Curriculum and Instruction*. Chicago, IL: University of Chicago Press.

Vygotsky, L.S. (1962) *Thought and Language*. Cambridge, MA: MIT Press.

Walsh, P. (1993) *Education and Meaning: Philosophy in practice*. London and New York: Cassell.

Watkins, C. (2005) *Classrooms as Learning Communities: What's in it for schools?* London: Routledge.

Watkins, C., Carnell, E. and Lodge, C. (2007) *Effective Learning in Classrooms*. London: Paul Chapman.

Weber, H. (2004) 'Reconstructing the "Thirld World"? Poverty reduction and territoriality in the global politics of development', *Third World Quarterly, 25*(1): 187–206.

White, J. (ed.) (2004a) *Rethinking the School Curriculum: Values, aims and purposes*. London and New York: Routledge/Falmer.

——(2004b) 'Introduction'. In White, J. (ed.) *Rethinking the School Curriculum: Values, aims and purposes*. London and New York: Routledge/Falmer, pp. 1–19.

——(2004c) 'Shaping a curriculum'. In White, J. (ed.) *Rethinking the School Curriculum: Values, aims and purposes*. London and New York: Routledge/Falmer, pp. 20–29.

——(2004d) 'Conclusion'. In White, J. (ed.) *Rethinking the School Curriculum: Values, aims and purposes*. London and New York: Routledge/Falmer, pp. 179–190.

Williams, R. (1961) *The Long Revolution*. London: Chatto and Windus.

Wood, A.T. (2008) 'What is Renewal? Why Now?'. In Goodlad, J.I., Solder, R. and McDaniel, B. (eds) *Education and the Making of a Democratic People*. Boulder, CO: Paradigm Publishers, pp. 29–45.

Yoshikawa, Shigeo (n.d) 'Background Information on the National Curriculum Standards in Japan'. Available at: www.ibe.unesco.org/curriculum/Asia%20Networkpdf/JAPAN.pdf.

Youdell, D.C. (2011) *School Trouble: Identity, power and politics in education*. London: Routledge.

Young, G.M. and Handcock, W.D. (eds) (1954) *English Historical Documents XII (1)*. London: Eyre and Spottiswoode.

Young, M.F.D. (ed.) (1971) *Knowledge and Control*. London: Collier-Macmillan.

——(1998) *The Curriculum of the Future: From the 'new sociology of education' to a critical theory of learning*. London: Falmer Press.

——(2006) 'Education, knowledge and the role of the State: The 'nationalization' of educational knowledge?'. In Moore, A. (ed.) *Schooling, Society and Curriculum*. Abingdon and New York: Routledge, pp. 19–30.

Zajda, J. (ed.) (2010) *Globalisation, Ideology and Education Policy Reforms*. Dordrecht: Springer.

Zhu, H. (2010) 'Curriculum reform and professional development: a case study on Chinese teacher educators', *Professional Development in Education, 36*(1–2): 373–391.

Index

Page numbers in *italic* indicate figures and those followed by a letter n indicate end of chapter notes.